CONTINUOUS QUALITY IMPROVEMENT IN THE CLASSROOM :

A COLLABORATIVE APPROACH

by

Robert Cornesky, Sc.D.

and

William Lazarus, M.A.

OCLC 33191471
Oct. 2001

CORNESKY & ASSOCIATES, Inc., 1995

First Printing August 1995

About the authors. . .

Dr. Robert Cornesky is the author or co-author of numerous books and articles on Total Quality Management and Continuous Quality Improvement for educational institutions. He has over 25 years experience in education across the nation. He has served as the Dean of a School of Science, Management & Technologies at Edinboro University of Pennsylvania and as a Professor and Dean of the School of Allied Health at Texas Tech University Health Sciences Center. Bob, the founding editor of the *TQM in Higher Education* Newsletter, is presently the editor and publisher of *The Chronicle of CQI,* a newsletter for continuous quality improvement in education. Bob's corporation specializes in TQM/CQI consulting for educational institutions. His address is 489 Oakland Park Blvd., Port Orange, Florida 32127; phone (800) 388-8682 or (904) 760-5866; Fax (904) 756-6755; E-Mail: TQM1BOB@AOL.COM

Other books by Robert A. Cornesky as author or co-author include:
Using Deming to Improve Quality in Colleges and Universities
Implementing Total Quality Management in Institutions of Higher Education
Total Quality Improvement Guide for Institutions of Higher Education
The Quality Teacher: Implementing Total Quality Management in the Classroom
The Quality Professor: Implementing Total Quality Management in the College Classroom
Quality Fusion: Turning Total Quality Management Into Classroom Practice
Quality Classroom Practices for Professors
Turning Continuous Quality Improvement Into Institutional Practice: The Tools and Techniques

Mr. William Lazarus has been a biblical historian for almost 40 years. He has lectured and taught courses on historical topics in Connecticut and Florida and has written several books on biblical history. He is a graduate of Kent State University (OH) University with a B.A. and M.A. in journalism. He has taught writing at a variety of universities and colleges including Yale, Embry-Riddle Aeronautical University, Cuyahoga Community College, and Daytona Beach Community College. He is also a contributing editor of *The Chronicle of CQI* newsletter.

Other books by William Lazarus include:

Nonfiction	Fiction
David's Legacy	*The Unauthorized Biography of Nostradamus*
Abraham's Journey	*The Last Testament of Simon Peter*
	Ghosts (Books 1 and 2)

TABLE OF CONTENTS

Table of Contents

LIST OF ILLUSTRATIONS

List of Illustrations

CHAPTER ONE: INTRODUCTION TO THE CONCEPTS OF CONTINUOUS QUALITY IMPROVEMENT

You've picked up this book because you want to bring Continuous Quality Improvement (CQI) ideas into your classroom. By doing so, you are joining an ever-increasing number of teachers from kindergarten through graduate school who believe that their students deserve a quality education.

The basic concepts have been proven at large institutions like Penn State University and smaller ones like Northwest Missouri State University and Samford University. Quality in education has become such an important concept that the Malcolm Baldrige National Quality Award, annually given to top U.S. companies that follow quality principles, is being expanded to include educational institutions.

But what is quality? How can anyone identify it? How can anyone institute it in a classroom? That's what this book is all about. We will show you how the concept was developed, some of the latest theories about quality and then take you step-by-step through the process.

Let's start with a basic definition. A quality classroom is one that **in which everyone in the class knows the objectives of the class and adopts a quality philosophy to continuously improve the work done to meet those objectives.** The general principles and tools of CQI encourage everyone in the classroom to identify inadequate processes and systems, and to recommend improvements. This occurs when teachers effectively cultivate the arts of active listening, analyzing, and implementing. **CQI is not a rigid set of rules and regulations, but a series of processes and procedures for improving performance.**

This understanding becomes the road map for everything that happens in the classroom. It is not surprising that the **first step** in quality management in the classroom is the co-creation of **a mission statement** and **a quality statement.** Once such statements have been established, they provide the focus of attention for the teacher, students, and other "customers" by placing them in control of learning.

Will CQI make your job easier? Yes and no. It won't reduce your workload or simplify teaching. Teaching is hard work and requires extensive preparation and energy. In CQI classrooms, all the hallmarks of good teaching (Seldon, 1985) still apply. The teacher must:

- Be well prepared for class
- Demonstrate comprehensive subject knowledge
- Motivate students to take charge of their own learning
- Be fair
- Be sincere and interested in the subject matter.

Good teachers also must exhibit these three characteristics (McKeachie, 1978):

1. Enthusiasm and willingness to make the course worthwhile
2. Objectivity
3. A sympathetic attitude toward the problems of the students.

What CQI will do is help you focus your attention on education instead of on discipline or other distractions. It helps you build a team with your students, encouraging them and exciting them. That will definitely make your job more challenging and rewarding.

One of the reasons that the CQI approach works is **because** it requires teamwork and collaboration. It also could change your teaching style. Here are some of the things a CQI teacher must do to achieve quality:

1. The teacher must engage the student in a discussion of the quality of the work to be done. S/he seeks and uses the input of the students. This cannot be done by lecturing the entire class period, but requires the art of listening and incorporating student suggestions into classroom teaching,
2. The teacher must demonstrate precisely what is expected of the student—this is the benefit of a course syllabus and CQI tools,
3. The teacher must ask students to inspect their own work, with the understanding that they know a great deal about how to produce quality work,
4. Finally, the teacher as a leader becomes a facilitator and coach who shows the students that s/he has done everything to provide them with the best tools and workplace as well as a non-coercive, non-adversarial atmosphere in which to do a quality job.

None of these ideas developed overnight, but have resulted from extensive research by noted social scientists.

In his book *Achieving Educational Excellence* (1985), Alexander Astin states that students learn by becoming involved. This means a student must devote a considerable amount of energy, both physical and emotional, to studying and interacting frequently with faculty and other students. Astin states "... if a particular curriculum ... is to have its intended effects, it must elicit enough student effort and investment of energy to bring about the desired learning. Simply exposing the student to a particular set of courses may or may not work."

Astin is wary about educational experiences which assign students to a passive role.

Seldon (1985) said that "students can appropriately be asked to rate those human interactive skills and characteristics that in and part of themselves do not promote learning but rather create an environment or affective situation that promotes and facilitates it."

Scholars like him argue that by using CQI and CQI tools, the teacher immediately gets the students involved in their own educational experience. As a result, from the first day of class, each student joins the teacher to look for ways in which each can continually improve.

The classroom processes have been examined through the eyes of business. Teachers essentially are managers with some basic requirements, including:

1. Assign work that is not boring
2. Manage workers (students) without coercion
3. Be aware that coercion begets coercion, and, as a result, learning and cooperation decreases
4. Be aware that empowerment of a student increases the number of students who will demonstrate effectiveness.

THE ELEVEN-STEP APPROACH TO CQI IN THE CLASSROOM

We have modified Byrnes and Cornesky's (1994) method to bring an advanced CQI approach into the classroom. Called Action CQI, it is a system's approach, that involves **eleven steps**. The steps are listed below with a brief summary. This book will devote a chapter to each point as we attempt to guide you on your quality journey.

1. The teacher must demonstrate leadership.
The teacher's role is that of a coach, collaborator, and team leader, rather than as a boss. S/he monitors the academic and social growth of every student, leading each into new areas of understanding and competence.

2. The mission, goals, and operational definitions of the class must be absolutely clear.
Teachers should have a clearly stated mission statement for each of their courses. All customers, including the students, should have considerable input for defining not only the goals, but also how the goals will be met. The students should be expected to master the stated terminal competencies of the course. They should also recognize the value in the content area being taught and its connections to other disciplines.

3. Most work must be pertinent and flow from the students through teams.
Much of the work teachers and students do can best be done as teams and must flow from student desire and student concerns. From the beginning, the work should be infused with student choice, design, revision, execution, reflection and evaluation. Teachers should take on some of the responsibility for assessing and ministering to the developmental needs of the students.

Students are trusted continually, and all are led to the point where they embrace responsibility.

4. Course content is connected to the community and the real world.
If teachers connect the content of a course to the campus community and the real world, students will be more willing to engage in meaningful discussions and projects.

3

5. The student is not only treated as a "worker," but also as a team member of the "research and development" department.

If the teacher considers himself to be the "manager" of the classroom, the student can be considered as the "worker" responsible for a large part of the product (learning). This concept means that the work is characterized by action as the students actively process information and complete the terminal competencies of the course.

A course should be designed so that after acquiring new information, students should be able to apply it to new course content in new ways. The atmosphere of constantly applying "research and development" techniques (the scientific method, critical thinking, logic, etc.) to routine class meetings should be firmly established.

When classes are run in such a manner, students will make mistakes. It should be clear to every student that mistakes will always occur when new things are tried—that's just part of "research and development."

6. Peer teaching, small group work, and teamwork are emphasized.

A constant feature in this book is the emphasis on peer teaching, small-group work, and teamwork. Every student should be involved in helping each other master the expected terminal competencies.

7. Students should have aesthetic experiences.

Teachers usually have many artistic examples that can be applied to not only their course, but to life in general. They should recognize the worth of aesthetic experiences and resist teaching practices that deprive students of the chance to use their imaginations. From these experiences, students develop their capacities to appreciate, refine, express, enjoy and to break away from restrictive, unproductive modes of thought.

8. Classroom processes should include reflection.

The teacher should mandate that at least five minutes of each class be set aside for reflection. This is an essential activity if the students and teacher want to consider how the present teaching and learning systems are to be improved.

9. All classroom systems should undergo constant evaluation.

We believe that the mastery of most terminal competencies should be evaluated by a variety of testing strategies. The teacher should ask: "In what ways will you prove to me at the end of this class that you have mastered the objectives we have designed?"

Students should be trained to develop portfolios and to monitor their own progress, and then they should devise their own improvement plans. Students should understand that the success of each student is the job of every other student, since working together will help advance society (and reduce prejudice).

If the student works closely with a teacher in developing his/her portfolio, the student will have a valuable resource to evaluate the learning experience. In addition, the portfolio, if kept on file, will provide the teacher with information that is often required for letters of recommendation.

10. New activities should constantly evolve from the old.
As the course progresses, newly acquired competencies should evolve gracefully out of the previous ones.

The students should understand that their quest for quality work is never ending and that the "product" of one class is nothing more than the "raw" material for another advanced "product."

The questions at the end of each class period, as well as at the end of each course, should be: "Now what? What do we know that we didn't know when we started out together? How can we use these skills and this information in some new, more complex and interesting ways? What's next?"

11. There must be an audience beyond the teacher.
The students should be recognized for their achievement by audiences other than the teacher. There are many ways to recognize students. One of our personal favorites is having an oral report of a research project by each team, usually during the evening hours, to invited community groups, business leaders, school administrators, and other faculty.

THE CQI MODEL

Each of these steps are linked so that they build upon each other. As you can see, we examine the classroom from four systems: 1) the **facilitation** system, 2) the **learning** system, 3) the **improvement** system, and 4) the **payment** (or reward) system.

Figure 1.0 shows the relationships between the various steps and the four operational systems within the CQI model.

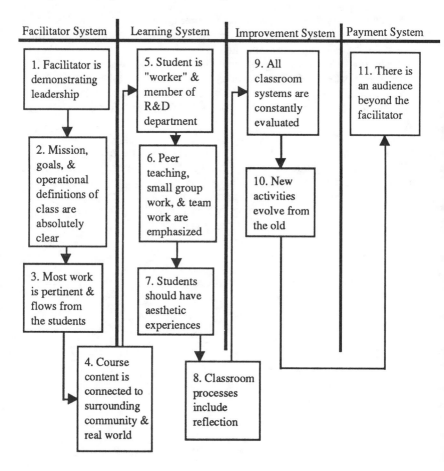

| Facilitator System | Learning System | Improvement System | Payment System |

1. Facilitator is demonstrating leadership

5. Student is "worker" & member of R&D department

9. All classroom systems are constantly evaluated

11. There is an audience beyond the facilitator

2. Mission, goals, & operational definitions of class are absolutely clear

6. Peer teaching, small group work, & team work are emphasized

10. New activities evolve from the old

3. Most work is pertinent & flows from the students

7. Students should have aesthetic experiences

4. Course content is connected to surrounding community & real world

8. Classroom processes include reflection

SOURCE

Where did CQI ideas originate? In business. When Dr. W. Edwards Deming first came up with his 14 points (Deming, 1982) for managing quality and productivity, he was not thinking about education. A noted professor of management in this country, he had been invited by Gen. Douglas MacArthur to come to Japan in 1947 as a business consultant. Deming's lectures to leading Japanese engineers and managers were enthusiastically adopted as Japanese industries struggled to recover from the devastating effects of World War II.

Flush with victory, American firms had rejected his revolutionary ideas about Total Quality Management (TQM) and CQI. Japanese companies, however, had developed an unwanted reputation for producing shoddy merchandise. To compete on the world market, the Japanese recognized the need for changes in their production methods. In time, Deming was able to test his theories in an entire country across a broad range of companies.

The results have been astonishing. By 1951, the Union of Japanese Scientists and Engineers had set up the Deming Prize for quality. Soon after, Japanese products became the quality benchmark for the rest of the world.

In 1981, after NBC broadcast a documentary on the success of Japanese car companies, Ford Motor Co. invited Deming to Detroit to run a series of seminars. Within a couple of years, Ford had added black ink to its books, and its products had begun to move up the various quality index ratings. General Motors held out longer, but succumbed to Deming's approach after wasting millions of dollars on robots in the mistaken belief Japanese success was tied to higher technology not quality management. In this decade, American companies, which once scorned TQM, increasingly have made "Quality is Job 1," as the Ford Motor Co. commercials once proclaimed. Deming's ideas are now standard in industry both in this country and abroad.

His concept is relatively simple. He stressed statistical process control (SPC), which essentially means that data must be collected before decisions are made. He argued that people must be treated humanely, and that workers are intelligent and want to do a quality job. That thinking essentially reversed age-old concepts of management-controlled procedures. Under Deming's guidance, Japanese companies developed "quality circles" in which employers and employees met as equals to solve problems and to smooth operations. In this country, companies like Xerox, IBM, Dupont, Chrysler and many others have followed suit.

In particular, Deming refused to blame workers for quality problems. Instead, he shifted the blame onto the manufacturing procedures which limit workers and create an atmosphere for poor quality. In doing so, he boosted morale and provided incentives for all company employees to work together toward a quality-oriented environment.

PRINCIPLES OF CONTINUOUS QUALITY IMPROVEMENT
His work, combined with the work of Philip Crosby and Masaaki Imai, among others, have created common elements that serve as the base of CQI (Byrnes, Cornesky, and Byrnes, 1992).

1. PROCESSES AND SYSTEMS
All of the combined tasks or steps necessary to accomplish a given result are defined as a process. Deming and Crosby emphasize that since management controls at least 85 percent of the processes and systems in which the employees work, most poor quality is the direct result of poor management.

Every work activity is a part of a process and system. It follows that classroom learning can improve only if the processes and systems in which the students learn improve. If teachers improve the processes and systems, they will receive better quality results and achieve higher levels of productivity from the students.

Most teachers inherit students trained by previous teachers in methods and procedures not directed towards the CQI philosophy. CQI instructors face the challenge of maintaining the strengths and eliminating the weaknesses of systems established by their predecessors. Most likely they face situations where anticipated results yield predictable attitudes and behaviors. This cycle of predictability is not only difficult to alter, but it also inhibits change towards quality (Byrnes, Cornesky, and Byrnes, 1992). This is illustrated in Figure 1.1.

Figure 1.1:   Process inhibiting change to quality.

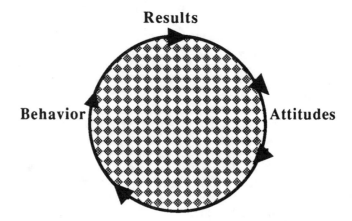

If we assume that the teacher controls 85 percent of the classroom processes and systems, each teacher can influence students to commit to quality. Students will most likely work hard if convinced that quality will be the result (Glasser 1990, p. 433). We agree with Bill Glasser's comment: "quality is contagious" (p. 435). If the teacher directs all of his/her energies toward improving the processes and systems for quality results and boosts the students' reception of the approach, we are confident that quality results will lead to an improved attitude, modified behavior, and, eventually, to a classroom culture directed toward achieving quality. An example of this process is displayed in Figure 1.2.

Figure 1.2: Process and results of introducing change to quality.

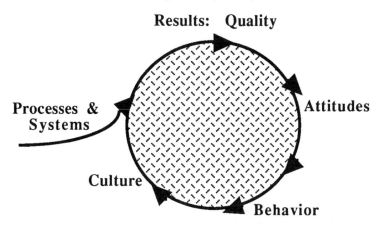

2. TEAMING

Teams and teamwork are extremely important in producing a quality service or product (including learning). Although hierarchy is needed within all organizations in order to avoid chaos, most classroom learning can best be accomplished across, not within, classroom (organizational) boundaries.

The informal power structure and the resulting culture in classrooms do not readily permit collegiality in a management system based upon hierarchy; however, properly done, teaming (cooperative and collaborative learning) is invariably found in classrooms producing quality work.

3. CUSTOMERS AND SUPPLIERS

Generally, the concept of customers within educational institutions differs from the private sector's definition because, in education, "repeat customers" are usually undesirable. It can be argued, however, that if parents, alumni and current students are well satisfied with their school experience, they will recommend the institution to others. Likewise, colleges and universities which are well satisfied with the high school graduates may admit additional graduates from that school. Thus, students, alumni, and employers do share some of the characteristics of traditional customers.

The customer/supplier relationship is very important for effective teamwork. Teachers must develop an understanding and appreciation of the concept in order to promote trust, pride, and quality. Central to applying the concept of quality in the classroom itself is the acceptance of the student's role in the customer/supplier relationship.

Likewise of prime importance is the removal of the top-down (boss-manager) model of management from the classroom. Instead, leadership training for all teachers and students should be undertaken so that everyone can reach her/his maximum performance. In fact, the decentralization necessary to stimulate effectively a customer/supplier attitude requires a participative atmosphere. Empowerment of all teachers and students is necessary for this atmosphere to exist within educational institutions. With empowerment comes trust; with trust comes pride-in-workmanship; and with pride-in-workmanship comes teamwork for Total Quality Improvement.

4. QUALITY BY FACT, PROCESS, AND PERCEPTION

Each of the quality proponents examines quality from at least three different perspectives: (1) by fact: does the product or service meet the specified requirements? (2) by process: does the process and/or system produce the product or service as intended? And, (3) by perception: are the customer's expectations met?

It is conceivable that a course can have quality by fact and of process, yet the perception of the customers, either the students or the employers, for example, may not think quality exists. In this case, quality has not been achieved. This is usually, but **not always**, the result of poor past performance.

5. MANAGEMENT BY FACT

All quality advocates emphasize the need for complete and comprehensive data prior to making major decisions. Several simple rules must apply in determining the mission of the course or even in setting out to improve a simple process: research data should be complete, accurate and made freely available to everyone. Information serves no purpose unless made available to those directly involved in the workplace, for at least two reasons: (1) when people know the facts, they can offer essential advice; and (2) they can call attention to a serious flaw in a developing plan, avoiding additional problems.

Whenever possible, decisions should be based on data rather than hunches. Data and facts have a tendency to uncover the root of the problem rather than the symptoms; thus, permanent solutions can be offered rather than quick fixes.

6. COMPLEXITY

All of the quality leaders realize the complexity of the processes and systems which produce a product or service.

Within a classroom setting, complexity can be defined as extra steps added to a process to deal with errors in the preceding educational experience of students, or to recover from errors occurring in the present classroom experience.

7. VARIATION

Every process involving humans and/or machines displays variation. In education, for example, we see wide variation/diversity in incoming students as well as in the teaching/learning process and in the quality of the graduates. Excessive variation, however, causes the processes and systems to be erratic and unpredictable. Mediocrity and generally poor quality result.

Since every process shows variation, no two products—components, services, reports, teaching effectiveness, or graduates—will ever be identical. The goal, therefore, is to increase the uniformity of the process. Universal involvement in studying processes and identification of potential sources of variation can accomplish this.

Once a system is under control, a teacher can determine common and special-cause variations by the use of simple statistics. Common-cause variation is the inherent variation of a system resulting from many small sources of variation. Special-cause variation is a large, sporadic variation unusual to the system under study. For example, the first football game of the year is likely to heighten students' excitability and distract them from their work. This would be considered a special-cause variations. An example of a common cause variation is boredom.

ΛΛΛΛΛΛΛΛΛ

Now you should understand how CQI developed and some of the basics of a CQI classroom. There's one more point that's important. It's called "benchmarking," or the study of similar individuals or programs which you want to emulate.

If you want to be a great teacher, then you need to see how great teachers function. In our travels throughout the country, we have had the opportunity to observe some of the finest teachers in action. Without exception, they practice, although probably unknowingly, the principles of CQI discussed above. Their techniques may vary, however, they do three things consistently:

1. They concentrate on improving the teaching and learning processes by using a plan-do-check-act (PDCA) cycle
2. They have the students work in collaborative teams using a PDCA cycle
3. They use a variety of CQI tools and techniques to assess the effectiveness of both teaching and learning.

We have taken these elements and combined them with the ideas engendered by CQI scholars to develop an action plan for bringing CQI into the classroom. The processes and procedures within this book are meant to be modified to meet the needs of teaching and learning. You will need to customize these concepts to fit your own needs and institutional goals. However, modifications are not advised until you understand totally the principles and approaches of CQI.

LET'S BEGIN

Your CQI journey must start with a commitment to the goals of a quality classroom. To achieve those goals, you will have to make several decisions, all of which are directly related to the CQI process.

- Accept the concept that the students and other faculty are your internal customers, and that future employers and society are your external customers
- Assume that all of your students want to do a good job, to succeed, to be proud of their accomplishments, and to learn
- Believe that you either control or influence 85 percent of the teaching and learning systems in your classroom
- Accept the fact that if a student does not pass your course that it is your fault, since you did not provide him/her with the appropriate teaching/learning system.

Before you decide to adopt these goals, take a few minutes and reflect on these fundamental principles of CQI. They are simple statements that require a strong commitment. To help you make your choices, we've developed a chart (below). You can use it to describe your personal beliefs underneath each of the following questions.

Fundamental Principles of the CQI Philosophy
Do you believe when a student can't learn and when you are not able to help him/her, there is a process problem in the system, and, as a result, you, as the manager, will have to remove the process problem (root cause)? My personal belief statement:
Do you believe that the teacher is most knowledgeable about his/her job? My personal belief statement:
Do you believe that everyone wants to do the job well and to feel like a valuable contributor? My personal belief statement:
Do you believe that more can be accomplished by working together as a team to improve the system, rather than by having individuals working to get around the system? My personal belief statement:
Do you believe that adversarial relationships between teacher and the students, or teacher and management are counterproductive? My personal belief statement:

When you have completed this form, you will be able to see exactly how your ideas match up with CQI and begin to focus your efforts toward creating a quality classroom. In fact, you'll see that moving toward CQI is your best decision.

The next step is to complete the self-assessment rating of the teaching and learning systems in your course. If you don't know where you are now, how will know when you've gotten anywhere? Use the form in tools and techniques section at the end of this book, beginning on page 241. This **Quality Teaching Index** will give you a baseline from which to begin your CQI journey.

Since CQI results are sometimes incremental, we suggest that you redo the assessment and compare the results with your student evaluations after each course. We know you'll really be surprised with the results.

FACILITATING SYSTEM

CHAPTER TWO: LEADERSHIP

When you take the first steps towards a quality classroom, you actually are doing something else you may not have considered: you are showing leadership. In CQI, leadership is of prime importance to your success. The teacher must demonstrate leadership.

But what is leadership? How do you define it? Why is it important? We'll look at several aspects of leadership in this chapter.

What's In It For Me?
Upon completing the chapter you will be able to:
- Develop a definition of your quality classroom
- Understand why it is necessary to "walk-the-talk" about quality if you want quality work from your students
- Understand the importance of Deming's system of "Profound Knowledge" as it applies to the classroom
- Recognize the importance of using a variety of teaching styles
- Recognize why it is important for you to have a self-improvement program.

THE IMPORTANCE OF LEADERSHIP
Leadership is the first category of the Malcolm Baldrige National Quality Award (MBNQA), the prestigious award given to American companies that develop high-quality standards. Without it, all else fails. This is demonstrated in Figure 2.0. Leadership is the "driver" of the quality system which requires "Information and Analysis" to produce a good "Strategic and Operational Plan," which in turn is a prerequisite for effective "Human Resource Development," all of which contribute to the success of the "Education and Business Process Management." Leadership causes the quality system to promote good performance results with the resulting goal of student and stakeholder satisfaction.

Figure 2.0: The dynamic relationships between the categories in the Malcolm Baldrige National Quality Award Pilot for Education.

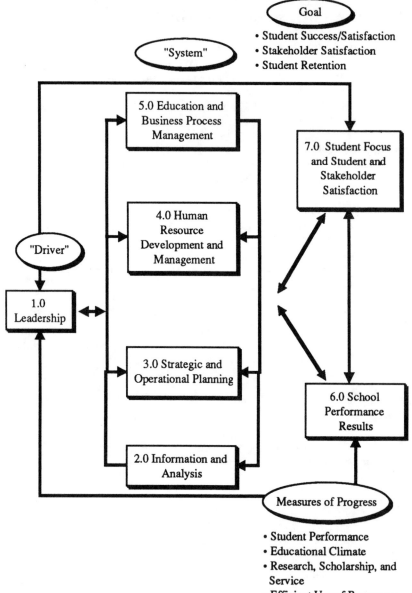

WHAT IS LEADERSHIP?

Leadership may also be the most difficult aspect of CQI to decipher, because it seems to imply that the leader must be strong. That might appear to be in direct contrast to the entire concept of empowering workers. However, all quality experts agree on the importance of leadership for quality. This means that as a quality teacher, you will want to take time to give shape and distinction to your own definition of quality. Not only must you understand what quality is; you will have to be able to articulate it in words that students and colleagues can understand. While CQI seeks to strengthen the extent of decision making and empowerment, it does not diminish the need for leadership to stay focused, set priorities and maintain the highest standards.

How do you achieve leadership in the classroom?

Take several minutes and reflect and record your responses to the following leadership questions.
- What is your definition of a quality classroom?

- Does your quality statement relate directly to the mission statement of the class?

- What have you done to communicate to your students **why** it is important for them to focus on quality results?

- Do your students understand the need to "do it right the first time?"

- Do your students understand why they must be customer focused?

- Do your students understand that in CQI theory that faulty processes and systems are the cause of most problems (and not a person)?

The answers can be articulated in a quality statement. This statement, like the mission statement, serves as a guideline for you and enables your students to understand where you and they are going and why. For example, let's assume that your department's mission statement is:

To prepare students with the knowledge, skills, and abilities necessary to become responsible and productive citizens in a global community.

Teachers within this department should articulate their quality statements within the context of the department's statement. A math teacher might have as her/his Quality Statement:

Quality work is defined by the ability to use logic, and to work individually and as teams to apply the mathematical concepts learned to real-life situations.

Take great care to prepare a quality statement, and then to articulate it to students and colleagues. Like your course mission statement, production of this statement can be a time-consuming process, but consider that it is the foundation for all that you will be doing within the classroom. Unless each of your students understands what you are seeking, how can you expect anyone to take an interest in following your lead?

A quality statement will slow you down. It will force you to be sure your students understand the quality concepts before you even start the course work. Avoid the temptation to "rush" into the course with the urge to cover the first chapter. It is exactly this rush to "get started" that has been at the root of teaching and learning failures for years.

Teachers who have been involved in quality teaching have learned that students need to understand "why" before they become interested in "how." You simply must resist the urge to dive into the course content rather than allowing students to understand the straightforward answers to 'why" they are in this class and "why" it is necessary for them to learn this content matter. In other words, students need to know how the information and skills gained in the class will be helpful and meaningful to their lives now and in the future. We will elaborate on this point in Chapter Five.

CQI teachers recognize that this level of understanding flips the motivation factor from external to internal. Successful teachers are experts at getting the students to recognize the basic worth and meaningfulness of any subject matter. This process may take a class period. (Some teachers have additional evening class meetings and/or office hours to discuss the "why-of-it.") You should not consider this wasted time, but rather time needed to build the foundation upon which a quality class can stand. Proponents of CQI teaching faithfully go through this process, since, in the end, students achieve more by the close of the academic term in a quality class than in a traditional setting.

The quality statement initiates the leadership process. It is not the only element in the mix. Leadership is what helps you in your role of coach, facilitator, collaborator and team leader, rather than as a boss. Leadership is the adeptness that directs you to monitor the academic and social evolution of every student, leading each into new areas of understanding and competence.

You **demonstrate** leadership qualities when **you** are able to:
- Bring students together into a cohesive group
- Establish trust among the students
- Convince everyone in the class to participate in establishing and/or refining the classroom mission
- Clearly elaborate on the course competencies necessary for students to achieve their personally desired goals
- Organize the class so that the students can think critically and resolve conflicts as they continue to be supportive of all other members of the class
- Create visibility for pride-in-workmanship
- Involve the students in community projects
- Constantly monitor and improve the teaching/learning system with input from stakeholders
- Evaluate the efforts of each student
- Help students to realize that they must constantly renew and improve upon their previous efforts.

Those personal traits are augmented by classroom leadership. You **exhibit** leadership qualities when your **classroom** shows the following:

- Every student knows how to use quality improvement tools to analyze and resolve problems
- Students know how to make the classroom run more efficiently and effectively and know how to do their jobs better as they work on improving day to day
- Every student is eager and willing to share information that will help improve the learning experience for everyone
- Every student makes many suggestions for process improvement during the semester, and 95 percent of the suggestions are implemented
- Students and instructors work collaboratively to create a learning environment totally free of fear
- Students and instructors experience the joy of learning together daily
- Students work together in teams, and each student contributes to the learning experience

Nor is your leadership role limited to the four walls of the classroom. Since leadership for quality emphasizes empowerment of workers and focuses on customer satisfaction, quality leaders also seek to inspire and lend support to suppliers—including previous teachers—in hopes they will bring CQI to their courses.

Your leadership role is an evolutionary process that becomes more refined as students, previous teachers, customers, and employers provide valuable, indeed irreplaceable, feedback that allows you to grow while your classrooms advance towards quality. Begin your role as a quality leader by finding ways to empower the students to become **partners** in the improvement process.

How do you accomplish that?

Take several minutes and reflect upon the following questions.

- What is a partner?

- What actions encourage partnerships?

- What actions discourage partnerships?

- What actions do you do that encourage partnerships?

- What actions do you do that discourage partnerships?

A CQI leader maintains high expectations and uses empowerment methods to gain student commitment to achieving them. S/he recognizes that having high expectations is not enough; you must know how you can demonstrate and help students achieve them.

This may pose a dilemma for teachers today since many believe "it takes so much more time and energy." True, CQI teaching does take time, especially in the beginning; however, the extra activities you devote yourself to are very different from those in a traditional setting. For instance, a CQI teacher pays careful attention to the need to show students examples of quality work. Students who have not experienced quality work will have little idea of what it looks like, let alone know how to accomplish quality. This is especially true of individuals who have previously struggled within the traditional top-down boss-management style classrooms.

The ability to create initial learning experiences for students that accommodate a variety of learning styles is essential for a quality classroom. To achieve greater knowledge and understanding, you must lead all students into becoming co-producers of additional learning experiences, each one building upon the preceding experiences and accommodating each student's preferred approach to learning. This represents a paradigm shift away from traditional approaches to education.

In effect, a quality teacher provides the leadership and assistance through mentoring, facilitating and coaching that allows each student to create and successfully carry out learning. The designated outcomes for each learning experience are established and agreed upon by all; however, the actual way in which the outcomes are reached can be left to the discretion of students and/or teams of students. All this takes place within the broad framework of the course content, but allows for individual differences, student empowerment and internal motivation.

WALK-THE-TALK

From the beginning, your leadership must reflect quality in every way. This is easier said than done. Once you begin your quality journey, you will be reminded daily how difficult, albeit exciting, it is. In short, there is no substitute for your displaying quality about every aspect of yourself or your actions both in and outside the classroom. You must "walk-the-talk."

Training students in quality begins before you ever enter the classroom. It starts with your commitment to becoming a CQI teacher, and it never ends. This is why it is so important to understand clearly what quality means to you. Anything less will surely leave you confused, frustrated, and disillusioned

Persistence is a very powerful habit. In fact, most successful people will rank this trait as one of their best. Maintain your quality vision. At the same time, be willing to alter the quality plan upward (never downward) your classroom bumps against outside factors that require flexibility. Take the posture that each time the students test your commitment to quality, they are giving you a gift. That gift is a constant reaffirmation of your belief and conviction that CQI is the way to higher academic achievement.

In fact, leadership for quality will begin to permeate everything you are and do. When you adopt a customer focus, you'll find yourself looking at all your activities and commitments from a different point of view. As a customer to many, you'll find yourself asking: is this quality? Once that happens, then you can be sure that you are well on the way to adopting a leadership role rather than boss-manager role.

With the customer focus and clearly defined ideas about what you want and expect, you will be able to align all classroom activities towards meeting your goal. If your goal is to have all students succeed at learning within your course, you must analyze all your course processes to determine if each process is in tune with your goal. If not, you have a critical determinant for a continuous improvement project.

Either you have a quality classroom mission statement with a customer focus or you don't. You cannot change according to the time of year. For instance, two weeks before the end of the term, you cannot dispense with your commitment to quality by thinking "I still have so much to cover." Your leadership commitment must be vital, strong, and totally focused at all times. Panicking at the end of the semester will not result in students' doing any more or any higher quality work. Don't let the curriculum get in the way of learning.

The need for you as the leader to **stay focused** cannot be understated. Quality leaders demonstrate through actions what they are about. Having a written statement about quality and then saying things that drive in fear will confuse students. Not only is it important that your actions and statements be focused on quality, but also your personal appearance. People recognize those individuals who "walk their talk" rather than "stumble their mumble" to be the true leaders. Quality is not something that relates simply to what we do between 8 a.m. and 3 p.m. each day.

The need for teachers to become quality role models has never been greater. It is an obligation of every teacher to be a role model, but the CQI Teacher sets continuously higher standards of excellence for himself/herself as well as for the students. Anything less will confuse students, making it more difficult for them to recognize quality and far less able to reach it.

The CQI Teacher becomes more involved, rather than less involved. S/he makes time to speak about quality at every opportunity and points out quality wherever possible. Your presence at community meetings or functions, or faculty meetings sends strong messages to external customers and suppliers. In fact, these sessions are viewed as important opportunities to keep the organization focused on quality.

The CQI Teacher aligns every aspect of his/her work with the stated mission and goals. Along with this alignment comes a need to study and understand how students learn. Quality leadership is predicated on an understanding of Deming's system of profound knowledge. Profound knowledge holds the key to unlocking the secret of quality for teachers and other leaders. Often a lack of understanding of Profound Knowledge is what is missing from leaders who attempt to build quality into their organizations only to have the organization fail.

PROFOUND KNOWLEDGE

Deming's system of profound knowledge appears simplistic. It states that in order to bring Quality Management principles and processes into the classroom the instructor must have a thorough understanding of four concepts: 1) an appreciation for a system, 2) statistical theory, 3) theory of knowledge, and 4) psychology. Let's examine each of these points briefly.

Appreciation for a system

Education is a system with many sub-systems and processes within the sub-systems. For example the school is one large system, and each level (school, department, program, course) represents a sub-system within the larger system. Within each system, numerous processes exist. The quality experts agree that anywhere from 85-90 percent of all problems within an organization are due to faulty processes and systems. Teachers control the system and, therefore, must be responsible for taking the lead in changing it. Teachers are managers of their course. It is imperative, therefore, that teachers **understand that by adopting a system's view, they must focus on improving processes and not results.**

You may be saying, "In my department I am evaluated on results and, therefore, must exert all my energy to covering the content and making certain the students learn." Don't confuse the issues of process improvement with student achievement. Inspection at the end (such as a test at the end of an academic term) is simply too late to discover there was a process flaw that kept everyone from being successful. Quality must be built into every process before high-quality results can follow. Quality classrooms focus more on process improvement while setting high-quality expectations. Results do follow.

ΔΔΔΔΔΔΔΔΔ

Training Activity

Here is an activity to help you get the power of processes and systems across to your students. We have used it to demonstrate these concepts from first-grade students to medical students and administrators.

Materials:

1 packet of four, 25-piece Puzzle Patch Puzzles © for ages 3-7. The packet can be purchased at Wal-Mart, K-Mart, etc. It is important that you purchase the packet rather than four separate puzzles as the four within a packet appear to be cut from a similar dye, and one of the frames can **almost** be interchanged with one or two of the others. You'll have to experiment with the puzzles beforehand. Label the puzzles Group 1 through Group 4 respectively.

Four stop watches.

Four 6.5 x 9.5 envelopes marked Group 1 through Group 3 respectively.

Procedure:

1. Ask the students to study each of the four puzzles.
2. After a few minutes ask them to give the puzzles to you. At this point break down the puzzles in front of them (at a distance far enough away that they cannot see the markings on the envelopes). Place two of the puzzles in their appropriately labeled envelopes (Group 1 pieces in Group 1-labeled envelope and Group 3 pieces in the Group 3 envelope). Then interchange the other two by putting

Group 2 pieces in the Group 4-labeled envelope, and Group 4 pieces in the Group 2-labeled envelope.
3. Establish 4 separate groups in each corner of the room. Assign 3 to 6 students per group.
4. Give a puzzle frame and a stop watch to each group.
5. Post or read the following:
   • The **purpose** (Classroom Mission) of this experiment is to see if you understand the concepts of **Continuous Quality Improvement principles** so that you can constantly **improve yourself, get a job and contribute to society.**
   • The **goal** is to work together as a team to complete **puzzles** in a timely fashion.
6. Ask them to discuss how they are going to approach the project and who will do the timing. Then when each group is ready, give its members the envelope (containing the pieces) that is marked to match the number on their puzzle. Tell the timer that s/he is to start timing when the envelope is opened and to stop the timing when the quality puzzle is completed. Then holler out **begin!**

Results and Discussion:

Usually, the students work together as four separate groups and not as a team as was instructed to meet the goal stated above. As a result, the two puzzles whose frames and pieces matched will be completed quickly and the product will be of high quality. The other two puzzles whose pieces did not quite exactly match the frame will not only be of poorer quality, but they will have taken substantially more time to "complete" as well. The discussion should revolve around the processes (pieces) and systems (frames) and people (students). No matter how hard the students worked with the processes that did not match the system, they could not do quality work. By the same token, those students who had the correct processes and system were able to accomplish similar results in much less time since they did not have to do rework. With college students, we inquire as to why they worked as four separate groups when the instructions were clearly to work as a team to complete **puzzles**, not puzzle. We have received a wide variety of interesting responses.

ΔΔΔΔΔΔΔΔΔ

A training activity as described above is one method to educate students about processes and systems. You can also demonstrate the power of processes and systems by using Flow Charts regularly to show how your classroom teaching and learning systems interact. One example follows, but we recommend that you refer to the appendix for more specifics on flow charting and for additional examples.

A Flow Chart is a common business tool that clearly demonstrates how one element in a system connects to another and how all aspects of the system are interrelated. As with any universal visual tool, flow charting has standardized symbols. One very functional and simple set of standards were described by Myron Tribus (1989). They are shown in Figure 2.1.

Figure 2.1: Standardized symbols for flow charting.

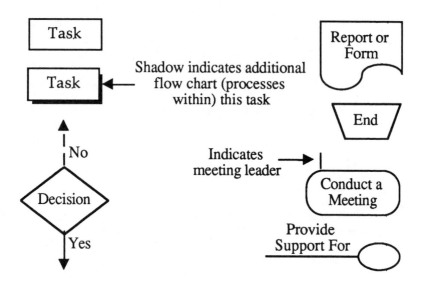

Let's create a Flow Chart for a mythical teacher, Mr. Waldon. The following are examples of flow charts showing the teaching/learning system of Mr. Waldon's approach to teaching ninth-grade students vocabulary before and after learning about the positive affect of teaming (Source: Byrnes, Cornesky, and Byrnes. 1992).

Figure 2.2:
Initial flow chart of Mr. Waldon's spelling
and vocabulary-testing system.

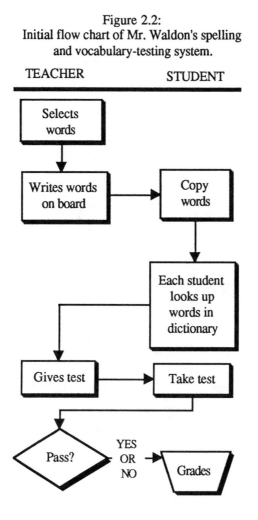

Figure 2.3:
Revised flow chart of Mr. Waldon's spelling and vocabulary-testing system.

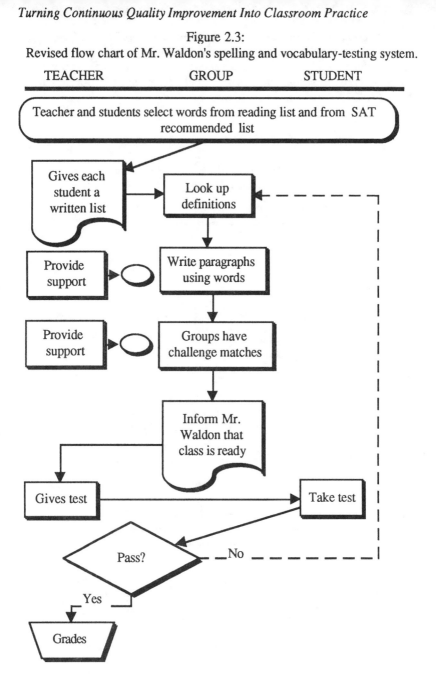

You can see the difference. The new system, empowering the students, will increase learning.

Statistical theory

Quality experts agree that the use of data is critical. Without it, we simply would not know what action to take for process change. When data is not used, we run the risk of tampering with processes while not knowing the real problem(s).

In many respects, the failure to use statistics and meaningful data when working within a system that deals with people has led to a decline in the existing teaching/learning process .

Understanding statistical theory means that you must understand the concept of variation. You should learn what makes a system stable and unstable. You should know the "common causes" of variation (and how they are often mistaken as "special-cause" variation), and the special causes of variation (and how they are often mistaken for common-cause variation). You should understand how improper tampering with the system can create bigger and more difficult problems than if you had done nothing.

In education, a fairly common cause of poor learning is student boredom, yet it is often treated as a special cause. Common causes are those things that regularly recur due to normal statistical variation of the system. Student boredom is probably one of the biggest contributors to students' dropping out and/or not passing a course. Still, many educators believe that boredom is the student's problem and not a process problem. As a consequence, no action is taken to collect data, discover root causes and implement an action plan for reducing boredom.

Special-cause variations of why students might be missing your class might include:

- A high absentee rate due to a flu epidemic
- The football team scheduled to play in a championship game
- The first snowfall of the year.

In order to fully understand the processes within the classroom, you will have to become familiar with simple statistical tools. They are not difficult to learn or understand. Even the various control charts can be made very easily through the use of computer software. An example of a np-control chart measuring the variation in the number of students not turning in homework assignments in an algebra class over a 30-day period is shown in Figure 2.4. The construction and interpretation of control charts are shown in the appendix. Without the data, statistical tools and a clear understanding of how to use them for process improvement, it is unsafe to assume that you can obtain top learning results through any of the classroom processes.

As you can see in Figure 2.4, the "system" was unstable because the "special-cause" variations. The number of students not completing the homework assignments were both above the expected number (UCL—upper control limit), and below the number that was expected (LCL—lower control limit).

The "common-cause" variations are those points between the UCL and LCL.

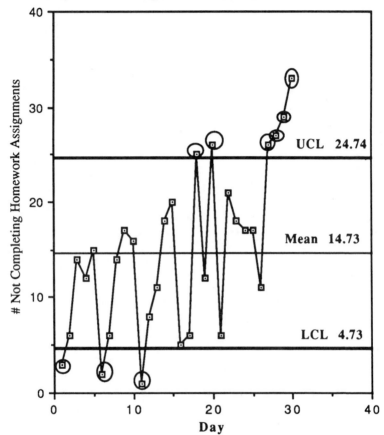

Figure: 2.4: np-control chart showing the number of students not doing homework assignments over 30 days.

With these statistics, we can see when the problem occurred and then link it to the variables affecting the system. Only then can we expect to make changes to improve quality in the classroom.

Theory of knowledge

Theory of knowledge means that teachers understand the impact of change on the system. This places the burden on the teacher to engage in a Plan-Do-Check-Act (PDCA) cycle prior to making any change. Therefore, in thinking about the classroom, we must remember that it is the way each of the processes interacts with the others that creates quality teaching and learning. Teachers who employ coercive tactics, even just with one or two students, alter the learning environment for everyone. Where fear is entrenched, people simply cannot do their best. Classrooms based on fear, ridicule, or humiliation are not places where students maintain a high interest or are eager to take educational risks to optimize their learning.

Psychology

Teachers must understand people and their basic needs: survival, love/respect, power, fun and freedom. Every human behavior seeks to satisfy one or more of these needs. If you don't pay attention to these needs, then neither students nor colleagues will respond in ways that optimize the efficiency and effectiveness of your course and/or department.

Students' needs include power, fun, and freedom. Give yourself another reality check. How much power do the students in your classes have right now? Do they have any decision-making power? If so, who has it— everyone or only some of the students? How much fun do you and the students have in class? How do you define fun? What about freedom? Do students in your class(es) have any freedom or must everyone do the same thing at the same time in the same way?

No one takes pride in doing work that is repetitive, dull or watered down. Students who are engaged in this kind of work view it as drudgery and may even begin to perceive your course as punishment. On the other hand, students who have the opportunity to tackle real life issues in a meaningful way (see Chapter Five), and then report results to an audience (see Chapter 12), will be more likely to take great pride in their work and see the joy of learning. Fun comes in many forms. It does not mean that one has to sit and laugh all day. There is a great deal of fun in knowing that you've accomplished a very difficult skill, or in creating new knowledge and reflecting with wisdom on your work (see Chapter Nine). Joy in learning comes from having fun in the process and knowing that you've accomplished something worthwhile. Pride in workmanship is crucial to optimizing learning.

A basic belief of the psychology category of profound knowledge is that everyone comes to class wanting to do a good job. Do you believe that every student comes to your class wanting to do a good job and that faulty processes keep everyone from being successful? This is what quality classroom teachers believe. We've found this concept to be a difficult one for many to accept.

Motivation of students occurs when:
- They feel respected
- The teacher provides many experiences for decision-making
- The learning environment is free of fear
- Learning experiences are meaningful to students.

Pride in workmanship comes from creating products that are meaningful and have a greater audience than the teacher. Students who are given roles of equal partners with their classmates and teachers will accomplish far more academically than you think possible. Motivation must be internal, rarely external. The carrot-and-stick approach rarely results in optimizing the achievement.

Psychology goes beyond the classroom and requires a wider scope of thinking. Everyone examines quality from at least three different perspectives. Each one is important, and you must learn to recognize the worth of all three. Each asks a different question of the teacher.

1. Does the product of the learning experience meet the specified requirements? (quality by fact)
2. Does the process and/or system produce the product as intended? (quality of process)
3. Are the customer's expectations met? (quality by perception)

Each of these poses an important question for teachers. First, quality by fact. Indeed, does the student's work represent quality and does it meet the specifications? This presupposes that you and the students all have a clear understanding of the specified requirements. This goes for every learning experience the students engage in. In later chapters, we will examine ways to determine this in detail. Second, quality of process. The question is: "Does the process allow every student to achieve the learning outcomes intended or are there process flaws?"

For the moment, let's look at the last issue, quality by perception. Here is where psychology enters the picture and is a major issue in education today. Many people believe that our educational system is sub-standard, including those schools and classrooms where students are doing excellent work (and there are many). In many instances, we have to overcome the negative attitudes or perceptions of these customers. If your customers believe you have an inferior product, then you will have to deal with this as if it were reality, because it is reality for those customers. In education, you must not only build in quality by fact and process, but you must also deal with the quality by perception issue. You cannot ignore it. By the same token, just about every survey of parents in the K-12 educational system believes that their schools are "above average," when, in reality, they are poor, at best.

We suggest that you take a couple of minutes and reflect on the following questions:

*   When is the last time you did a comprehensive survey of your stakeholders (students, other teachers, and employers)? Are you confident that you asked the "right" questions?

*   When are you going to do a survey to determine if your class has quality by fact, of process, and by perception?

The same type of mental exercise extends into personal teaching methods. Recognition and understanding don't always translate into action, so care must be taken to integrate one's personal, preferred teaching style with other teaching styles. Using different teaching styles can be difficult because many of us were reared in an educational system that focused on one method over the others—typically the lecture method.

You can understand the problem clearly by considering the following examples. Imagine a physician who returned from the grave after 100 years and observed an operation. S/he would realize that some sort of healing process was being performed, but s/he would also know that s/he could not take the place of anyone in the room. To further illustrate, imagine a manufacturer who returned after 100 years. S/he would not be able to comprehend the production processes which often involve robotics and statistical process control methods. By the same token, a teacher who returned after 100 years would see little difference in how the students were being taught (with the possible exception of technologies) and s/he would not feel uncomfortable in most classroom settings. Just as times have changed in industry and medicine, teachers must realize the need for change in classroom strategies.

CONTINUOUS QUALITY IMPROVEMENT

Since leadership cannot be sustained without on-going education, you must maintain a high degree of continuous improvement. Continuous improvement comes from reading, attending conferences, seminars, and workshops about quality as well as about your discipline; keeping active in professional organizations; visiting other educational institutions and classrooms; and communicating with your internal and external customers. Engaging in "Total Quality" obligates you to continuously seek out opportunities to provide quality leadership to students and colleagues.

Actually, a quality leader by definition allows CQI principles and processes to permeate every aspect of his or her life. A CQI Teacher seeks ways to influence others to adopt quality standards. Some obvious ways to do this are through presentations and a willingness to share information and ideas. Another perhaps less obvious way, is to become a better listener. By being an active listener, you send a signal to others of your desire to understand their point of view and their needs. As Stephen R. Covey (1989) says, seek first to understand, then to be understood. Once you know this, it becomes easier to seek agreement through collaboration and agreement on alternative (win-win) solutions.

THE FIRST STEP TO CLASSROOM LEADERSHIP

The first step to classroom leadership is to have your classroom mission statement, goals, and operational definitions clearly defined so that the academic integrity of your course is never in question. This is the subject of the next chapter.

ΔΔΔΔΔΔΔΔΔ

The following is a check sheet to help you implement the CQI Action technique into the classroom.

FACILITATING SYSTEM

Step 1:   You are demonstrating leadership.
- √   Develop a definition of a quality classroom.
- √   Walk-the-Talk about quality.
- √   Understand Deming's system of Profound Knowledge.
- √   Use a variety of teaching styles.
- √   Have a CQI program for yourself and your students.

FACILITATING SYSTEM

CHAPTER THREE: MISSION, GOALS, AND OPERATIONAL DEFINITIONS

If you are going to be successful with CQI, you need to know where you are going and then set goals. The mission, goals, and operational definitions of the class must be absolutely clear.

What's In It For Me?
Upon completing the chapter, you will be able to:
- Establish your course mission statement
- List the benefits of developing personal and student goals for your course
- Identify ways of co-creating the mission, goals, and operational definitions of the course with the students
- Discuss why it is important to align your course mission and goals with those of your school and/or your department.

Let's begin with the basics. With your students, write:
1. A classroom mission statement
2. Quality goals
3. Operational definitions for demonstrating quality goals.

Let's look at each element in turn, starting with the classroom mission statement. What is it? Why do you need one? What do you do with it once you have one?

MISSION STATEMENT
A mission statement essentially defines the purpose of your work. In it, you explain exactly the principles that underline your classroom activities. You need one as a map to guide you toward your quality destination. It gives you and your students a clear view at a very fundamental level of what the basic goals and academic integrity of your class are, and it should reflect a shared vision between your institution, you, and your students. Teachers without a clear mission statement have little or no idea of their goals in either the short or long term.

The concept of a mission statement is supported by the best selling book by Covey, *The 7 Habits of Highly Effective People*. Covey found that the first three habits of highly effective people are:
1. **Be Proactive**
2. **Begin with the End in Mind**
3. **Put first things first**

Covey's first three habits are closely aligned with Deming's (1982) first point: **Create a constancy of purpose toward improvement of product and service.**

As you begin your CQI journey, you should **be proactive** by having a firmly established view of your course mission. Then each of your class meetings can **begin with the end in mind.** Knowing were you are going will force you to have adopted short- and long-range plans to implement your mission statement and to improve upon it through years of "research and development." You will, in effect, be **putting first things first.**

Without having a constancy of purpose clearly evident through a clearly defined mission statement and a plan to implement it, you will be driven by reactions to immediate concerns. In addition, you will have the tendency to move in a random fashion in order to satisfy any immediate needs rather than to resolve the root problem causing the concern.

Developing a mission is not as easy as it may seem. If your mission is to teach world geography, you may feel that you are being successful in spite of the fact that 50 percent of your students are not learning. If no one learns, however, you can't claim to have taught. Remember, schools don't exist for teachers to teach, but for students to learn.

Teachers must focus away from teaching and towards learning. Quality teachers lead students and facilitate the learning process. The interaction between teacher and learner must be shifted so more responsibility for learning is placed on the student, and more facilitating is done by the teacher.

Teachers should take an initial leadership role in creating the learning environment. As the course progresses, however, teachers should gradually increase the leadership responsibilities of **all** students. Students should become partners in co-creating the learning experiences and in establishing a learning environment where everyone can succeed. As the teacher exerts less control, s/he should mentor students to become more active in their own learning.

Let's assume the teacher has carefully reflected and determined his/her classroom mission to be:

> To teach about the world so all students can understand how the regional, national, and international economies are related in order for the students to advance our society.

This mission statement can be improved dramatically by the addition of another phrase which would inform the student "what's in it for them." Most great mission statements answers the "why" question at least three times. In the above mission statement, the "why" question is answered twice. Let's add in a third "why" answer.

> To facilitate learning about the world (**WHY?**) so all students can understand how the regional, national, and international economies are related (**WHY?**) in order for the students to advance our society (**WHY?**) *and lead productive lives.*

Now, this is a much better mission statement since **learning** replaces teaching as the primary purpose. In addition, the reasons why the learning is important are stated, including the answer to the question of "what's in it for me?"

Now construct your own classroom mission statement.

My Classroom Mission Statement is:

Is your classroom mission statement aligned with the institutional mission?

Once you have carefully written your mission statement and reflected upon it, you should consider how it might be improved. You should record how you put "first things first"—the important and urgent activities you do to support your mission statement, and the relatively unimportant and not urgent things you do which impede your mission statement. What are your opportunities for improvement? Place your thoughts and observations into the following table.

Things I do to enhance my mission statement are:

Actions I will take to ensure that I continue to do these things:

Things I do that impede my mission statement are:

Actions I will take to overcome these things:

The mission statement sets you on your quality journey; it does not give you a way to determine when you have achieved any results. That's where quality goals come in. They are the second requirement for a CQI classroom and reflect "terminal competencies," the expected results students should achieve before they leave your class. You develop them to set a standard by which you will judge your success.

QUALITY GOALS

Create quality goals for each of your classes and for each unit of study within your course by spelling out what students should have learned or the skills they should have mastered by the time your class ends.

This is not a solitary exercise. You should discuss these goals with other people (called "stakeholders" in CQI jargon) who are affected by your class. That would include potential employers as well as instructors who will get your students after they leave your class. Students must be part of the process, too. After all, they have a major stake in the class. Believe it or not, the students will actually add goals. Rarely will they request that you remove one.

Goal writing should be done in teams, with regular double-checks following a plan-do-check-act (PDCA) cycle (also known as the plan-do-study-act (PDSA) cycle) described in Chapter 9. Students commonly find this exercise challenging and enjoyable.

The goals are designed to be **measurable**, to give you a clear picture whether or not you achieved them. In context of business, they are akin to "product specifications." They must be met before either a student is assumed to have mastered the competencies and/or skills of your course. As students understand this concept, they also learn that quality factors are product specifications for each learning experience. These are the fundamentals that will ultimately determine whether or not they have achieved quality. Students will quickly learn that the only acceptable outcome of any learning experience is quality.

OPERATIONAL DEFINITIONS

Now that you've written your mission statement and created quality goals, you need to generate operational definitions for demonstrating your quality goals. An operational definition is a very precise statement of what is expected to meet a quality goal and is a prerequisite for collecting data and evaluating results. Operational definitions are appropriate for every process or system that is to be improved as well as for every goal to be obtained. Each operational definition has to be accepted by the teacher and students, but operational definitions must be flexible enough to be changed if the classroom process, system, or a quality goal is changed. Each operational definition should have student input as how they expect to demonstrate a competency.

These definitions are important because, if they are not followed carefully, then the results will be less than the best. The best example that we've heard was from a seminar given by Margaret Byrnes who stated that the operational definition is like the recipe for meeting the goal of baking the world's best cake.

OTHER SUGGESTIONS

You have now been introduced to the first three steps on the CQI journey. These three elements—mission statement, goals and operational definition—actually represent a far wider circle of quality tools.

As you go through the process of creating these elements, your students will be introduced to such tools as teaming, PDCA cycle and variation. They will learn about quality goals which are the course competencies. And they will set operational definitions by pinpointing steps that have to be taken and/or the things that have to transpire to demonstrate that the quality factors have been obtained. Consequently, students will be able to start your class learning about quality and CQI principles, in addition to the content of your course, regardless of the subject. This sets the stage for a quality learning experience.

You can stress the value of these procedures—most of which will be alien to your students (and yourself)—by looking toward Covey's findings. The author states (p. 151) that important matters have to do with results. *If something is important, it contributes to your mission, your values, your high-priority goals.* If you don't have a clear idea of your classroom mission, goals, and the results you would like to have your students achieve under your leadership, you will react to what seem like **urgent** matters, including some that are actually unimportant.

Once you have completed these tasks, you have a clear guide to move further along your quality path. You also have something to compare to: a self-improvement program that will help you reduce the behaviors that impede progress towards your mission and increase the supporting behaviors. By comparing your activities with your mission statement, goals and operational definitions, you can reduce any behavior that doesn't help you move the students toward your quality destination. Just as you may occasionally need help to align your progress towards your mission, so will your students. Be patient with yourself and with each student.

You now have to shift beyond the confines of your classroom. To complete your initial phase, familiarize yourself with the terminal course competencies that are expected by your colleagues. After all, your course is part of a curriculum that was (or should have been) designed by faculty members who considered the needs and requirements of internal and external customers.

That information is the final element for creating terminal competencies for your course and to determine how best your students can achieve and demonstrate the mastery of those competencies.

We recommend that the terminal competencies of your course be displayed prominently in the classroom and in the class syllabus. The purpose of all this is to impress upon you and your students the importance of the terminal competencies, especially in terms of your mission and hopefully, the way work is assessed. It is far too easy to lose sight of the required terminal competencies. Of course, CQI teachers view terminal competencies as minimal standards and never as ultimate goals.

Posting the competencies help students keep abreast of expectations. They can see for themselves where they are exceeding expectations and where they are falling behind. That relieves you of the burden of threatening any student who is not living up to expectations and developing ways of assisting them.

When students co-create the goals and the way they will learn, you will discover that competencies can be reached in ways you have not thought of. This beautiful blend is the result of students' becoming very highly motivated. The teacher's job becomes much easier, since students become focused. Of course, there is never enough time for you to accomplish everything that you would like to do during the term. Just resign yourself to that fact, especially if the students want to do additional work on a project or take another direction in solving a problem.

With each learning experience, you and students together determine which competencies will be achieved when the experience is finished. It may take some time for you to put all the additional competencies on a chart, but the time is well spent since students will be able to keep track of their own progress.

While we recommend tracking competencies, we remind you that the focus of the classroom experiences must remain on processes and not on the competencies. Through the co-creation of learning experiences, learning can become such a joy for students and teachers alike that you'll undoubtedly discover that achievements will soar far beyond your original expectations.

That doesn't mean you should consider diluting the process to speed things up or to direct students where they may not want to go. The whole idea behind co-creation of the learning experience is that students and teachers together determine the way(s) competencies will be achieved. There are infinite ways to master the same competencies, so allow yourself and the students to have fun while determining what road to take. Remember, not everyone has to take the same road. Students learn best in different ways, and there may even be instances when you have six or more different ways to achieve the end.

By maintaining a clear constancy of purpose and by having a written mission statement and a set of measurable goals, you will be able to align all classroom activities and to work with students, colleagues, and other stakeholders to build quality into every process within your course. By building quality into each process, you will see a much higher level of achievement for all students. And all of you, together, can enjoy the fun of learning.

ΔΔΔΔΔΔΔΔΔ

The following is a check sheet to help you implement the CQI Action technique into the classroom.

FACILITATING SYSTEM

Step 1:   You are demonstrating leadership.
  √ Develop a definition of a quality classroom.
  √ Walk-the-Talk about quality.
  √ Understand Deming's system of Profound Knowledge.
  √ Use a variety of teaching styles.
  √ Have a CQI program for yourself and your students.

Step 2:   The mission, goals, and operational definitions of your course are absolutely clear.
  √ Establish a course mission statement.
  √ Develop quality goals for the course.
  √ Co-create mission statement, quality goals and operational definitions with the students.
  √ Align course mission and goals with those of the institution (program/major).

FACILITATING SYSTEM

CHAPTER FOUR: PERTINENT WORK FROM STUDENTS

In the previous chapters, you were introduced to CQI and learned why you must lead your students into a quality environment. This chapter will explore ways to create teams to accomplish your quality goals.

That naturally leads to questions about what is the value of teamwork? What is the relationship of teams to CQI? How can you set them up, get them to function properly and guide them to achieve optimum results? How do you demonstrate that teams do improve learning? How do you obtain necessary feedback?

What's In It For Me?

Upon completing the chapter, you will be able to:

- Break down barriers between you and your students
- Understand why it is important to have the students co-create the learning experience
- Recognize the importance of teamwork in problem solving and decision making
- Understand why it is better to create interdisciplinary learning activities
- Recognize the importance of reverse feedback for improving the teaching system
- Appreciate the functions of quality classroom teams
- Understand the difference between cooperative learning and collaborative learning.

WHY TEAMS?

CQI is based on teamwork. That's because classwork can be completed more completely and with a higher retention level through the existence of teams that flow from student desire and student concerns. From the beginning, the work is infused with student choice, design, revision, execution, reflection and evaluation. You are responsible for assessing and ministering to your students' developmental needs, not demanding and lecturing.

Most problems that arise during classroom activities are solved in collaboration with students. When a student asks, "Here's a situation that just came up. I don't know what to do about it. What should I do?" the teacher turns the question back to the class to wrestle with and solve, rather than simply answering it. Students are trusted continually, and all are led to the point where they welcome responsibility.

DAY 1: FORM TEAMS AND BREAK DOWN BARRIERS

To achieve a high level of success, you need to start as soon as your class meets for the first time. Read them the mission statement you have already developed. Then, start working with the students to refine your mission statement so they can understand and "buy into" your goals.

This essentially answers the **why** question for students. Often, students don't know why they have to learn something. If students don't know the answer to the **why** question, they frequently will not be eager participants. Some students may be reluctant learners or even unmotivated. However, just the opposite is generally true. Students who know the relevance or the **why** of any learning experience can become internally motivated learners.

Some teachers have a tendency to answer the **why** question by responding with some version of "you'll need to know this when you graduate." In colleges, this may work for students who have to take a national exam in order to practice their profession, such as nurses. That rarely works for other students, especially high school students who need more immediate pay-off.

It usually stuns students when teachers ask them questions like, "Why are you taking this class?" However, the responses you'll get will tell you a great deal about the way you'll need to work with the class and even with certain students. In response to the question: why are you here? a teacher may get a range of answers from:

- My parents made me go to school
- So I can get good grades and go to college or medical school
- So I can get an 'A'
- Because I want a degree
- Because I want to get a good job.

Obviously, you'll want to continue asking **why** until students respond with something about learning. Once they realize they are there to learn, your motivational battles are over. As you know, you cannot motivate students to do anything they don't want to do. To get students beyond the range of answers listed above, you'll want to ask "why" to each of their responses. For instance, if the original answer is "So I can get an 'A'," ask why do you want/need an 'A'?

One effective way of getting students to begin the buy-in process is simply to ask them to participate. Give a verbal invitation. For reluctant students, you may wish to work through a classmate to make additional contact. Either way, you'll need to make sure that everyone knows:

- The potential benefits
- What's in it for them and for the class
- The various connections and expertise that would be available in a team
- The commitment that will be required if they are part of the team.

The quality classroom teams provide insights and suggestions for students and teacher, they administer classroom surveys, they focus on process improvement, and they implement many of their own suggestions (Laugher, 1992). They do not dictate course content nor should the teacher always equate "the customer is always right" mentality with the student.

When establishing teams, you should talk about the concept of teaming with the students. You are setting the stage for the entire academic term by letting the students know that each of them is vital to the group and that each is important and has special gifts and skills that others do not have. Include yourself in this discussion as you are a part of this team effort. Set a warm, friendly, classroom climate right away.

Engage the students in conversation about teams—what makes a great team, what makes a poor team, etc. Draw examples from baseball, football, basketball, debate, theater performances, etc. Most students can identify or have some ideas about teamwork. From the questions and examples that arise, you can easily stimulate discussion about what it takes to have a great team.

Using quality classroom teams also can be difficult and time consuming. But you can increase the success of the teams by:

- Making yourself a part of the team
- Providing a fast feedback mechanism for the quality teams
- Being involved in quality teams and awakening in the students a sense of responsibility for their own learning.

Teamwork is a great teaching strategy, but it is not a panacea. It comes with problems, just as with any teaching method. Your students should also be informed that teaming has the potential to produce problems—but we suggest that you minimize the negative aspects about teaming and inform them that as problems arise, you and the class will handle them together.

More traditional teachers become uncomfortable when problems appear within the classroom. However, by focusing on the process rather than the outcome, the entire class can come together to resolve almost any problem. Generally, when students are encouraged to resolve their own problems, the result is far superior and more long-lasting than if problems are resolved from other sources. This is an important point for CQI teachers and one that requires the belief that all students want to do a good job, but that the system keeps them (and the teacher) from being successful. (Of course, this is not always true.)

One of the problems that is constantly brought out by the students is the "lack of communication" between team members. We suggest that you acknowledge this potential problem by pointing out that when two people communicate, two communication pathways exist: one from person A who communicates to person B; and the second from person B who communicates to person A. However, when three people communicate, six pathways exist as shown in Figure 4.0.

Figure 4.0: The communication pathways when three people are involved.

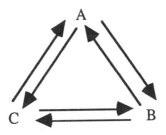

Then, to emphasize the importance of teamwork and communication, we suggest you introduce the formula for the number of pathways which is: $N(N-1)$. Therefore, when three people are in a group, they will have $3(3-1) = 3(2)$ or 6 communication pathways. A team of nine people will have $9(8)$ or 72 communication pathways. So a team of nine people is more likely to have communication problems than a team of two or three; however, the students must be aware that in the real world, company teams of nine people are not unusual.

One approach to teaming is to share a problem-solving model with the students. This means that each team understands that (just like in the real world) there may be times when people don't communicate properly and the job isn't getting done. In this case, as in all others, the group has to take responsibility for resolving any problems. Thus, the teacher's role changes from boss-manager to mentor and facilitator. Students can and should be responsible for working through most classroom problems.

One way to approach this is to educate students about one of the many problem-solving models. One possible plan-do-study-act (PDSA) model might very well consist of the following steps:

Step 1: A problem is identified by either the teacher or someone in the class.

Step 2: A convener is chosen to select a team to address the problem.

Step 3: A meeting is held.

Step 4: The problem is clearly stated.

Step 5: Facts are gathered and studied.

Step 6: Solutions are suggested.

Step 7: Consequences of each solution are considered.

Step 8: Decision for change is made.

Step 9: Change is implemented and the results are recorded and studied.

Classes which are taught and regularly practice something like this PDSA model are more successful at staying focused on the task and getting the "job" done with minimal problems. These are classrooms where students function quite nicely while the teacher is working with an individual or another team. The students do not require constant supervision. In fact, the more students practice their own problem solving, the more empowered they become, leading to greater self-confidence and sense of responsibility for their own behavior.

Another way to engage students as problem solvers while working in teams is to include the use of quality improvement tools shown in Table 4.0 and described in the appendix.

Table 4.0: Several extremely useful Continuous Quality Improvement tools to identify and rank problem "processes" and/or "systems" in classrooms. All of these tools are fully explained in the appendix.

Affinity Diagram
- Used to examine complex and/or hard to understand problems
- Used to build team consensus
- Results can be further analyzed by a **Relations Diagram**

Cause and Effect Diagram (Fishbones)
- Used to identify **root causes** of a problem
- Used to draw out many ideas and/or opinions about the causes

Flow Charts
- Give a picture of the processes in the system

Force Field Analysis
- Used when changing the system might be difficult and/or complex

Histogram
- A bar graph of data which displays information about the data set and shape
- Can be used to predict the stability in the system

Nominal Group Process
- A structured process to help groups make decisions
- Useful in choosing a problem to work on
- Used to build team consensus
- Used to draw out many ideas and/or opinions about the causes

Pareto Diagram
- Bar chart that ranks data by categories
- Used to show that a few items contribute greatly to over-all problem(s)
- Helps teams identify which processes/systems to direct their efforts

Relations Diagram
- Helps teams analyze the cause-and-effect relationships between complex issues
- Directs teams to the **root** causes of a problem

Systematic Diagram
- Used when a broad task or goal becomes the focus of a team's work
- Often used after an **Affinity Diagram** and/or **Relations Diagram**
- Used when the action plan needed to accomplish the goal or the task is complex

---

For example, Mr. Lake, a chemistry teacher in a Florida community college, was unhappy with the quality of laboratory reports. He briefly explained the **Cause and Effect Diagram** (CED) and how it might be useful to get at the root cause(s) of the problem. After describing the problem on a CED and positing it and notes in the chemistry laboratory, he obtained the following comments from the students and other chemistry faculty members (see Figure 4.1).

Figure 4.1: A Cause-and-Effect Diagram showing the perceptions of Mr. Lake's students as to why they are doing so poorly in chemistry lab.

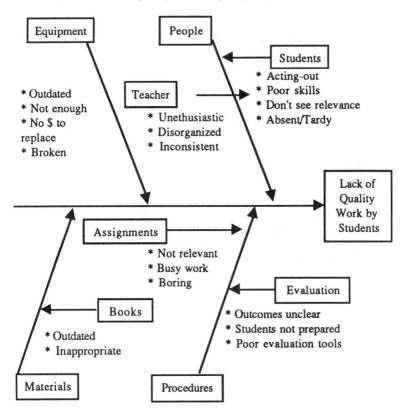

Armed with this information, Mr. Lake formed a classroom quality team to address the "procedures" category and eventually resolved his concerns.

The process also works on a wider scale. At Samford University in Birmingham, Alabama, Kathy Baugher has had enormous success teaching student teams to work with instructors to continuously improve teaching and learning. Students from quality teams help instructors make changes in their courses that enable more students to comprehend the material being covered. Baugher has published a manual entitled LEARN (Baugher, 1992) that guides student team members to (1) Locate an opportunity for improvement, (2) Establish a team, (3) Assess the current process, (4) Research causes, and (5) Nominate a solution. In contrast to traditional course evaluations that are given at the end of a class and which furnish generic information for use in future classes, student teams provide continuous evaluation throughout the class that can assist the instructor in improving learning opportunities for current students.

At Delaware County Community College (DCCC) in Media, Pennsylvania, Mary Ann Heverly has reported excellent results with faculty using the LEARN model (1994, Personal Communication; Contact Mary Ann Heverly, director of Institutional Research, Delaware County Community College, 901 S. Media Line Road, Media, PA 19063-1094; PH: 610-359-5138; fax: 610-359-5343; E-Mail: mheverly@dccc.edu

At DCCC, a major initiative was launched to support CQI efforts in the classroom using the LEARN model. The steps in the model take the teacher and the student team members through an entire PDCA cycle, and the process forces the students to collect data from the entire class and not just from a small, vocal, possibly nonrepresentative segment of the class.

The student team uses brainstorming to identify characteristics that may be interfering with student learning. Then they develop a survey based on the input. The data gathered are used to plan changes to improve classroom processes. Noteworthy is the fact that the LEARN cycle begins early in the semester so currently enrolled students actually experience the benefits.

Some positive results reported by the faculty were:
- Students take an active role in analyzing the teaching process and how it affects them
- Students became more responsible for their learning
- There was a greater cohesiveness among the students
- There was evidence of improved learning.

Some negative results reported by the faculty:
- Finding time to set up the various phases of LEARN
- Some faculty members had difficulty of adapting the model to their class
- Some faculty reported that it was difficult to "cover" the curriculum while integrating LEARN
- Some faculty had difficulty in sharing power with the students.

Regardless of the approach you take, teams do work. The following histograms (Figures 4.2 and 4.3) show the changes that occurred in the grading patterns when football players studied as individuals and when they studied as a group (team) prior to taking tests in a science class. Results like these are consistent from grade school to medical school.

Figure 4.2: Histogram showing the distribution of grades for a science class before studying as a team.

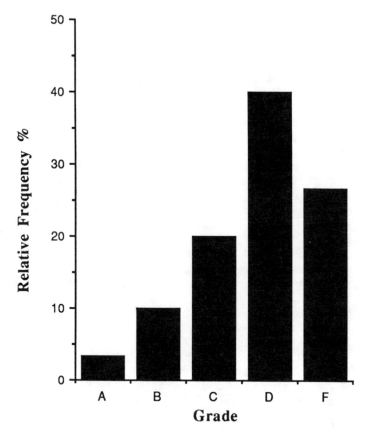

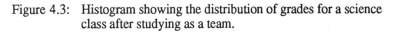

Figure 4.3: Histogram showing the distribution of grades for a science class after studying as a team.

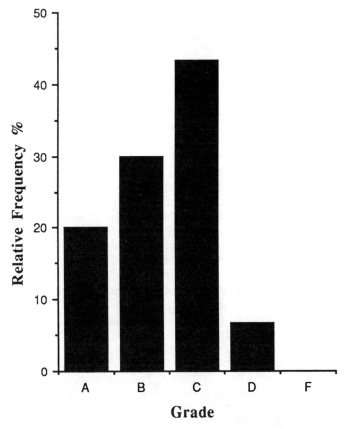

Please refer to the appendix for instructions on how to prepare and interpret histograms.

ΔΔΔΔΔΔΔΔΔ

Training Activity
The Power of Teams 1

Here are two interesting methods to demonstrate the power of teams to improve quality and productivity. We have used them to illustrate teaming concepts from first-grade students to post-graduate students.

Materials:
25-piece Puzzle Patch Puzzles © for ages 3-7.
Stopwatches.

Procedure:
1. Ask the students to team up in pairs. Distribute a puzzle and a stopwatch to each pair. Ask the students to observe their puzzle closely with the understanding that one of the students will reconstruct the puzzle while the other will observe him/her and time the effort.
2. After a few minutes of observation, ask one student in each group to break down the puzzles and to mix up the pieces thoroughly and then reconstruct them while their partner times the effort.
3. Repeat the exercise having the other member of the pair reconstruct the puzzle while his/her partner records the time.
4. Record the time and then construct a Histogram using the relative frequency data and approximately 30 second intervals.
5. Establish four separate groups of 3 to 6 students per team.
6. Give a puzzle and a stopwatch to each group.
7. Ask them to first discuss how they will work together to construct the puzzle as a team. Have them work out their own procedures.
8. After a few minutes, ask the group to break down the puzzles and to mix up the pieces thoroughly and then reconstruct them while one member times the effort.
9. Record the time and then construct a Histogram with the data at approximately 30-second intervals.

Results and Discussion:
The results invariably show a bimodal histogram when each student worked separately—apparently some students have great difficulty in visualizing shapes—while the team data usually shows a symmetrical bell-shaped curve representing a "normal" distribution. Team data also shows that by working together that the results were done more quickly. Question the students as to why these differences occurred and if teaming was really effective. (One thing you will quickly discover is that the students say it was "fun" to work in teams.)

HISTOGRAM #1: Distribution of times to complete puzzle as individuals.

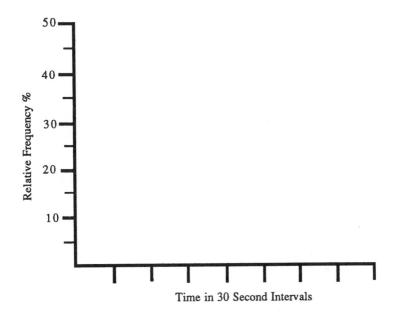

HISTOGRAM #2: Distribution of times to complete puzzle as teams.

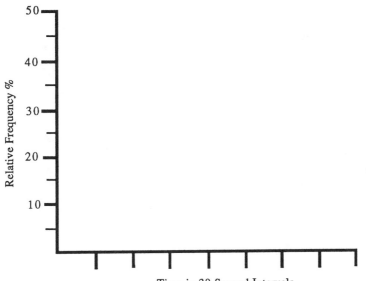

Training Activity
The Power of Teams 2

Materials:
Two decks of cards with all face cards removed.
Stopwatches.

Procedure:
1. Ask the students to team up in groups of 7 or 9. Ask each group to pick a "Leader" and a "Timer." Ask half of the groups to leave the room as this experiment will be done in two different ways.
2. Distribute a stopwatch and a combined set of the two decks which were thoroughly shuffled to each of the groups still in the room. Inform the students that each group has a thoroughly shuffled set of cards that has two decks with all of the face cards removed.
3. Inform the group that they must remain silent while the Leader distributes an equal number of points (an ace counts as 1 point) to each member of the group including him/herself and the Timer. After laying the ground rules, tell them to begin timing the effort. Remember, there is to be no conversation at this point. Record the times to accomplish these efforts.
4. Ask the second group to enter the room and then repeat this exercise with the following modification: **Ask the group to work as a team** and distribute an equal number of points to every member of their team including the Leader and Timer. Record the results. Permit the first group to observe the others working, laughing, and talking as they go about their task.

Results and Discussion:
The results invariably show that teaming was more effective (done quicker) and a lot more fun.

ΔΔΔΔΔΔΔΔ

Research has shown a positive relationship between the quality of the decision and the quality of interaction between the members of the team. This direct relationship is shown in Figure 4.4.

FIGURE 4.4

RELATIONSHIP BETWEEN THE QUALITY OF THE DECISION AND THE QUALITY OF INTERACTION

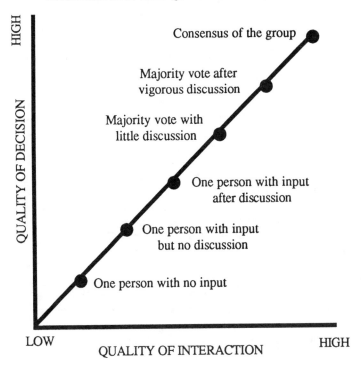

More evidence of the value of teams has turned up in recent years. The Graduate School of Business at the University of Chicago started to implement CQI in certain classrooms in 1989. In 1991, the school started a course **The Laboratory to Achieve Organizational Excellence: Improvement of Teaching, Curriculum and Research**. Faculty experimented with different techniques to improve their teaching. Students acted as consultants and helped the faculty participants (Bemowski, Baugher, 1991). During the first year, 11 faculty members worked with students and student teams on improving their courses (Bateman and Roberts, 1993).

COOPERATIVE AND COLLABORATIVE LEARNING
The concept of teams spills over into another area of education, **cooperative** and **collaborative learning**. The terms are often used interchangeably, but there is a significant difference. Cooperative learning is

53

noncompetitive learning in which the students are rewarded for working on teams to accomplish a common goal or project and where the traditional authority structure is maintained. Collaborative learning is always cooperative learning, but the student is expected to challenge the traditional authority structure and to become more of a critical thinker. Cooperative learning is possible in the K-12 system, whereas collaborative learning is probably best implemented in higher education.

Cooperative learning links teamwork to pertinence. As a teacher, you not only want, but plan to make all of your class work pertinent to the subject. But is it? Or could you enhance the pertinence and the learning experience?

Pertinent work refers to real-life information. It must include learning fundamentals, but its appearance in the classroom can be negotiated and collaboratively determined by students and teachers. For example, when teaching "Environmental Science" to freshman biology majors, it might be better if you create a joint venture with teachers in speech, English, and, perhaps, economics, so that these students could **speak** on environmental issues, **write** on environmental issues, and measure the impact **economically** on environmental issues. This would mean, however, that the students and the teachers would have to coordinate their teaching schedules if such a cooperative learning experience were to be established. This concept is known as "Learning Communities," and it will be the wave of the future as students learn more and retain more.

One successful adventure of pertinent work occurred in the laboratory science courses at California State University in Bakersfield. Under the leadership of Jack Coash, dean of Natural Sciences and Mathematics, "Inquiry Learning" was introduced under a National Science Foundation grant. In the project, teams of students regularly determine a laboratory project that they wanted to do over the semester. The projects are pertinent to their major or interests. For example, in the "General Microbiology" course, a group of nursing students chose to examine the quantity of air-borne bacteria in hospital rooms before and during the making of beds. Another group of premedical students tested the antibacterial effectiveness of various mouthwashes by taking cultures before and after gargling for various periods of time. A group of environmental science majors determined the number of coliform bacteria in various streams as a function of rain and temperature.

One of our favorites was a group of art majors who wanted to "paint" the soil. They permeated canvases with various types of selective microbiological media and then sprinkled various soil samples over the canvas. They incubated the canvases in their bathrooms under high humidity conditions. The growth consisted of various molds and bacteria of various colors—each was unique. They preserved their "art" with hair spray and displayed it at a regional art show where they won first prize. Regardless of their projects, all groups had to learn the basics of sterile techniques, plate counts, dilutions, use of the microscopes, staining, preparation of selective media, etc., prior to getting their project approved by the professor.

In preparing some kind of classroom experience that will encompass interdisciplinary activities and relate directly to the specified competency of your course, your students will need to know what is expected of them.

- **Why are we doing this?** The reason must be compelling for everyone, otherwise they will not "buy in" and will resist teaming efforts. We recommend that the goals for each learning experience be written collaboratively by students and teacher, and posted in the classroom. The goals can also be written with the quality factors and operational definitions.

- **What are the quality factors (goals) we will look for?** Limit the quality factors to the top two or three. Be certain to work with the students so everyone understands that these goals (competencies) will be judged, and that once the students achieve the quality factors, they can move on to other things—but that everyone must reach quality. Here you can emphasize the importance of working together. This will be discussed in greater detail in another chapter. As students progress, a quality factor you might want to routinely include is **cycle time.** How much time will be given to any learning experience? A CQI classroom seeks to continually improve the learning experiences while reducing cycle time. Thus students advance more rapidly in a quality classroom.

- **Create operational definitions on how we will assess our results?** If you were going to tell someone specifically how to create "an excellent oil painting," what would you say? What are the key elements or ingredients that are necessary to achieve the "best?" Beginning art students will need more guidance than senior art majors. Begin by seeding the list with one or two obvious particulars and then allow the students to come up with others. You'll need to guide them through this, particularly when first starting the Continuous Quality Improvement process. If the students don't come up with all the fundamentals (or learning objectives), then you should add to the list by stating that you are a part of the group, too. For that reason, you are adding these elements. Once this is fully developed and understood by all, post the operational definitions along with the quality factors and mission statement.

For each process that was targeted for improvement, complete the following form.

PROCESS IMPROVEMENT GUIDE

Quality Improvement Team Leader: _____

Date: _____

Mission:
Quality Factors (What are the goals?):
Operational Definitions (What is necessary to achieve the Quality Factors?):

ELIMINATE CONFUSION

Prior to beginning any learning experience then, students are given a copy of the Mission, Quality Goals and Operational Definitions. This **eliminates any confusion** that might arise about the assignment or requirements.

By reaching into your own experiences, you might be able to plant the seeds of creativity for learning experiences. Begin with something exciting and not too complex, but that everyone can relate to.

Wouldn't it be fascinating to study the economics of either an environmental issue or a health issue and how it might affect the local economy as well as the state, region, or national economies?

The learning outcomes that can be generated from the question(s) are limitless. Imagine the reading, writing, research, speaking, listening skills involved. Imagine the data gathering, charting and graphing, statistical analysis and other mathematical skills that can be learned. Imagine the scientific discovery methods, problem solving, critical thinking, and new knowledge possibilities. Students majoring in mass media or communications can create brochures, write newspaper articles, hold press conferences, lobby their state and national legislators, and testify before public groups. They may even want to team up with a national organization interested in saving the planet. With an interdisciplinary approach, students can learn a phenomenal amount, maintain a high degree of motivation, achieve far beyond their expectations, and maybe most importantly, will feel empowered that they've done something significant; that the assignment was not merely "work" from a textbook, but truly significant.

When an assignment is completed, and the quality factors are met, students and teachers debrief. Here is one example of a simple debriefing form after a learning experience.

How Helpful Were These Resources?

Class _____   Semester _____
Period _____   Project _____

For this competency, we used the following resources:
    Lecture   Field Trip
    Textbooks   Video
    Library books   Computers
    Discussion   Other
    Newspaper - Magazine Articles

Please rate each on how much it helped you complete the learning experience:
    E = excellent, couldn't have completed it without it.
    G = good; was a big help
    O = okay; didn't help much
    W = waste of time; was no help whatsoever

Method	RATING			
	E	G	O	W
Lecture				
Textbooks				
Library Books				
Discussion				
Articles				
Field Trip				
Video				
Computers				
Other				

What suggestions do you have for improving this learning experience?

When students have completed the debriefing sheet, the quality team or teacher can collate the responses by using the debriefing check sheet. This information can improve all subsequent learning experiences. For example, if 40 percent of all students rated the lectures "okay," while an equal percentage rated them good or excellent, you would want to pursue with the students what was helpful and what wasn't. Many of us identify with our work and become defensive when students offer criticism or make suggestions. We caution you to resist doing that when you ask students to help. If you ask and they are honest, which is what you hope for, don't become defensive. Be grateful for any help that comes. In this case, the lectures may require some alteration to become more effective for all the students.

If, for example, more than 40 percent of students think the textbook is a waste while 45 percent were lukewarm about its worth, you might either want to change textbooks or limit the required reading. Don't ignore what the students have said. They will continue to view you with goodwill as long as they can see that their suggestions are being taken seriously and changes are being made.

Keep the course mission statement in the forefront of your mind throughout these experiences. Remember that every action taken within the classroom should support the mission statement and goals.

Other ways to debrief after any learning experience are discussed in chapter ten. The above method may be helpful to teachers as they proceed on their own continuous improvement journey.

Quality classrooms are distinguishable in several ways. Teachers engage students continuously in co-creating the learning experiences. Work that is assigned has meaning to the students and real-world connections. Each learning experience grows upon the others and results from students and teacher debriefing and analyzing the previous assignment before creating the next.

Teachers in CQI classrooms do not resolve problems in isolation but they work together with students, knowing that the collective wisdom of the group is much greater than their own. Students become empowered, more self-confident, eager life-long learners who care about the class as a whole and are willing to assist others as needed.

Responsibility for learning rests with each student, the teams, and with the class as a whole including the teacher. Everyone contributes to expanding the thinking of the group and works together to create exciting, efficient learning experiences.

Debriefing is really one method of getting feedback from your students. There are other techniques used in conjunction with debriefing which will obtain the necessary information.

FEEDBACK

One of the highly used and successful outcomes by Bateman and Roberts (1993) was in the use of **Reverse Feedback** surveys given at the end of each class period. Typical questions included:
- How much did you get out of today's class?
- What was the most important thing you learned?
- What was the muddiest point?
- Comment briefly on the helpfulness of the reading assignment
- How much did you get out of today's class?
- What one thing can the instructor do to help you?
- What one thing can you do to improve your future learning?

These **fastback** surveys pointed to problems that previously gone undetected and which could easily be cured, such as the writing on the board or the quality of the overheads, or the inclusion of additional case studies. In addition, the instructors provided the students with a fast response to the surveys. This procedure tends to draw the students and faculty closer together in improving the teaching and learning systems. It also required substantial time and effort by the teachers in reading the responses, but the payback in avoidance of rework has been large for both the students and the teacher alike.

There are other ways to obtain information from students than by conducting post-class surveys. The following was adapted from a 1992 report by Laura Vernon, staff writer, Brigham Young University (BYU). After being trained in CQI-like techniques by faculty in a special center, certain faculty and students at BYU have had their teaching and learning systems evaluated by one or more of the following techniques:

1. Faux Student—during the class, a student observer takes notes as if a member of the class and then returns the notes to the teacher.
2. Recorder/Observer—the student observer records in writing what went on in the classroom in terms of time spent on boardwork, questions asked, and small group discussions.
3. Filmmaker—the student observer videotapes the class for the teacher to view privately or with the student observer.
4. Interviewer—the teacher leaves the class while the student observer interviews students to assess how well they are understanding the concepts.
5. Primed Student—the teacher meets with the student observer prior to class to give pointers about what to look for.
6. Student Consultant—the teacher asks the student observer to act as a consultant by noting the class member's receptivity, attentiveness, participation and understanding of a concept.

Here is another, perhaps even more powerful evaluation tool created by John Huntley, professor, Department of English, The University of Iowa. He designed a software program called the **Quality Evaluator** (QE), a HyperCard™ program for Macintosh computers, to help peer groups (students) and the group leader (teacher) evaluate the relative quality of their work. As a result, the QE sensitizes team members to recognize quality in the work they inspect and motivates them to pursue CQI in the work that they do. The tool is dynamite and, in our opinion, can be used constructively in classroom teams from middle school to graduate school.

The QE uses a four-step process:

Step 1: Set Up.

The teacher generates individual QE packets which are then distributed to each member of the team.

Step 2: Inspection, Comment, and Discrimination.

Members of the team review, comment on, and sort out the materials to be evaluated. Items are sorted from a relatively "better" and relatively "worse" compared to relatively "middle." These sorting rules prevent bias, eliminate skewed judgment and underwrite fairness. Members write their comments and judgments in their individual QE stacks, which are then returned to the teacher.

Step 3: Tally, Discrimination, and Report.

The teacher tallies the incoming data, re-balances the group's judgments regarding differences in relative quality, and prepares feedback reports for members of the group.

Step 4: Consider, Interpret, and Confer.

Group members receive their reports and formulate constructive ways to respond to the anonymous perceptions stimulated by having participated in a cycle of peer evaluation.

Of course, feedback simply cements the partnership between you and your students.

ΔΔΔΔΔΔΔΔΔ

Training Activity
The Principles of CQI

Teamwork is a key component of CQI and one which can be used to link up with other elements, as demonstrated through this activity. With it, we can demonstrate the following principles of CQI:

1. Processes and Systems
2. Teaming
3. Customers and Suppliers
4. Quality by Fact, Process, and Perception
5. Management by Fact
6. Complexity
7. Variation.

We have used this activity to demonstrate these concepts with sixth-grade students to MBA faculty and administrators.

Materials:
2 packets of four 25-piece Puzzle Patch Puzzles © for ages 3-7. The packet can be purchased at Wal-Mart, K-Mart, etc. Label the puzzles Group 1 through Group 8 respectively.

Eight stopwatches.

Eight 6.5 x 9.5 envelopes marked Group 1 through Group 8 respectively.

Procedure:
1. Ask the students to divide into groups of 4-5 people.
2. Post the following:
   • The **purpose** (Classroom Mission) of this experiment is to see if you understand the concepts of **Continuous Quality Improvement principles** so that you can constantly **improve yourself, get a job, and contribute to society.**

61

        • The **goal** is to work together as a team to complete puzzles in a timely fashion.

3. Give each group a frame without the pieces of the puzzle and a stopwatch. (You will have broken down the puzzle and will have placed approximately 15 to 20 of the pieces into their appropriately marked envelope, but you will have randomly mixed in pieces from other puzzles. So the Group 1 envelope will contain 15 to 20 pieces of the Group 1 pieces and may contain pieces from the rest of the groups. The students are not to know this.)

4. Ask them to discuss how they are going to approach the project and who will do the timing. Then when each group is ready, give the members the envelope (containing the pieces) that is marked to match the number on their puzzle. Tell the timer that s/he is to start timing when the envelope is opened and to stop the timing when the quality puzzle is completed. Then holler out **begin!**

Results and Discussion:

At first, the students work together as separate groups and not as a team as was instructed to meet the goal, *i.e.* to work together as a team to complete puzzles in a timely fashion. But, someone will notice that they have pieces that belong to another group's puzzle. As a result, people begin to run back and forth (suppliers and customers) and the entire class acts as a team to match the pieces (processes) with the appropriate frame (system). Finally all of the puzzles will be completed and the results will show quality by fact, of process, and by perception. Furthermore, the different times will demonstrate the concepts of complexity and variation. Ask the students to discuss the following principle of CQI:

1. Processes and Systems
2. Teaming
3. Customers and Suppliers
4. Quality by Fact, Process, and Perception
5. Management by Fact
6. Complexity
7. Variation.

ΔΔΔΔΔΔΔΔΔ

WHAT HAVE WE LEARNED BY USING QUALITY TEAMS?
Once you've brought students into your partnership, you'll find they have a higher level of interest, motivation, and achievement results. While the concept of partnering with students may seem foreign, it is in fact a perfect melding together of notions about teaching and learning. That is, we learn best when we believe the task fulfills a need, is achievable even though it may represent a quantum leap, and will be fun. Otherwise, boredom, disinterest, and resistance may result.

If this concept is so obvious, why do so many teachers resist changing the instructional format to include students as full partners? One idea may be that we teach the way we were taught. CQI is gaining an immense following, but few current teachers have been taught through this method. In the next generation, the question may be why anyone preferred the teacher-boss concept.

ΔΔΔΔΔΔΔΔΔ

The following is a check sheet to help you implement the CQI Action technique into the classroom.

FACILITATING SYSTEM

Step 1: You are demonstrating leadership.
- √ Develop a definition of a quality classroom.
- √ Walk-the-Talk about quality.
- √ Understand Deming's system of Profound Knowledge.
- √ Use a variety of teaching styles.
- √ Have a CQI program for yourself and your students.

Step 2: The mission, goals, and operational definitions of your course are absolutely clear.
- √ Establish a course mission statement.
- √ Develop quality goals for the course.
- √ Co-create mission statement, quality goals and operational definitions with the students.
- √ Align course mission and goals with those of the institution (program/major).

Step 3: Most work is pertinent and flows from the students through teams.
- √ Break down barriers on day one by refining the course mission statement with the students.
- √ Have students co-create learning experiences.
- √ Stress the importance of teamwork in problem solving and decision making.
- √ Define quality and what it means.
- √ Create interdisciplinary learning activities.

FACILITATING/LEARNING SYSTEM

CHAPTER FIVE: COURSE CONTENT AND THE REAL WORLD

In the previous chapter, we touched on how to connect classrooms together to liven the learning experiences. In this chapter, we'll investigate that approach much further as we encourage you to tie your course content to the community in addition to the real world.

Upon completing the chapter, you will be able to:

- Demonstrate to students the connections between the course competencies and the real world
- Understand why it is important to have students analyze the learning assignments
- Understand why it is better to implement student suggestions on improving the learning system.

WHAT'S IN IT FOR ME?

As a teacher, you are well aware that students rarely see much of a link between whatever they do in the classroom and their careers. Indeed, education used to be predicated on the concept that students went to school to be educated. Upon graduation, they would find a job in their field of interest and learn their trade there. A 1969 survey founded that most students felt that way.

A similar survey in 1970, after the shootings at Kent State University in the spring, showed a shift in attitude. They were in college, student participants said, to prepare for a career. However, nothing changed in the classroom to reflect this new attitude. As a result, even today, students interviewed about their future rarely say they believe what they are learning in classes has any relationship to their future career plans.

We all know that when presented with something we are not interested in, there is little incentive to learn about it. No matter how much someone tries to convince us, if we cannot imagine that it will add any value to our lives, we simply have a tendency to reject it. Occasionally, someone with great influence over us can persuade us to try something. Sad to say, that is rarely the case between students and their teachers outside of their major. An excellent teacher may be able to persuade some of the students to become involved because s/he works so hard at making "it" interesting. However, far too many teachers become burned out, while far too many students still see no added value to the subject matter. Thus, we are left with teachers viewing students as unmotivated and not interested in learning.

If we carefully examine this phenomena, however, a different picture emerges. It is human nature to continue learning. Humans are very complex. We spend our days learning new skills and abilities that we believe will bring us respect, love, survival, happiness and enjoyment. As we grow and develop, we learn to act and react to outside influences (usually significant others) who give us feedback on our behaviors. The need to love and be loved, and the need for respect, lie at the core of what drives our behavior. Thus, by the time a youngster reaches college, behavior patterns are well established, based on the reaction of parents/guardians, grandparents, siblings, etc.

Students don't lose their enthusiasm for learning—they simply lose their enthusiasm for being told what to learn, when to learn it, how to learn it, and where to learn it. Students who appear unmotivated in class are seldom "vegetables" who sit in front of the television. They are often very active learners outside of class, but are not afforded the opportunity to learn in ways that meet their preferred learning styles. In fact, we penalize students whose learning styles are a mismatch with our preferred teaching style.

The interesting thing about teaching and learning styles is that you may be teaching, but some students are not learning because your approach may seem like a foreign language to them. Sadly, these students get further behind and are often punished for something over which they have no control. These are the students who have so many failures that they are stripped of their self-esteem and drop out of school.

What looks like an unmotivated student may really be a student who may have been denied the right to learn in ways that are interesting and exciting. We believe there is no such thing as an unmotivated learner. Rather, there are many students who are no longer motivated to be compliant in a system that does not recognize their worth as individuals. One glance at students when they are out of class reveals that they are continuously learning. Unfortunately, they are picking up behaviors and ideas that we wish they would avoid.

One thing is very clear: Most students start school eager to learn. By the time they reach the second or third or fourth grade, many say they hate—not dislike, but hate—school. The same is true about college: students come eager and ready to learn, but approximately 50 percent drop out because, for the most part, they dislike school. These students are responding to a system they view as uncaring by not caring themselves, since it probably hurts less that way. Students make a very strong statement that the system has failed by virtue of their behaviors. Absenteeism, tardiness, disrespect for teachers and all forms of authority are all expressions of dissatisfaction with the system.

If you have a sense that students are not responding enthusiastically to an assignment that you have poured your heart and soul into, then the first thing to do is ask the students to analyze the problem for you. Approach it from the perspective that you need their help since you cannot figure out why they are still unresponsive to the wonderful assignments.

ATTACH THE LEARNING EXPERIENCE

It is absolutely crucial to attach every learning experience to the student's world. You can do this three ways:

1. Based on the required and recommended competencies, have students consider ways they would like to learn so you can co-create the

learning experiences together. A competency is a goal; therefore, ask them to define the ways that they would like to demonstrate that they have achieved the goal, *i.e.,* the operational definition. You may have to prepare a computer spreadsheet to make a matrix of the competencies, although this can be done manually. Down the rows list the competencies. In a 15-week semester you could have listed 30 to 50 terminal competencies. Across the column headings are the levels of learning based on Bloom's Taxonomy: knowledge, comprehension, problem-solving, analysis, synthesis, and evaluation. You may have to individualize the matrix for each student. The student should be given the opportunity to document meeting each goal by a variety of ways, including in a portfolio of finished work at each cell in the matrix. You can give a higher grade to those students who master a higher proportion of competencies (goals) at higher levels such as analysis or synthesis.

2. Interact with colleagues and create a cross-curricular approach to learning, thus making each learning experience meaningful to the students. The "Learning Community" approach, in our opinion, has become the best teaching/learning system for the future.

3. Be prepared to answer the **why** question as it relates to why students need to learn your subject matter; be certain to ask students **why** they are in your class.

CQI teachers are much better at engaging in cross-curricular activities ("Learning Communities") than average teachers. It makes sense to approach learning holistically rather than in isolation as it most often is presented.

For example, have you ever encountered a math problem that was just a series of numbers completely unattached to "something?" Think about how limited it is to be teaching this way. Mathematics and the logic underlying it should become a part of all education, not just reserved for the classroom setting. The same can be said for communication skills, science, and even physical education. For example, the Department of Biological Sciences at Carnegie-Mellon University once sponsored a senior seminar called "Anatomy and Physiology in Motion." It was actually Martha Graham performing and explaining modern dance. It was a huge success.

Have you ever considered how much physical education relies on the principles of anatomy, physiology, psychology, mathematics, physics, geometry, and kinesiology? Yet, there are not many attempts to integrate this into most physical education courses. Interestingly, we consider book learning to be academic, but applied knowledge is often viewed as vocational. Without application, what is the lesson to be learned?

Even Shakespeare and the works of other masters can be taught so that there is meaning for each student's life. The classics are the author's way of problem resolution, and classics deal with situations that are still happening to students today. Humanity is still fraught with inequity, and there are abundant examples throughout the great works of literature.

Therefore, whatever your subject matter and your curricular interests, you must work from the supposition that they can be brought to the students' world, can increase their motivation to learn and at the same time decrease drop-out rates.

Doing more of what you've always done will get you more of what you've always gotten. The question is: are all the students being successful and are they all internally motivated to do high-quality work?

You can begin the process of attaching the learning experience with a reluctant group of students through a tool called a **Force Field Analysis**. The tool was developed by Professor Kurt Lewin at the University of Iowa. He received a federal grant to find a way to change meat-buying habits of American housewives during World War II. His research led him to a method of identifying forces that may inhibit the recommended change, increase it or do both. Once the target is identified, a team can study it and use the analysis to make the necessary adjustments.

In a classroom, the entire class can get involved. In that way, the analysis can boost quality while students analyze their study efforts. In addition, it can be used as a tool by individual students to reflect on their habits that can lead to success. By increasing the forces driving the change, or by decreasing the forces inhibiting the change, or both, a task force can recommend actions to bring about the change successfully. Recent studies indicate that you will have more success if you concentrate most of your efforts on decreasing the restraining forces. The following example was taken from Byrnes, Cornesky, and Byrnes (1992).

Case Study

Mrs. Moore heard that thematic units represents an effective teaching technique for second graders. She thought it might work in her class and wanted to consider it. At the same time, she recognized there could be problems with the approach.

So, she formed a task force comprised of parents, colleagues, the principal and herself to study the feasibility of such a change. The group met to discuss the topic and selected a facilitator. The facilitator recorded observations and helped keep the discussion moving. They brainstormed elements they thought would drive the process or restrain it. Each person who generated an idea was asked to explain its importance. No criticism was allowed. In some cases, ideas were combined when they shared similar traits. Others were eliminated or grew in importance during the discussion. Then, the task force listed each point in order of importance. By doing so, the members effectively gave a relative value to each item. It's also possible to assign points to the items.

After the driving and restraining forces were recorded, discussed and prioritized, the task force recommended steps that should be taken in order to effect the desired change. These suggestions were designed to enhance positive points and defuse the negative ones. The full process is outlined in the table below.

FORCE FIELD ANALYSIS

Recommended Change: Infuse Thematic Units into Classroom

Driving Forces (+)	Restraining Forces (−)
	Alters the curriculum (-5)
Students respond enthusiastically to this approach (+1)	Teacher isn't knowledgeable about thematic units (-1)
	Requires the teacher to think about the curriculum differently and plan alternative activities (-4)
Interrelates many aspects of the curriculum (+3)	Teacher lacks the skill to create instructional materials for thematic units (-6)
	No incentive for teachers to try new ideas in their classes (-2)
Accommodates many different learning styles (+2)	School lacks resources for teachers to create materials (-3)

RECOMMENDED ACTIONS:
1. The administration should provide funding for the teacher to attend a workshop on Thematic Units. (This would address the #1, #4, #5, and #6 ranked restraining forces and the #2 and #3 ranked driving forces.)
2. This teacher should be encouraged to implement Thematic Units and present her plans and outcomes before the entire faculty. (This would address the #2 and #5 restraining forces and all driving forces.)
3. Teachers who agree to share their Thematic Unit plans will receive money from the PTO for creating additional instructional materials. (This would address the #2 , #3 and #6 restraining forces and #1 and #3 driving forces.)
4. This teacher can become a lead teacher within the building, training colleagues in the use of Thematic Units. (This would address restraining forces #2,#4, #5, #6.)

Once the various forces were addressed, Mrs. Moore could confidently begin the move into a thematic approach.

This tool works well in conjunction with related CQI tools and shares many of their traits, including brainstorming, selection of a facilitator, team members have an opportunity to discuss without criticism and members are encouraged to build on the ideas of others.

ΔΔΔΔΔΔΔΔ

The following is a check sheet to help you implement the CQI Action technique into the classroom.

FACILITATING SYSTEM

Step 1: You are demonstrating leadership.
- √ Develop a definition of a quality classroom.
- √ Walk-the-Talk about quality.
- √ Understand Deming's system of Profound Knowledge.
- √ Use a variety of teaching styles.
- √ Have a CQI program for yourself and your students.

Step 2: The mission, goals, and operational definitions of your course are absolutely clear.
- √ Establish a course mission statement.
- √ Develop quality goals for the course.
- √ Co-create mission statement, quality goals and operational definitions with the students.
- √ Align course mission and goals with those of the institution (program/major).

Step 3: Most work is pertinent and flows from the students through teams.
- √ Break down barriers on day one by refining the course mission statement with the students.
- √ Have students co-create learning experiences.
- √ Stress the importance of teamwork in problem solving and decision making.
- √ Define quality and what it means.
- √ Create interdisciplinary learning activities.

FACILITATING/LEARNING SYSTEM

Step 4: The course content is connected to the surrounding community and the real world.
- √ Demonstrate the connectedness between work and the real world.
- √ Ask the students to analyze the learning assignments.
- √ Begin CQI tool and team training for the students.
- √ Implement student suggestions on how best to improve the learning system.

LEARNING SYSTEM

CHAPTER SIX: WORKERS AND RESEARCH AND DEVELOPMENT

To this point, you have been leading your students toward quality, building teams and preparing the various statements that guide your class. Now it's time to bring your students more completely into the process. The student should be treated as worker and a member of your research and development department.

WHAT'S IN IT FOR ME?
Upon completing the chapter you will be able to:
- Understand why it is important for the students to have a historical overview of the quality movement
- Discuss and analyze the importance of the Plan-Do-Check-Act (PDCA) cycle in the teaching, learning, and continuous improvement systems.

WHAT'S WRONG WITH TRADITION?
Although you want to create a quality classroom, you are probably still lecturing to your students. Not only is that the traditional way to provide information, it's also the easiest. More progressive teachers do vary their teaching styles and attempt to make the subject matter interesting; however, far too many still adhere to the strict lecture method. In a way, the approach is understandable. Students see you as the provider of information that they are supposed to learn. It's difficult to get them to shift their roles, to become "empowered" to choose their own educational path.

That's particularly true on the college level. Instructors have built-in limitations. They are experts in their fields and become boxed into their particular subject matter. College programs are divided up into various subject areas, isolating instructors and giving them little or no reason to interact with colleagues. Some colleges have included a teaming in the classrooms, but only a few are also using an interdisciplinary approach, called "Learning Communities," to learning. Ironically, even K-12 teachers have successfully introduced thematic units into their classrooms.

The paradigm shift of applying CQI to the teaching and learning systems requires dramatic re-thinking, moving away from traditional teaching methods and opening doors between departments, colleges and other institutional units. However, unless we all think differently about education, the tendency will be to continue to re-create a poor system.

STUDENTS AS WORKERS
We can start by re-examining the role of students. In quality systems, students are viewed as both primary customers and workers within the system. That is, students are expected to perform the assignments or the work within the processes leading to the system the teacher has created.

Below is a deployment flow chart showing an assignment in a traditional classroom.

Figure 6.0: Deployment flow chart of a typical classroom assignment.

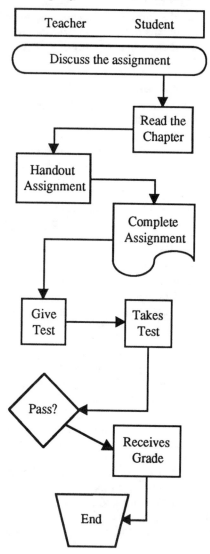

Deployment Flow Chart

You can see from the Flow Chart that there is no room in the processes within this system for students to evaluate their activities or the way they are supposed to achieve the end product which, in this case, is to pass the test after having mastered the material. Compare this Flow Chart with Figure 2.3 on page 26, which has a feedback cycle for those students who did not pass the test. In the Figure 6.0, if there is a mismatch between teaching and learning styles, a student in this class will be unable to function optimally. If the materials are not adequate, students will be unable to achieve optimally. If the assignment does not have relevance to the student's world, or if s/he doesn't understand how learning this particular skill fits into his/her future, the student will have little incentive to conceptualize and assimilate the material. None of the above is an indictment of the teacher, but rather each represents a system flaw that could be resolved with input from the workers. The quality experts believe that workers are in the best position to make suggestions for improvement. Since students must produce assignments within the rules that are controlled by the teacher, they fit that definition.

Even teachers recognize that student roles often don't allow them to fulfill that function. That's because these teachers are usually the ones who have to remain in control and cannot act in a facilitative role which enables the students to be active self starters. In the control spectrum, these teachers usually are in the "Do To" to the "Do For" range, but they think they are in the "Do With" or the "Enable" range, as shown in the following figure.

Figure 6.1: The roles teachers and students have within the control spectrum range.

Control Spectrum			
TEACHERS			
DO TO	DO FOR	DO WITH	ENABLE
Master	All Knowing Provider	Expert/Coach	Facilitator Intellectual Provocateur Mentor
Slave	Passive Recipient	Learning Participant	Active Self Starting Learner
STUDENTS			
			from Tribus, 1991

Teachers who work too closely to either the "DO TO" or the "DO FOR" range usually have a classroom system that resembles the deployment flow chart shown in Figure 6.2 on page 74.

Figure 6.2: Deployment flow chart of a teacher who thinks he is coaching or enabling students.

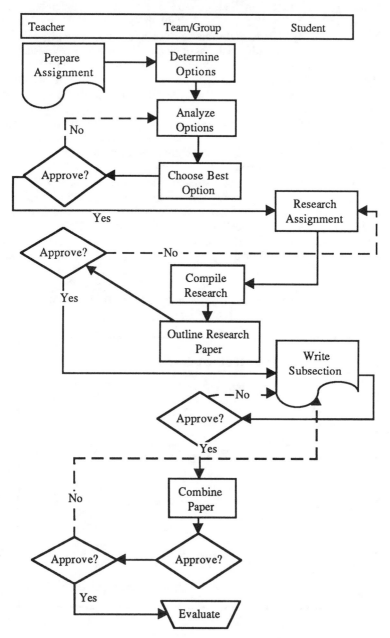

As you can see in Figure 6.2, the teacher is the person who not only prepares the assignment, but who also is involved in no less than three separate approval processes. In addition, s/he determines what student will do the particular research assignment, thus removing the responsibility of the "team" to apply the appropriate peer pressure to do a quality job. In Figure 6.3, another deployment flow chart shows the processes of a teacher who is actually coaching and enabling students.

Figure 6.3: Deployment flow chart of a teacher who is coaching and enabling students.

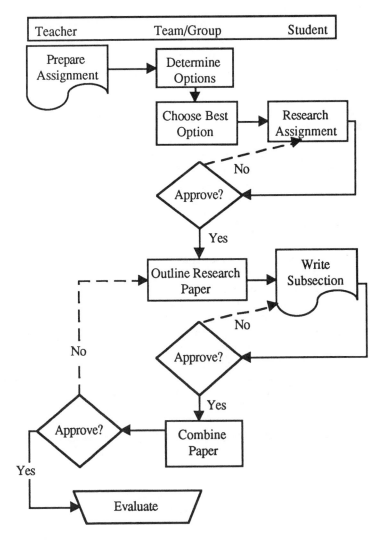

In the above example, the teacher lets the group/team not only determine the best option to meet the assignment, but s/he also empowers the group to assign the research and subsection writing as well as to approve or disapprove the quality of each team member's work. In addition, the teacher, as part of the team, is involved with the students in doing the evaluations. They are actually doing a plan-do-check-act cycle on their own work.

STEPS TO SYSTEM IMPROVEMENT

We suggest that you begin your course with an introduction to quality management theory. This overview is necessary because students need to realize why you have chosen to have quality classroom teams and to teach differently. Everyone over 30 can understand the story about Japan and the products they produced as being junk. But what about students today? For the most part, they grew up in a world where Japanese products have been revered for their quality, reliability, and technology. Few students can recall when Japanese products were considered inferior, so the brief history lesson about quality is important.

Along with that, we recommend a brief discussion about what has happened in our country with our major corporations. Some students, perhaps not the youngest, can relate very well to stories about the auto industry, television, video games, computer chips, etc. If you are unfamiliar with these stories, do some research. Students will be fascinated (depending on the way you tell the stories), and many can relate because their parents may work for one of those companies, or may work in a retail store that sells televisions, etc. You'll need to put the quality story into context for the particular age group your working with, so they can link the information to their own lives.

Follow this discussion with a general conversation about quality and what it means to do quality work. Then, move the students into a discussion about things that make it easier to learn and things that make it more difficult. You may get some excellent clues right away from the students as to what can be done to help make it better. Let the students know that you are serious about asking them for help. You might want to talk about an experience you had in school where no matter how hard you tried, you just couldn't understand something.

Sometimes, teachers, especially college professors, are afraid to ask students for help because they think the students will turn on them. Perhaps they are more afraid that they will hear, perhaps for the first time, that they are not a success. This must be tied to our fear of evaluation. We have put teachers, especially college professors, in the position of being the "expert" for so long, that it is frightening for them to think that they may not know all the answers.

In a quality classroom, action is rarely if ever taken without first analyzing root causes of problems and embarking on a PDCA cycle for process improvement. As we mentioned in Chapter 1, great teachers consistently do three things:

- They concentrate on improving the teaching and learning processes by using a PDCA cycle
- They have the students work in collaborative teams using a PDCA cycle

- They use a variety of CQI tools and techniques to assess the effectiveness of both the teaching and learning.

Let's look at a training exercise that can demonstrate the power of collaborative learning and the PDCA cycle.

ΔΔΔΔΔΔΔΔΔ

Training Activities

The Power of Team Learning and the Plan-Do-Check-Act Cycle—The Foam Ball Exercise

The following activity is a real eye opener to those who doubt the value of team learning and the PDCA cycle. We have used this activity with all age groups.

Materials:

1—3 inch diameter Nerf (Sponge) ball for every team of 4-7 people
1 stopwatch for every team

Procedure:

Ask the students to divide into teams of 6-9 people. Then demonstrate the expected exercise. Ask one person of a team to act as a timer. Then instruct the other members of one team to form a large circle. Give a Nerf™ ball to one of the persons and ask him/her to gently throw the ball to someone in the circle and at which time the timer will begin. When s/he has done so, tell the person with the ball that s/he must pass the ball to another person who has not as yet caught the ball. Instruct the next person in the same manner. After the last person has caught the ball, inform him/her to pass the ball back to the person who originally started the activity. Ask the timer to stop the activity and record the time.

Post the following for all to see:

Purpose: To work together as a team to:

1. Decrease the cycle time necessary to complete the task just assigned
2. Collect data and plot the results to demonstrate increased productivity

Directions:

1. Every person must touch the ball in an agreed upon order
2. Not more than two people may handle the ball at any given time
3. One person is to time and record each trial
4. Every team must try to improve the process at least 15 times
5. The group must graphically plot the results in a **Run Chart**

<u>Results and Discussion:</u>

What usually happens is that the group has a 20- to 30-second first trial. Then they make the circle tighter and pass the ball quicker, sometimes dropping the ball and increasing the time. Then they realize that if they rearrange the circle so that they can pass the ball in a single direction that their time decreases. Then someone usually figures out that if the first person just holds the ball and lets the others touch it, that the team can further decrease the time. At this point, you may have to suggest that it might be better if one person moves while the others hold their hands still that perhaps the time can be decreased further—and it will. Finally someone will recognize that if the others simply line up their fingers closely on a table top that the starter can simply run the ball over the fingers quicker than the timer can start and stop the watch. (At this point you may want to see if there are any piano players doing the timing, since their reaction times are generally better.) It is not uncommon to have a final time of less the 1/10th of a second. The **Run Chart** will generally take the following shape.

Figure 6.4: A typical Run Chart obtained during a PDCA cycle and the foam ball exercise.

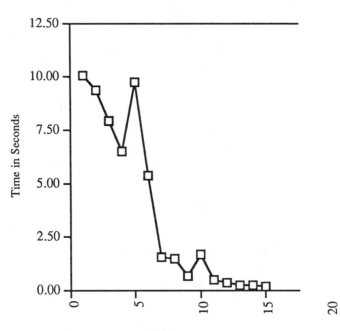

A WORD ON TRUST

As you can see, students are able to make decisions that improve their learning with just some guidance. How can we translate that knowledge into a classroom setting. The learning experiences in a quality classroom are characterized by student action, rather than passive receipt of processed information. Students are continually led into new work and unfamiliar territory. Once skills are "won," they must be reapplied to new problems in new ways.

In this configuration, students always operate at the edge of their competence. Therefore, it must be clear to them that a mistake is not a failure, but an attempt at innovation. They must realize that positive, constructive scrutiny of those mistakes by the rest of the class can only occur in an atmosphere free of fear where students never have to risk embarrassment.

Trust and respect remain the foundation upon which a quality classroom can be built. If the foundation is weak, progress will be sporadic and lead to frustration, and, eventually, disenfranchised students will opt out. A quality classroom cannot be built in an atmosphere of distrust.

Trust within the classroom means students can:

- Take "learning" risks without fear of being shamed
- Express their opinions about the learning experience without fear of being punished, ridiculed, or ignored
- Be responsible for solving problems
- Focus on learning without a coercive atmosphere.

Trust within the classroom means teachers can:

- Allow students to co-create the learning environment and learning experiences
- Release the "need" to control
- Focus on leadership
- Develop and use students' problem solving skills so more time can be spent learning
- Seek data from internal and external customers freely and use it as a basis for improvement.

Fear is an overwhelming issue for all students. The more fear invades the classroom, the less willing the students will be to work together. Building trust among students isn't as easy as it might seem. Bias and prejudice are factors that also must be overcome. Students who have experienced put-downs are going to be understandably less willing to take risks than others.

We are not suggesting that every learning experience has to be a team effort, but that teaming become a routine part of education. There can and should be opportunities for students to engage in individual research as well, and the two experiences need not be at odds with each other.

WHAT ABOUT STUDENTS WHO REFUSE TO PARTICIPATE?

You will undoubtedly find situations where some students simply refuse to work with others. These may be students who present themselves as being "tough." These situations always create a dilemma to teachers: if you crack down on the student, you create fear and relinquish any hope for a quality classroom; if you don't, you allow these students to demolish opportunities for quality.

Patience and understanding are your biggest allies. We recommend that you find ways to develop a rapport with stubborn students and see if they'll eventually share with you some of the reasons for not wanting to team. Whatever you do, **never** embarrass or humiliate a student. It will be nearly impossible for you to establish a good rapport and engage him/her as part of the team or class because s/he simply won't trust you.

You can engage some of the more reluctant students more readily when you have students solve problems as a group.

As in all learning experiences, allow time to reflect and debrief after every group exercise. Students may not be accustomed to having reflective time to talk about the problems they encountered and how they would improve the process, if there were time to repeat it. The debriefing sessions are as valuable as the actual activity. You are establishing a ritual for the class to follow as you move through the semester. You'll want students to feel comfortable expressing their opinions in an effort to improve every single process. This is a key factor in engaging students as research and development experts. In essence, you are asking them to portray that role every time you debrief and engage in the Plan-Do-Check-Act cycle.

ΔΔΔΔΔΔΔΔΔ

The following is a check sheet to help you implement the CQI Action technique into the classroom.

FACILITATING SYSTEM

Step 1:   You are demonstrating leadership.
- √   Develop a definition of a quality classroom.
- √   Walk-the-Talk about quality.
- √   Understand Deming's system of Profound Knowledge.
- √   Use a variety of teaching styles.
- √   Have a CQI program for yourself and your students.

Step 2:   The mission, goals, and operational definitions of your course are absolutely clear.
- √   Establish a course mission statement.
- √   Develop quality goals for the course.
- √   Co-create mission statement, quality goals and operational definitions with the students.
- √   Align course mission and goals with those of the institution (program/major).

Step 3: Most work is pertinent and flows from the students through teams.
- √ Break down barriers on day one by refining the course mission statement with the students.
- √ Have students co-create learning experiences.
- √ Stress the importance of teamwork in problem solving and decision making.
- √ Define quality and what it means.
- √ Create interdisciplinary learning activities.

FACILITATING/LEARNING SYSTEM

Step 4: The course content is connected to the surrounding community and the real world.
- √ Demonstrate the connectedness between work and the real world.
- √ Ask the students to analyze the learning assignments.
- √ Begin CQI tool and team training for the students.
- √ Implement student suggestions on how best to improve the learning system.

LEARNING SYSTEM

Step 5: The student is treated as a "worker," but s/he is also considered a valuable team member of the "research and development" department.
- √ Re-examine the role of students: Discuss quality systems with students and why they are viewed as both primary customers and workers within the educational system.
- √ Give the students an historical overview about the quality movement and discussed examples.
- √ Discuss the PDCA cycle and root causes of problems.
- √ Discuss the importance of "trust" in a quality classroom.

LEARNING SYSTEM

CHAPTER SEVEN: PEER TEACHING, SMALL GROUP
                 WORK, AND TEAMWORK

In the last chapter, we talked about the importance in teamwork, the PDCA cycle, and why the students have to consider themselves as "workers" who are responsible for the quality of their own work. In this chapter, we'll look into allowing students to evaluate, assesses and encourage their peers to higher achievement. The hard part may be overcoming their fears and personal animosities as you encourage peer teaching, small group work, and teamwork.

WHAT'S IN IT FOR ME?
Upon completing the chapter you will be able to:
- Engage the students in both team and individual activities
- Provide guidelines and opportunities for students to assess each others' work
- Understand how the systems' approach to teaching and learning reduces fear in the classroom
- Encourage students to provide peer tutoring.

THE LARGER PICTURE
In quality classrooms, you and your students see yourselves as part of a single unit. You are not the giver of information; you are sharing with your students just as they are sharing with you. Everyone in your class has a sense of the need to work together and help each other.

Teams within the classroom can take several forms. There are probably unlimited numbers and purposes of teams within the classroom. We will elaborate on several.

A **Quality Improvement Team** (QIT) functions to collect suggestions for improvement from other students, teachers, parents, and administration. You might want to change this group every three weeks. There are various ways to select this group, but give everyone in the class an opportunity sometime throughout the term. It's important not even to hint that only "certain" students will be selected. Invest everyone right away in the realization that this is their classroom and that each person has an important role to play. As the names are selected, post them in a prominent place along with the period of time to be served. Next time, be certain not to include any names that were selected during the first round, and so forth until everyone (or almost everyone in large classes) has had a turn.

The importance of this team is to maintain the suggestion box, and/or to collect suggestions from students or teams throughout the semester. These are read with the teacher, and a determination is made how to proceed. Encourage students to make suggestions for improvement and post the names of students whose suggestions are implemented.

The team can select a leader who reads to the class any suggested improvement recommendations. Students are then polled to prioritize which suggested improvements they want to implement.

A **Quality Leadership Team** (QLT) provides over-all leadership to the class. Students are randomly selected from the entire class. The team probably functions best with only four or six members. They, too, should rotate monthly so several groups in the class have the opportunity to participate. They collect data and use quality improvement tools to post the information so everyone can see where improvement takes place and where efforts for improvement still need to be looked at. The QLT works in tandem with the Quality Improvement Team and often bring ideas forth based on the data they've collected.

The team members work together to determine who will take responsibility for specific duties, what type of data needs to be collected, what form it will take, where it will be posted, and when and how they will report to the class. **By working together like this, you eliminate the scourge of the classroom—cheating.** There's no reason for anyone to cheat, since you are all working together toward an agreed-upon goal. Students are led by their teacher and classmates to know where and how to access information which becomes more important than memorizing facts.

The idea that memorization isn't important chills some teachers. They can't imagine a teaching method that does not build on basic information. Neither can we. CQI does not eliminate the need for a knowledge foundation. It simply is learned differently. Students are not asked to memorize names, dates, facts and figures that are nice for trivia contest but have little use in real life. Instead, they learn where to access the information as they need it and apply it to real-life projects that do have meaning.

Consider that most information can be gleaned from using a dictionary, a calculator, a map, or a book, and now a CD ROM. Doesn't it truly make more sense to have students learn to use the tools of learning that can open up the entire universe to them as they need it, rather than have them memorize some facts to store in their short-term memory to regurgitate on a test?

CQI changes the classroom orientation by insisting on an answer to the **why** question. Why are we leaning this? You and your students must understand why you are studying something. No one will resist learning something that has meaning; resistance increases when something has no meaning. Some students, of course, will go along with whatever you ask. The other students, however, can't be ignored. When they understand the value of what they are being asked to learn, they will join with the rest.

Here is an excellent example of how one academic department and a professor in Arizona answers the **why** question. Let's look at sections taken from the department's Orientation Manual and her syllabus.

Orientation Manual: We want every student to understand what the Biology Department expects of them and what every student can expect of us. It is our ultimate goal to improve student learning so we create learning experiences that are related to real world experiences. This is our main focus, our uniqueness, and our position. Learning drives our entire curriculum and learning is our highest mission.

Class Syllabus: The following are the drivers of my course.

Class Values and Philosophy

I believe that <u>Our Students</u> are the most important part of our institution. I will operate my class so that I provide our students with the best educational experiences that I can. <u>Students</u> are my greatest resource, and I will treat my students in all classes with fairness and respect. However, students are expected to buy-into my <u>class tradition</u>: In all we do, we strive to be the best.

My Classroom Credo

My classroom is a place where the genuine care and learning environment of my students is my highest mission. I pledge to provide the finest personal service for my students, who will always find a friendly, warm and yet, refined atmosphere.

You are the Expert

Be aware of events and things the we are doing in the Course. Inform people about activities in all areas. This not only makes good conversation, but it also makes them feel good about the College. Be aggressive about sharing that information with other people.

Anticipate Needs

Stop to help people who look like they need help and go beyond the minimum expectations. Help those with a bewildered look on their face. Remember, it is not cheating to help another person learn.

Measure and Monitor Teaching and Learning

- *Ask for Student Comments*
- *Complete the Rating Cards at the End of Every Class*
- *Study with Focus Groups*
- *Ask Students What I Can Do Better*
- *Ask Students What They Can Do Better*
- *Ask Students and Me What We Can Do Better*

To be Successful and Keep Your Sanity in This Class
- *You need to genuinely like people*
- *You need to like working and serving people*
- *You need to accept the challenge*

You can see the emphasis on self-help and working with other students. Those are key components of CQI, too.

In previous material, we have stressed teamwork. That's because it represents a different approach to traditional teaching. But it is not the only approach. Not every student learns that way. Besides, students can derive great benefits from working independently. After all, students must learn to follow a task through from start to finish by themselves. Some students have so many creative thoughts running through their heads that they are unable to focus on anything long enough to complete a task. Learning to follow through and accomplish the goal is vital to success in life. Therefore, we recommend teachers find a way to mix the learning experiences, so that students spend part of each day working independently from a team or partner.

Independent work does not mean that you abandon the idea of peer teaching, having fun, or working on meaningful experiences. You can draw students quickly into the educational process by making learning as much fun as possible. Students know what they enjoy. All you have to do is ask them.

Individual learning experiences can also be integrated with peer teaching and pairing. Part of this experience is teaching students to assess their work as well as the work of their peers. Assessing truly is an art, and one that requires facilitation and mentoring by the teacher. Students often can be cruel with those they somehow view as less intelligent, inept or otherwise "inferior." Those students treated as inferior also have difficulty evaluating classmates they view as "superior." Helping both sets of students comprehend the importance of valuations and use them wisely can become a difficult and tricky issue, one that requires a great deal of sensitivity for teacher and students. By the way, this happens at **all** levels of education—from kindergarten to graduate school.

Peer assessment and/or self-assessment are skills that can be taught and, once implemented, can yield great rewards for students. However, you must realize that if the students have any fears of receiving a lower grade because of self-assessment, it will be impossible for them to be honest in their assessment. Analysis of this makes perfect sense, since we generally do not willingly engage in things that we know will bring harm to us.

It is not difficult to imagine the sensitivity that must be used when broaching the subject of self-assessment and peer assessment. However, it is a key concept in a quality classroom due to the vast advantages that can derive from its use. For example, students who can assess their work develop a tremendous ability to know how much more is required of them to complete the task. These students understand the concept of continuous improvement and are not concerned when others complete the task sooner. Furthermore, when students become comfortable with their peers assessing their work, they soon realize how important and valuable it is to gain feedback from another person. Too often, especially in writing assignments, the writer has difficulty viewing his work from another perspective. By using peer and self-assessment techniques, we can move students forward in creating much more refined works.

Begin the training process by discussing the value of assessments. Help the students understand the value of a fair, honest assessment. Lead the students to understand that being unduly harsh will undermine the process. They will gradually see that personal attacks or biases only defeat the purpose of producing a quality product. They should understand that the goal is to create quality, not to tear down one person at the expense of another. The quality of the "process," "system," and/or "product," are being evaluated critically, **not** necessarily the person(s) involved.

The next step is to provide everyone with some guidelines for assessing each other's work. The best way to keep peer assessment out of the personal realm is to remind students of the operational definitions and quality factors already agreed upon by the group. Use those as the guide (rubric).

There really shouldn't be any questions (not many for certain) because the operational definitions must be measurable. For example: *The use of good paragraphs* is not an operational definition since "good paragraph" cannot be measured. How would one know necessarily what a good paragraph was except to mentally take a paragraph apart and analyze it. The result of your analysis does create operational definitions.

The class will be able to do this, but you may need to prompt the students somewhat in the beginning. We suggest that after students complete the peer assessment rubric, they write some comments and suggestions for improvement. Afterwards, provide time for peers to reflect with their partner about the comments and the rubric. This can be the most valuable part of the experience. Students learn excellent communication skills, and they also become mentors for their partners. It is this synergy of students working together to make greater gains than they could have achieved independently that is so exciting for students and the teacher. Indeed, the reward of using this approach is not simply that individual students make greater gains, it is in seeing how students come to value each other in completely different ways. They begin to view each other as resources rather than simply social partners.

To facilitate this process, it is a good idea to generate some samples and have students practice. Your samples can become more complex as students have had practice with the more obviously flawed one(s). After each practice run, engage students in a conversation about how they've scored it and the comments made. Have them compare responses and provide samples until students become familiar with the format and begin to get consensus on scoring. Always remember to review the operational definitions prior to giving out the sample.

Peer assessment has another almost immeasurable value, too. That is, by assessing others' work, your own improves. Just as research has shown that one of the best ways to learn something is to teach it, the same value comes from assessing others' work. Though we know this to be true, few actually use this technique in the classroom. Many teachers have students correct the objective tests of others, but this is not what we are recommending.

The peer-assessment method is very powerful and a natural outgrowth of the concept of Continuous Quality Improvement. It is based on measurable operational definitions and gives students real guidelines for assessing without making personal attacks. This also teaches students the value of accepting constructive criticism gracefully. In a real sense, the students are not criticizing; they are assessing each other's work for quality.

By the time the student is ready to turn in the product of any learning experience for assessment by the teacher, there should be almost no doubt about whether it is quality. Indeed, the teacher is in the position of asking the student if s/he has met all the quality factors. If the answer is "Yes," then the product is accepted. If the answer is "No," then the student can ask the teacher for an assessment and recommendations for improvement. Students then go back and continue working until all quality factors are met. In a quality classroom, the only acceptable product is **quality**.

PEER ASSESSMENT REVISITED

John Huntley, professor, Department of English, The University of Iowa, has designed a software program called the **Quality Evaluator** (QE). A HyperCard™ program for Macintosh computers, it is designed to help peer groups (students) and the group leader (teacher) evaluate the relative quality of their work. As a result, the QE sensitizes team members to recognize quality in the work they inspect and motivates them to pursue CQI in the work that they do. The tool is dynamite and, in our opinion, can be used constructively in classroom teams from middle school to graduate school. Please refer to Chapter 4, page 79, for a description.

Regardless of your CQI approach or what you do, you cannot succeed with peer evaluations unless your students lose their fear of criticism. We have talked about the need to eliminate fear in a classroom as it relates to your teaching methods. In this case, you need to understand that students are just as frightened of what their classmates will say or do to them. Fortunately, there is a simple method for reducing fear as it relates to peer criticism: reduce the dependency on grading. Students must be weaned away from passivity in their learning and become much more proactive. Passivity can come from fear.

In the past, educators have successfully trained students not to evaluate their work, but to create products solely for the teacher ("customer") and to become totally dependent on the teacher for information about their success or failure. Clearly, the result of a fear-driven class is not only devastating to the success of the whole, but also to the achievement level of students. Teachers who operate in a fear-based culture probably wonder why all of their students are not motivated.

It is important to reduce fear as much as possible to optimize the learning experience. Some teachers fear that anarchy will ensue if they enlist the student's help in resolving classroom process problems. Nothing could be farther from the truth, provided that students trust you and respect you. Of course, without trust and respect, you'll never be able to come close to a quality classroom. That's why those issues were addressed earlier. If you are following quality guidelines in all your efforts and are living up to the standards you set, your students will trust and respect you.

The question remains of how to coexist within a system that forces you to give grades and have students become comfortable with self-assessment and peer assessment. There is really no good answer to that question, probably because as long as grades are involved there will always be a lingering element of fear (and prayer) in the classroom. But some things can help.

For one thing, for each learning experience it is essential that a timeline be established so that everyone can understand the logical cycle time for completion. Within that timeline, make it clear to students that they are free to have peer evaluations at any time along the way, as often as they'd like. Encourage students to assess themselves along the way, too. Reduce the dependency on you, to the extent possible, by letting students know that you will be available for guidance and mentoring, but that it is important for them to engage their peers as well. Peer assessments help everyone since the assessor learns as much as the one being assessed. Therefore, assessments are a valuable part of the learning process.

What do you do while your students are evaluating each other? Your role shifts from lecturer to guide (coach, leader), being aware of which students are "stuck" and need guidance. This means you maintain an active role in facilitating and mentoring. Teachers within a quality classroom rarely have time to sit idly while their students are working. Certainly if a general trend becomes apparent, the teacher will grab the opportunity to work with a group of students and/or the entire class in clarifying a point or providing further guidance. Perhaps it is a common, frequent grammatical error that students are making. The teacher might rightly assume that when this was taught, these students did not learn it well enough to apply it to other situations. In such a case, the teacher would be wise to provide students with several examples of proper usage. There should be no shame or blame here, but a Quality Teacher will take note, and at a later date do some investigating to determine where the breakdown in learning occurred. Although we will not discuss this in detail, we recommend that when students repeatedly show deficiencies from previous classes that the teacher take any such information and recommend a cross-functional team of faculty to work together to improve the process in order to build quality into the students' education. Since this might become a sensitive point for some teachers, it is important to find a way to present the information without shaming or blaming the previous instructor.

PEER TUTORS

Another example of students working with other students is peer tutoring. We really like the idea of having students help others. It provides a very strong, positive experience for all students, especially those who are having difficulty understanding.

Another advantage of using peer tutors is that many times, students respond better to their peers, or in one-on-one situations. Studies have shown that students are more patient with their peers and can achieve far better results. A rapport can be developed that will pay dividends well beyond one assignment. Once again, it is crucial that all students are trained in some basic principles of peer tutoring. That has to be done to ensure that no one uses coercion or other abusive tactics. Another is that the student being tutored must do the work and not the tutor. Sometimes, students become impatient and want to do the work for their friend. In such cases, the tutor must understand that the one being tutored does not really make many learning gains.

Before engaging in any peer-tutoring activities, you'll want to gather the class around and generate a discussion about how to optimize the effectiveness of the tutors. Ask students for suggestions about what is most helpful to them and be certain to include some things like being friendly, calm, soft-spoken, etc.

Another very effective technique when you have both older students and younger students in your class is to have older students buddy up to tutor younger students. This works well on two fronts: (1) it makes the older student feel important and useful, and (2) it gives the younger student a support system beyond the class. Often, a rapport develops that extends beyond the classroom. Thus, young students develop bonds with older students. This technique often makes students within the class feel that they share a common goal or purpose. As a side benefit, older students often have work or study habits which might rub off on their less experienced classmates. By the way, this applies to all levels of education—from elementary school to graduate school.

ΔΔΔΔΔΔΔΔΔ

The following is a check sheet to help you implement the CQI Action technique into the classroom.

FACILITATING SYSTEM

Step 1: You are demonstrating leadership.
- √ Develop a definition of a quality classroom.
- √ Walk-the-Talk about quality.
- √ Understand Deming's system of Profound Knowledge.
- √ Use a variety of teaching styles.
- √ Have a CQI program for yourself and your students.

Step 2: The mission, goals, and operational definitions of your course are absolutely clear.
- √ Establish a course mission statement.
- √ Develop quality goals for the course.
- √ Co-create mission statement, quality goals and operational definitions with the students.
- √ Align course mission and goals with those of the institution (program/major).

Step 3: Most work is pertinent and flows from the students through teams.
- √ Break down barriers on day one by refining the course mission statement with the students.
- √ Have students co-create learning experiences.
- √ Stress the importance of teamwork in problem solving and decision making.
- √ Define quality and what it means.
- √ Create interdisciplinary learning activities.

FACILITATING/LEARNING SYSTEM

Step 4: The course content is connected to the surrounding community and the real world.
- √ Demonstrate the connectedness between work and the real world.
- √ Ask the students to analyze the learning assignments.
- √ Begin CQI tool and team training for the students.
- √ Implement student suggestions on how best to improve the learning system.

LEARNING SYSTEM

Step 5: The student is treated as a "worker," but s/he is also considered a valuable team member of the "research and development" department.

√ Re-examine the role of students: Discuss quality systems with students and why they are viewed as both primary customers and workers within the educational system.

√ Give the students an historical overview about the quality movement and discussed examples.

√ Discuss the PDCA cycle and root causes of problems.

√ Discuss the importance of "trust" in a quality classroom.

Step 6: Peer teaching, small group work, and team work are emphasized.

√ Engage the students in activities that emphasized teaming and making learning fun.

√ You and your students understand why you are studying a particular aspect of your course.

√ Engage students to work independently away from the team, but encourage them to report the results to their peers.

√ Provide guidelines and opportunities for students to assess each others' work.

√ Encourage each student to ask you for an assessment and recommendations for improvement.

√ Emphasize the systems approach and regularly asked the students how we can reduce fear.

√ Provide students with the opportunity for peer tutoring.

√ Elaborate upon the types of quality teams.

√ Introduce the students to additional CQI tools and techniques.

LEARNING/IMPROVEMENT SYSTEM

CHAPTER EIGHT: AESTHETIC EXPERIENCES

You've introduced quality into your classroom. You've got your students working together in teams, appraising each other's work, serving as peer counselors and striving to learn on their own. What's left to do?

How about bringing something extra into the classroom? something that will make classes even more interesting and boost student creativity? How about introducing culture into education? How about providing the students with aesthetic experiences?

WHAT'S IN IT FOR ME?
Upon completing the chapter you will be able to:
- Engage the students in activities that encourage imagination
- Understand why it is important to discuss art, music, nature, relaxation, world events, and controversial topics.

DOMAIN AND NON-DOMAIN KNOWLEDGE
Creativity is the cornerstone of progress. Creative people take knowledge, expand and develop it, generating new ideas for future generations to build upon. Not everyone is creative, of course. But, CQI provides an avenue to enhance your students' creativity and boost the learning experience. In addition, you will instill the kind of pride that encourages students to do quality work.

Even simple questions can open horizons into creative thinking: what would the world be like without any prejudice...or what will travel be like in the year 2020? These and similar questions force our brains to reach outside our current paradigms and build on our current knowledge to create new knowledge. Speculation is one of the first steps to discovery.

Creativity involves a portion of knowledge. Knowledge is usually divided into two categories, domain and non-domain. Domain knowledge is related to the skills required to function properly in one's job. It can be taught by the company which employs the worker. It can be noncreative, rote learning, so a worker can handle the required tasks. Its antithesis is called non-domain knowledge. This knowledge helps people develop new ideas, to do their work creatively.

Both types of knowledge exist in the classroom. Domain knowledge involves the material necessary to understand and work within the subject area. Non-domain knowledge is the extra material that allows students to take great joy or pride in their work. Part of what drives human beings is the desire to create new knowledge as well as new ways of doing something. You can enhance that process by building creativity into every learning experience.

This can be done simply by asking students how they want to learn. Left to their own devices (with some guidance from teachers), students will become more creative, take more learning risks, and value the experience more. Students may want to develop a play around classroom material, or turn it into a game. The actual approach does not matter as long as it is creative.

What CQI elements are involved with a creative exercise?

• Teamwork. Creative projects commonly require a variety of people. At Kent State University, for example, instead of the usual lectures in a required, typically dull journalism law course, the instructor let the students design their own learning technique. They put "truth" on trial before a judge and jury of their own choosing, researched legal precedents, assigned roles to a prosecutor and defense and spent five weeks setting up and then presenting the trial. The instructor served to guide research and provide direction, but did not interfere with the process. Then the rest of the class— who were involved with other, related projects —assessed the results.

• Peer assistance. In any creative project, students must work together. They share ideas, "brainstorm," expand each other's knowledge,

• Peer assessment. Creative projects are presented to the class, allowing nonparticipants to comment and evaluate.

• Supplier education. Such projects open doors to other teachers. They can be presented school-wide, or to other students. That encourages other teachers to seek creative avenues for educating.

• Cooperative education. Because a creative project rarely can be confined to a single study area, the projects often involve many teachers and support facilities. At Governors State University (Ill.) University, for example, what could have been a rote historical survey course was turned into "The History of Medicine, Art, and Literature." It was team taught with a professor of art and a professor of health science. Not only were the students interested in looking at the advances in these disciplines, but the instructors also learned a great deal by participating in the course.

• Fun. Students enjoy creativity. They look forward to coming into class and learning. The more creative the project, the more involved they become.

• Future learning. The knowledge learned remains part of the student, unlike a lecture that is noted and forgotten after a test.

There is no limitation to what can be done. You might develop a few ideas and offer them to students who have trouble getting started. That will initiate the conversation. Divide the students into groups and let them play with various ideas until they reach a consensus. Every great breakthrough starts with an idea.

Students who have regular opportunities to stretch their imaginations continue to use these skills and eventually become better communicators and more critical thinkers. These skills must be nurtured and allowed to grow, never stifled.

Even controversial topics can be broached in this method. A debate can open eyes; so can the creation of a board game or other creative approach. They will diffuse emotions without reducing learning.

AESTHETICS IN YOUR COURSE

Creativity helps bridge the gap between culture and education. The two are often seen as separate entities. Indeed, when schools cut back to save money, they tend to reduce cultural programs in an effort to preserve "educational" classes. However, understanding and appreciation for culture has to be an integral part of education.

An educated person displays a keen interest in a wide variety of topics and has an appreciation for art, music, theater, and nature. Traditional courses don't do a very good job of nurturing students holistically, even though we all recognize there is much more to life than the cognitive activities. Quality classrooms are able to engage students in a broad range of activities and demonstrate how they interface with each other.

The systems approach to learning emphasizes that nothing exists by itself, but that everything is a part of a larger whole. We must provide many opportunities for students to understand the connections within their world and the universe of what we are teaching. This presupposes that we have spent time exploring the world beyond our subject matter.

It's possible to bring cultural elements into any project and enhance an appreciation of the culture. For example, a biology lesson could include the sounds of whales and an explanation of the music involved. Art can work well with geometry or chemistry. All good art has deep roots in reality and knowledge.

What if you created a learning experience that encompassed one or more of the great artists with music of the period, history, psychology, and great authors; and then study the era from a contemporary perspective? What lessons could be learned from doing that? What if your students did some research on contemporary music and the influence of history and culture on it? What might once have been viewed as a "drag" by students who had to sit through art history or music history classes could turn into an exciting experience and might forever alter the students' appreciation for the arts.

We live in an isolated world in which many students find themselves separated from the cultural stimulation that enhanced the lives of their parents and grandparents. Today, with the pressure to grow up and the "instant gratification" from television, many students don't even read a newspaper. Studies indicate readership is down and that most people today get their news via television. Video games have replaced more sedate activities like chess and bridge. Movies have outlasted literature. In many ways, movies have become modern literature.

Cultural components bring at least one other element into the mix, one which enhances life completely. You and your students live with far too many stresses and not many opportunities to relieve them. They need to be free to learn and to experience joy in learning. Therefore, we suggest the use of reflection time for students to relax. Look at a painting, listen to music, stretch the mind with creative activity while resting the rest of the body.

Even Covey (1989) recognized the importance of self-renewal: his seventh habit is to "Sharpen the Saw."

△△△△△△△△△

The following is a check sheet to help you implement the CQI Action technique into the classroom.

FACILITATING SYSTEM

Step 1: You are demonstrating leadership.
- √ Develop a definition of a quality classroom.
- √ Walk-the-Talk about quality.
- √ Understand Deming's system of Profound Knowledge.
- √ Use a variety of teaching styles.
- √ Have a CQI program for yourself and your students.

Step 2: The mission, goals, and operational definitions of your course are absolutely clear.
- √ Establish a course mission statement.
- √ Develop quality goals for the course.
- √ Co-create mission statement, quality goals and operational definitions with the students.
- √ Align course mission and goals with those of the institution (program/major).

Step 3: Most work is pertinent and flows from the students through teams.
- √ Break down barriers on day one by refining the course mission statement with the students.
- √ Have students co-create learning experiences.
- √ Stress the importance of teamwork in problem solving and decision making.
- √ Define quality and what it means.
- √ Create interdisciplinary learning activities.

FACILITATING/LEARNING SYSTEM

Step 4: The course content is connected to the surrounding community and the real world.
- √ Demonstrate the connectedness between work and the real world.
- √ Ask the students to analyze the learning assignments.
- √ Begin CQI tool and team training for the students.
- √ Implement student suggestions on how best to improve the learning system.

LEARNING SYSTEM

Step 5: The student is treated as a "worker," but s/he is also considered a valuable team member of the "research and development" department.

√ Re-examine the role of students: Discuss quality systems with students and why they are viewed as both primary customers and workers within the educational system.

√ Give the students an historical overview about the quality movement and discussed examples.

√ Discuss the PDCA cycle and root causes of problems.

√ Discuss the importance of "trust" in a quality classroom.

Step 6: Peer teaching, small group work, and team work are emphasized.

√ Engage the students in activities that emphasized teaming and making learning fun.

√ You and your students understand why you are studying a particular aspect of your course.

√ Engage students to work independently away from the team, but encourage them to report the results to their peers.

√ Provide guidelines and opportunities for students to assess each others' work.

√ Encourage each student to ask you for an assessment and recommendations for improvement.

√ Emphasize the systems approach and regularly asked the students how we can reduce fear.

√ Provide students with the opportunity for peer tutoring.

√ Elaborate upon the types of quality teams.

√ Introduce the students to additional CQI tools and techniques.

LEARNING/IMPROVEMENT SYSTEM

Step 7: Students should have aesthetic experiences.

√ Encourage students to use their imagination daily.

√ Discuss the importance of art, music, nature, relaxation techniques, meditation, diet, and exercise with one or more students.

√ Discuss news headlines and/or controversial topics with one or more students.

√ Gather specific data to evaluate and improve creative experiences.

IMPROVEMENT SYSTEM

CHAPTER NINE: CLASSROOM PROCESSES INCLUDE REFLECTION

As you can imagine, a CQI classroom can be a busy place, with students involved in various projects, actively counseling peers, critiquing the work of their colleagues, researching, working in teams and making presentations.

But one thing often is forgotten in the bustle of work: students need time to think. Therefore, your classroom processes should include reflection.

WHAT'S IN IT FOR ME?
Upon completing the chapter you will be able to:
- Develop various instant feedback forms to measure the effectiveness of the teaching and learning systems
- Understand why it is important for the students to reflect on the relevance of your course work to real world issues
- Understand why it is important to reflect on your course mission, goals, and operational definitions to meet the goals.

Seldom within the educational setting do either teachers or students have time to reflect on their work or their goals or their accomplishments. We seem to focus on the "doing" of things rather than "why" we are doing them. It's not easy to take the time. You probably complain that you have no time to think, no time to pause and reflect on the teaching/learning process or about the progress the class or individuals are making. Yet, without adequate reflection time, you may be perpetuating some aspect of learning that needs to be improved. How can you tell if you don't take a moment or two to study it?

We must give serious thought to the necessity for reflection. In the Plan-Do-Study-Act (PDSA) cycle (also known as the Plan-Do-Check-Act or PDCA cycle), the planning phase is crucial—see Figure 9.0. It is the phase that provides the foundations for every process and includes reflection on cause and effect as well as on the study of current processes for "best practice." Without adequate reflection and planning, you will reduce chances of building additional quality into the processes that make up the activity of the classroom. At the same time, you will delay the imposition of quality in areas that may need improvement.

Figure 9.0 P-D-S-A Cycle

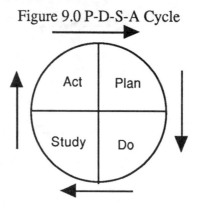

Most faculty spend 50 to 60 hours a week doing work for their institution. They are constantly preparing and/or revising lectures, reading about the advances in their area of specialization, writing grant proposals, doing research, advising students, participating on department, school, and institutional committees. Some are actively involved in providing services for their community and/or their national organization. They attend meetings in order to keep themselves professionally developed.

Most teachers would probably agree that they take little or no time to reflect on their mission and goals and performance in the classroom. Most would probably agree that some processes are not working optimally and that if they obtained help from students and/or colleagues, the learning environment as well as learning experiences could be improved.

How, then, do you find the time? What can you do to expand the clock?

For starters, you can invite some help into the process.

INSTANT FEEDBACK
In a quality classroom, teachers encourage their students to help them reflect on various classroom processes each day. This might be called "fast feedback," or debriefing, or simply reflection time. The essence of this is that teachers cannot possibly carry the entire burden for learning, nor should they. Shared responsibility and shared decision making is one of the tenets of quality. For example, a fast feedback form for a computer class might look like this:

Table 9.0: Fast Feedback Form

Activity	Too Fast	—	OK	—	Too Slow
Data Base	5	4	3	2	1
Word Processing	5	4	3	2	1
Spreadsheet	5	4	3	2	1

With a simple glance, you can recognize who needs help and which student(s) would benefit from some peer assistance.

During the next class, you can reorganize the class into groups with at least one student who was excelling at the particular activity and one who was having some difficulty. In this way, students could help each other and the teacher could be of greater help to the entire class by moving between groups.

Here's a variation on the idea. In a statistics class at Western Illinois University, instructor Eric Ward completes his 15-week class in five weeks. The students who showed competency in the subject, then help the remaining students while Professor Ward repeats the material. He debriefs the students at 10 weeks and repeats the process. By this time, about 66 percent of the class are helping the remaining students grasp the concepts. Ward does not have to drain himself to obtain minimal result. He has help. And the level of learning is remarkably high with every student guaranteed assistance.

To increase the learning curve, you might ask your students for more general information about what they need to make the activities more interesting or to help them learn.

Teachers of mathematics in our colleges and universities should probably present one concept (one problem) each day, and it should almost always be a real world problem. Students should work in teams to resolve the problem. Each students should first attempt to solve the problem on their own, writing down the logic of steps in their portfolio or diary. Next, the team should discusses the problem with the members comparing their notes. By getting into the habit of writing their thinking down, students will more readily learn the logic errors they've made and they will be able to self-correct many of them.

Table 9.1 presents a fast feedback form from a statistics class.

Circle the number that best represents your thoughts on today's work.

1 = Strongly Agree   2 = Agree
3 = Somewhat Disagree   4 = Disagree

1. I understand the logic of today's problem.

     1   2   3   4

2. I could apply this logic to another situation.

     1   2   3   4

3. This class is moving at a good pace for me.

     1   2   3   4

Signature (optional):

_____

All teachers would do well to allow their students to give them continuous feedback much like that suggested above. Unless we know (specifically and systematically) what difficulties the students encounter, how can we possibly know how to create a better learning environment or learning experience?

Do not feel limited by the forms. Ask other questions, change those on the form. Experiment until you find a way to get useful feedback from your classes. Every teacher will want to experiment with these ideas and with practice discover how to ask questions that provide the best information in a short amount of time.

We recommend that students be given the option of signing their names so that the teacher can provide them with the help needed. If a third or more of the students report that the class is moving too slow or too fast, the teacher would be wise to find a way to accommodate them. The optimum response comes when most of the students answer the question about pace by circling the no. 2 response. After the students get accustomed to fast feedback, you can random sample students rather than the entire class.

Never underestimate the power of students' help. They reflect on classes often outside of school and/or during class when you may surmise they are daydreaming. They are the ones working in the system and, therefore, are in the best position to offer assistance about ways to build quality into the system or process.

Just as it's important for you to reflect on your teaching and the success of your approach, students need time to reflect. Rarely do we provide opportunities for students to participate in any reflection about their work or the work of their team or classmates. By not doing so, in essence, educators perpetuate the short-term recall and pay little attention to the larger questions that arise with learning experiences. These experiences require students to do research and create new knowledge. Whenever one is engaged in creating new knowledge or testing a new theory, reflection is a critical step.

Students who engage in regular reflective time also seem to gain insights into their own lives and behaviors in the context of the larger world. This leads to goal setting and valuable lifelong skills. This self-assessment requires each student to reflect on her/his behavior and performance for the week and to set personal goals. The results from this type of activity have kept the students more focused, thus allowing them to learn more each week. Students like the idea of having to write personal goals and engage in some reflection and self-assessment. In fact, some students report they have their families and friends engage in goal setting.

We're not suggesting leaving a few minutes in a class for idle conversation. Students need direction and information, just as you do, for reflection to have any value. A CQI tool, like a **Force Field Analysis**, can serve as an instrument for gathering data for reflection. Such tools commit them to reflect on behavior and habits leading to success or failure. You might want to include regular times for your students to complete a **Force Field Analysis** of their efforts to improve the overall quality of the class. Or this could become part of a total class effort led by the quality leadership team, and the students could also engage in **Cause-and-Effect Diagrams** (CED).

The method or continuous quality improvement tool you select is not nearly as important as taking the time to include reflection as a routine part of the quality classroom. Students and teachers both can benefit from this activity. We suggest that students fill a notebook with the story of their Continuous Quality Improvement journey. Such a notebook can be filled with pages of **Force Field Analyses, CED,** etc. The material can become part of the portfolio and serve as evidence—to themselves as well as for parents and teachers—that they've grown in their reflective ability and improved their performance as a result.

Other feedback methods using trained students were discussed in Chapter 4. The method you choose does not matter. It's the reflection that counts.

ΔΔΔΔΔΔΔΔΔ

The following is a check sheet to help you implement the CQI Action technique into the classroom.

FACILITATING SYSTEM

Step 1: You are demonstrating leadership.
- √ Develop a definition of a quality classroom.
- √ Walk-the-Talk about quality.
- √ Understand Deming's system of Profound Knowledge.
- √ Use a variety of teaching styles.
- √ Have a CQI program for yourself and your students.

Step 2: The mission, goals, and operational definitions of your course are absolutely clear.
- √ Establish a course mission statement.
- √ Develop quality goals for the course.
- √ Co-create mission statement, quality goals and operational definitions with the students.
- √ Align course mission and goals with those of the institution (program/major).

Step 3: Most work is pertinent and flows from the students through teams.
- √ Break down barriers on day one by refining the course mission statement with the students.
- √ Have students co-create learning experiences.
- √ Stress the importance of teamwork in problem solving and decision making.
- √ Define quality and what it means.
- √ Create interdisciplinary learning activities.

FACILITATING/LEARNING SYSTEM

Step 4: The course content is connected to the surrounding community and the real world.

√ Demonstrate the connectedness between work and the real world.

√ Ask the students to analyze the learning assignments.

√ Begin CQI tool and team training for the students.

√ Implement student suggestions on how best to improve the learning system.

LEARNING SYSTEM

Step 5: The student is treated as a "worker," but s/he is also considered a valuable team member of the "research and development" department.

√ Re-examine the role of students: Discuss quality systems with students and why they are viewed as both primary customers and workers within the educational system.

√ Give the students an historical overview about the quality movement and discussed examples.

√ Discuss the PDCA cycle and root causes of problems.

√ Discuss the importance of "trust" in a quality classroom.

Step 6: Peer teaching, small group work, and team work are emphasized.

√ Engage the students in activities that emphasized teaming and making learning fun.

√ You and your students understand why you are studying a particular aspect of your course.

√ Engage students to work independently away from the team, but encourage them to report the results to their peers.

√ Provide guidelines and opportunities for students to assess each others' work.

√ Encourage each student to ask you for an assessment and recommendations for improvement.

√ Emphasize the systems approach and regularly asked the students how we can reduce fear.

√ Provide students with the opportunity for peer tutoring.

√ Elaborate upon the types of quality teams.

√ Introduce the students to additional CQI tools and techniques.

LEARNING/IMPROVEMENT SYSTEM

Step 7: Students should have aesthetic experiences.

√ Encourage students to use their imagination daily.

√ Discuss the importance of art, music, nature, relaxation techniques, meditation, diet, and exercise with one or more students.

√ Discuss news headlines and/or controversial topics with one or more students.

√ Gather specific data to evaluate and improve creative experiences.

IMPROVEMENT SYSTEM

Step 8:   Classroom processes include reflection.

√   Develop instant feedback form with students in order to measure classroom processes.

√   Distribute instant feedback forms in order to examine classroom processes.

√   Reflect on my mission, goals, and classroom processes.

√   Set time aside for students to reflect on the relevance of course work to real world issues and encouraged them to discuss their perceptions.

√   Develop self-assessment and goal-setting instruments with students.

IMPROVEMENT SYSTEM

CHAPTER TEN: CONSTANTLY EVALUATE THE
                SYSTEMS

Your students understand CQI principles and seem to be learning. But are they? How can you tell? How can they help you become a better teacher? This chapter will explain why obtaining data is important and show you techniques for using your students to get the necessary information to help you constantly evaluate your teaching and learning systems.

WHAT'S IN IT FOR ME?
Upon completing the chapter you will be able to:
- Do a self-assessment on the effectiveness of your classroom systems
- Understand why it is important to have a professional work plan based on the mission and goals of your school and department

THE IMPORTANCE OF DATA
CQI is based on data. If you discover through your research that some educational procedure is accomplishing its goals, you can emphasize it and use its lessons to help improve other areas. If something is not working, you can analyze the problem through a variety of CQI tools, find the root cause and work out strategies to eliminate the problem. That also means you and your teaching methods must be assessed and evaluated. And that has to be done by the students. All research has shown that the only statistically valid assessments of teaching effectiveness are student ratings.

That assessment is integral to CQI—the constant assessment of your teaching and learning systems. All of that is logical, but when the process deals with humans, nothing is easy.

The biggest problem is fear: your fear of a negative evaluation, fear of administrators who are reluctant to conduct proper assessments, fear students feel when asked to provide an evaluation. Perhaps we can cope with it by understanding why we need to conduct the evaluations.

We think all mortals will agree that no one is perfect. If you accept that, then you can probably also agree that improvement is much faster when the environment is free of fear and fosters growth and continuous feedback. If you can't measure your teaching system, you can't control it, and you can't improve upon it. Hard data must be collected to measure the effectiveness of the teaching and learning systems in your courses.

You can ask administrators and your peers to conduct evaluations. Some people want or need everyone to like them. These are people who don't like the process of having to do classroom visitations for the purpose of evaluating the teacher and become uncomfortable with the idea that they may say something to hurt the teacher's feelings. Such people may rate every teacher the same—either excellent in all categories, or above average in all categories. It is doubtful that people with this type of personality would rate all teachers "average." These kinds of evaluations are not helpful. In their zeal to make everyone appear to have the same competencies, these evaluators do not assist the teacher. In effect, they contradict the exact purpose of the evaluation. For the most part, however, peer and administrative evaluations are minimally useful.

Good leaders allow people to take risks, to make mistakes and then learn from them, and encourage those who are struggling by helping provide what they need to improve. But this cannot be done without hard data—remember, one of the principles of CQI is "management by fact."

On the other hand, when a dedicated administrator or peer go into the classroom and takes notes, s/he makes many teachers nervous. Some instructors even become hostile with the thought that others dare to make any judgments based on one or two observations, especially when done by people who are not trained in the complicated methods of assessment. In essence, we have created a beast when it comes to assessing teacher performance. In many institutions, the evaluation process become a hotly contested negotiating point and has resulted in less-than-desired results, no matter what format the assessment takes.

In many colleges and universities, peers do evaluate each other. This makes professors nervous because they wonder who made the select few "gods," and the approach leads to isolation for those chosen to be the evaluators.

The reality is that the negative aspects of the present system of teacher evaluations far outweigh the good that might come from engaging everyone in a **continuous assessment** model that uses hard data to demonstrate that effective learning has occurred.

For all practical purposes, therefore, that leaves only students as evaluators. You will appreciate the evaluations, because they will make you a better teacher. Naturally, this is a paradigm shift: you are used to rating students; you probably aren't used to being rated. Nevertheless, student evaluations serve the valuable function of guiding you to improving quality. That's your goal and the goal of this book. Students are the ones who are the recipients of that quality approach; their opinions and observation have to matter.

We're not talking about end-of-the-semester evaluations many schools now use so students can grade their instructors. Such surveys may be used to work out merit and other raises. They may be the source of awards and recognition. However, many quality experts agree that ratings and yearly evaluations for raises or merit pay are destructive to the organization as they decrease morale and sense of stature. Individuals who are made to feel as if they are contributing less and not receiving any help from the system to improve their performance are likely to have lower self-esteem, produce less and be angry. (That's why merit raises serves as an inexpensive way of getting all of the teachers mad at each other.)

We're talking about ongoing, daily or weekly surveys that provide instant feedback about individual projects, lectures and lessons.

Your fear probably kicks in at this point. It shouldn't. We recognize that asking students questions about the classroom education process does carry some risks. You will be analyzed, and your efforts will be criticized.

That's a strange position to be in. Teachers have become used to doing all the planning, creating, and teaching with only the scrutiny of the department chairperson (or peer review team) several times per year—if their name falls into the evaluation cycle for that year. This method has suited many teachers perfectly, except when the reviewer makes some suggestions for improvement. Then they become defensive and view the review as punishment rather than an opportunity for positive growth.

You can't do that with student surveys. If you examine the classroom carefully, you will recognize that students, as "workers" within the system, are in the best position to help improve it and build quality into each process in the beginning. You will also realize that you cannot get along without regular feedback from your students. Once you try this, and can let go of any sense of defensiveness or personal attack, you will discover the merits of allowing students to help.

We suggest that you examine your fears in relation to having students help assess the teaching and learning processes. A word of caution: if you ask students for help in assessing the teaching and learning processes, then you have to be ready for whatever they say and listen without judgment. The minute you become defensive or try to explain, they will realize that you aren't really serious. If that happens, you will have some problems with the students because you'll have broken the trust bond between you, and it will take a long time to repair. Remember, the purpose of any teaching should be to optimize the students' learning. School isn't about teaching; it is about learning.

We strongly urge you to reach out to your students. Explain to them what you're doing and the necessity you see in doing regular evaluations. Unless every one of your students is currently operating at 100 percent efficiency, there is room for improvement.

DEBRIEFING

Evaluations or "debriefing" can take many forms. It is always important to do some type of debriefing after every learning experience, especially if your goal is continuous improvement. It takes just a minute or two but can yield very powerful and invaluable information for teachers. Student members of your quality leadership team can assist with the tabulation efforts. That process might take them 10 minutes for a class of 30 students. As they become more familiar with the debriefing sheet, students can reduce the time needed to tabulate the responses. It certainly is more powerful to have students do as much of this as possible, but if it is too frightening for you, then you can tabulate it yourself. Either way, in a very short time, you will obtain feedback that you can use to alter the resources, materials, and lecture you used.

Be prepared to consider what, if anything, you'll do if one-fourth or one-third of all students say your lectures are no help at all? We recommend you drop whatever sense of ownership you feel about those carefully prepared lectures and let go of them, or at a minimum modify them and continue to ask for feedback on their usefulness. Sometimes too much of ourselves is wrapped up in what we do, and for teachers, often, that is our lectures. Remember the purpose: optimize students' learning. If the lectures are not helpful, then don't lecture and be relieved that your students have felt they could be honest with you.

Other debriefing efforts can be in the form of fast feedback, which is used daily to assess how students felt they progressed that day in completing the learning experience. Fast feedback approaches depend on the class and the type of students. Structure your questions to solicit responses that will prove the most helpful for the following day. Some teachers prefer to use a very open-ended approach, others prefer questions that use a Likert Scale, and others a 'Yes/No' response. Questions using the Likert Scale can be especially enlightening if they are worded correctly; otherwise, you may not get the kind of information you need.

Whenever you use fast feedback, start by asking yourself what you need to know in order to improve the teaching/learning process for all the students. You don't need to know the names of all respondents, but it certainly would help you provide some assistance to students who indicate they need help. If anonymity is important to the students, then it would be wise to comply with their wishes. We recommend that you leave signature optional and stress that if students are having difficulty then you can best help if you know what their specific needs are.

Like most things having to do with quality, honest answers are predicated on trust. It takes a tremendous amount of trust for students to feel totally free to respond honestly rather than with what they think will please the teacher. Too often in many of our colleges, professors withhold respect from students who are honest with them. When you ask for feedback, be willing to listen and remember the **purpose** for asking: **to get data that can be used to improve the teaching and learning systems**. The most effective teachers are those who seek and use suggestions from students since doing so enhances trust, pride, cooperation, and teamwork.

STUDENT DEBRIEFING

As with teachers, students need to debrief as well. The format should be determined based on the type of learning experience the students just completed. Debriefing may start as an individual or team effort and then progress to the class as a whole. It may be formal, as in having students complete a questionnaire, or informal by having discussion follow some sort of format. In either case, results should be recorded and analyzed for making decisions about future projects, learning experiences, team selection, materials, etc.

With informal debriefings, we recommend that a student be selected (providing leadership opportunities to all students) to lead the discussion based on a selected format. Typical interview questions that a student quality improvement representative might ask of the class might be:

- The thing I liked best about this learning experience was:
- The thing that I didn't like was:
- The best thing about my group was:
- The thing I'd like to change about my group was:
- These kinds of learning experiences are:
- The thing(s) I learned from this is/are:

Have a student write all responses on the board to determine the most critical problem(s). This information can be used to set parameters for the very next learning experience.

PORTFOLIO AND SELF-ASSESSMENT

As your course moves more toward CQI, teach the students to perform regular self-assessments. This is usually something new for the students, and you'll need to teach your students some ways to do it. One of the first things you'll want to do is post the quality factors and operational definitions and also be certain each student has a copy for each learning experience. These provide the guideposts for students as they determine whether or not they've achieved quality. Everything that is done in the classroom should be under the guise of the quality factors and operational definitions.

How can assessment help you improve the quality in your class? Below is a Pareto Diagram with the results of a survey directed to the students who dropped out of a particular professor's **Introduction to Philosophy** course. If we add the "unfair tests" category to the "poor teaching" category and consider it a single category, we can safely state that over 50 percent of the dropouts can be contributed to bad teaching. Safe to say that these are the kinds of data which neither the teacher nor the students want to really face.

However, by having these data, either the administration and/or the teacher can now take steps for corrective action. After using additional CQI tools such as **control charts**, **run charts**, surveys, and **cause-and-effect diagrams**, perhaps the root cause(s) of perceived "poor teaching" can be eliminated. The solution might be as simple as instituting collaborative learning techniques along with more group discussion, or very complicated. Either way, the problem will be addressed and, hopefully, resolved.

You can obtain this important information daily and/or weekly through a variety of methods, but all methods should contain some form of data collection. It is critical to the Continuous Quality Improvement of the class, and its importance must not be overlooked. In fact, without it, your course is not likely to improve as quickly, if at all.

Figure 10.0: A Pareto Diagram displaying the reasons students dropped
Intro. to Phil. course during the past three years.

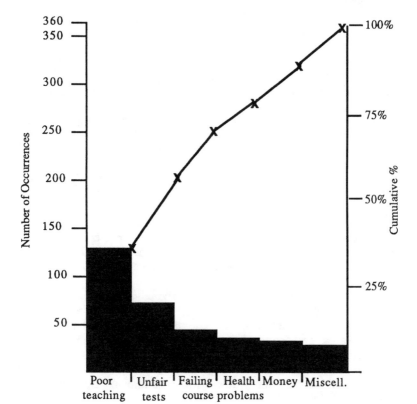

Dr. Emil Stubs is a chemistry teacher at a large, inner-city community college. Whereas the average failure rate for the **Organic Chemistry** course at the college was nearly 33 percent, Dr. Stubs' course had an average failure rate of 8.1 percent. In addition, his students always did much better in the department's standardized final exams and were much better prepared for transfer into the neighboring university. A newly hired chairman was under the impression that Dr. Stubs' classes had the same high failure rate as the rest of the department, but when he was presented with the control chart shown in Figure 10.1, he was forced to change his mind. When asked why he had such a high failure rate (i.e., "Special-Cause" Variation) in the third quarter of 1991, he was able to show that he had to undergo serious surgery and was hospitalized for four weeks. His classes were covered by his colleagues during his hospitalization.

Figure 10.1: A p-Control Chart showing the percent of students failing Dr. Stubs' Organic Chemistry course by term from 1988 to 1995.

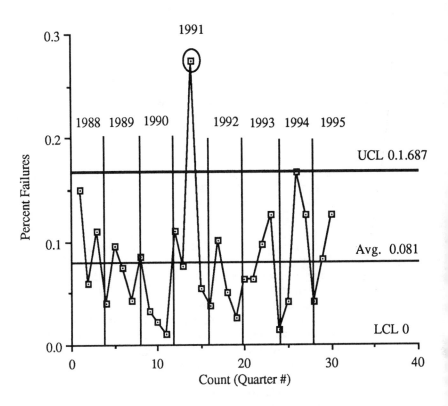

Several uses of control charts are presented in the Appendix.

Now that you can see the value of measurements, how can you demonstrate it to your students? Here is an activity that will help.

ΔΔΔΔΔΔΔΔΔ

Training Activity

A Two-Hour Activity to Demonstrate How Quality Can Be Improved With Better "Technologies" and The Use Of Control Charts In Measuring Quality Improvement

(Adapted from James A. Alloway, Jr., "The Card Drop Shop," *Quality Progress*, July 1994, 99-104.)

The following activity is a eye opener to those who doubt the value of the PDCA cycle and the introduction of new technologies to increase quality and the use of control charts to measure this increase. We have used this activity with college level students, but it probably can be modified for middle school and high school students.

Materials:
10 playing cards, 10 IDL binder clips (0.25 inch capacity), 50 paper clips, and a 8.5 x 11- inch sheet of paper per group of 4-6 students.

Procedure:
Ask the students to divide into teams of 4-6 people. Then demonstrate the expected exercise: Place the sheet of paper on the floor. Take a playing card and hold it between your thumb and middle finger perpendicular to the floor. Extend your arm at shoulder length and drop the card trying to land it on the 8.5 x 11- inch sheet of paper. Repeat with the other nine cards.

Post the following for all to see:
> **Purpose**: To work together as a team to minimize life-cycle costs and meet or exceed customers' requirements through optimizing designs and minimizing variation all in an environment of CQI.

> **Customer Requirements (cannot be changed):**
> 1. All of the playing cards are to be on target—but they are willing to accept the product if "deviations are not too bad." However, they will accept only those cards that are touching the paper as acceptable quality.
> 2. The playing cards are to be held between the thumb and middle finger perpendicular to sheet of paper on the floor. The cards are not to be bent, and they are to be dropped one at a time with the arm extended and from shoulder height.
> 3. All activities must be held away from walls, and the cards must not touch anyone or anything during the fall.

> **Directions: Round 1**
> 1. Every group is to drop 10 cards, trying to land them on target.
> 2. Record the number of failing to land on target.
> 3. Repeat four more times and record the failures for each trial, *i.e.*, those that are not touching the paper.
> 4. The group must do the calculations and graphically plot the results in a **np-control chart**. (This is an attribute chart used when the characteristic under study has a definite yes/no answer and the subgroups are of equal size. In our case, the sample size was 10 and we recorded the number that failed to land on the paper. **NOTE: the number of subgroups in our example was five**—we dropped the 10 cards only five times. It is important to emphasize that in real life we need a

minimum of 25 subgroups to construct a control chart, but since time for this demonstration is limited, we are going to do the calculations with a subgroup of five.)

Calculations:

1. Average # of failures = total # of failures ÷ # of subgroups
   = total # of failures ÷ 5
   =

2. Upper Control Limit = Average + 3 $\sqrt{\text{Average} (1 - [\text{Average} + n])}$

3. Lower Control Limit = Average - 3 $\sqrt{\text{Average} (1 - [\text{Average} + n])}$

Directions: Round 2

Have each group's members use their imaginations and apply the IDL binder clips ("new technology") to the cards before dropping them. Repeat the procedures as in Round 1 dropping 10 cards five times and recording the number of failures per trial. Do the calculations and construct another np-control chart.

Directions: Round 3

Have each group's members use their imaginations and apply the paper clips ("new technology") to the cards before dropping them. Repeat the procedures as in Round 1 dropping 10 cards five times and recording the number of failures per trial. Do the calculations and construct another np-control chart.

Results and Discussion:

We suggest that you lead the discussion by asking the students if the "quality" of the end-product increased significantly with the use of new technologies, i.e., the binders and paper clips. Then you could ask them to consider the costs of the binders versus the paper clips and the cost of labor needed to apply the binders and the paper clips. This is also a good place to discuss the concepts of value analysis and cost reduction.

Ask the students to compare the np-control charts for each of the rounds. What do they show? Are there any differences? A typical np-control chart pattern that results from the activity is shown below. Note the reduction in the UCL's and LCL's and averages when the "new technologies" are added to the product (cards). Also note that the range between the UCL and LCL is less in each round, demonstrating less variation.

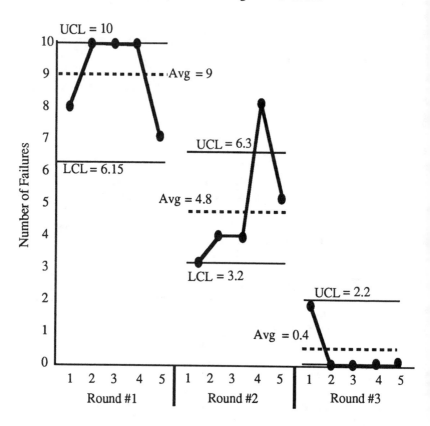

You can see that the "technology" increases quality, but that can only be determined by data collection and assessment.

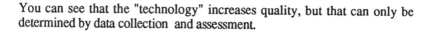

By now, you realize how important assessments are. They will help you boost your skills, improve your classes and inject more quality into the educational system. You simply need to get regular feedback from your students. After all, they are in the best position to help you improve the quality of your teaching.

However, there's no reason why you can't assess your own effort. We have developed a survey based on the Malcolm Baldrige National Quality Award Criteria to help you engage in a yearly self-assessment. This tool is in the Appendix. This **Quality Teaching Index** will give you a baseline from which you can begin to alter your approach to education. Since CQI results are sometimes incremental, we suggest that you redo the assessment after each course and compare the results with your student evaluations. We know you'll really be surprised with the results.

ΔΔΔΔΔΔΔΔΔ

The following is a check sheet to help you implement the CQI Action technique into the classroom.

FACILITATING SYSTEM

Step 1:   You are demonstrating leadership.
    √   Develop a definition of a quality classroom.
    √   Walk-the-Talk about quality.
    √   Understand Deming's system of Profound Knowledge.
    √   Use a variety of teaching styles.
    √   Have a CQI program for yourself and your students.

Step 2:   The mission, goals, and operational definitions of your course are absolutely clear.
    √   Establish a course mission statement.
    √   Develop quality goals for the course.
    √   Co-create mission statement, quality goals and operational definitions with the students.
    √   Align course mission and goals with those of the institution (program/major).

Step 3:   Most work is pertinent and flows from the students through teams.
    √   Break down barriers on day one by refining the course mission statement with the students.
    √   Have students co-create learning experiences.
    √   Stress the importance of teamwork in problem solving and decision making.
    √   Define quality and what it means.
    √   Create interdisciplinary learning activities.

FACILITATING/LEARNING SYSTEM

Step 4:   The course content is connected to the surrounding community and the real world.
    √   Demonstrate the connectedness between work and the real world.
    √   Ask the students to analyze the learning assignments.
    √   Begin CQI tool and team training for the students.
    √   Implement student suggestions on how best to improve the learning system.

LEARNING SYSTEM

Step 5: The student is treated as a "worker," but s/he is also considered a valuable team member of the "research and development" department.
- √ Re-examine the role of students: Discuss quality systems with students and why they are viewed as both primary customers and workers within the educational system.
- √ Give the students an historical overview about the quality movement and discussed examples.
- √ Discuss the PDCA cycle and root causes of problems.
- √ Discuss the importance of "trust" in a quality classroom.

Step 6: Peer teaching, small group work, and team work are emphasized.
- √ Engage the students in activities that emphasized teaming and making learning fun.
- √ You and your students understand why you are studying a particular aspect of your course.
- √ Engage students to work independently away from the team, but encourage them to report the results to their peers.
- √ Provide guidelines and opportunities for students to assess each others' work.
- √ Encourage each student to ask you for an assessment and recommendations for improvement.
- √ Emphasize the systems approach and regularly asked the students how we can reduce fear.
- √ Provide students with the opportunity for peer tutoring.
- √ Elaborate upon the types of quality teams.
- √ Introduce the students to additional CQI tools and techniques.

LEARNING/IMPROVEMENT SYSTEM

Step 7: Students should have aesthetic experiences.
- √ Encourage students to use their imagination daily.
- √ Discuss the importance of art, music, nature, relaxation techniques, meditation, diet, and exercise with one or more students.
- √ Discuss news headlines and/or controversial topics with one or more students.
- √ Gather specific data to evaluate and improve creative experiences.

IMPROVEMENT SYSTEM

Step 8: Classroom processes include reflection.

√ Develop instant feedback form with students in order to measure classroom processes.

√ Distribute instant feedback forms in order to examine classroom processes.

√ Reflect on my mission, goals, and classroom processes.

√ Set time aside for students to reflect on the relevance of course work to real world issues and encouraged them to discuss their perceptions.

√ Develop self-assessment and goal-setting instruments with students.

Step 9: The teaching and learning systems are constantly evaluated.

√ Use a modified Malcolm Baldrige National Quality Award Criteria to judge the effectiveness of your classroom processes.

√ Refine your professional work plan and based it on the mission and goals of my department and school.

√ Discuss your professional work plan with your supervisor.

√ Constantly interview and survey students as to the effectiveness of the teaching/learning system.

√ Teach students additional CQI tools, including the use of portfolios for self-assessment.

IMPROVEMENT SYSTEM

CHAPTER 11:   NEW ACTIVITIES

Because CQI is a flexible approach to teaching, it provides opportunities for expanding and developing, of building on ideas that evolve in the classroom. This chapter will look into ways to capitalize on the new ideas that emerge from your classroom discussions. In addition, we will discuss how to organize the input you receive from the stakeholders and include it in your course as new activities constantly evolve from the old.

WHAT'S IN IT FOR ME?
Upon completing the chapter you will be able to:
- Facilitate activities that arise during the learning activities
- Co-create new learning activities that emerge during classroom activities
- Reaffirm that all classroom processes and procedures are student-focused.

KNOWLEDGE EVOLUTION
In quality classrooms, there is never an absolute end to learning. Instead, learning experiences simply evolve one from another, and the flow of knowledge continues to build with new concepts being introduced in a wave-like fashion. You can see how this contrasts sharply with traditional classroom methods.

In the traditional model of learning, one concept is introduced. Lessons are directly related to it, and work is assigned to develop an understanding of this one concept. Then, students take a test to determine if they have learned the material. Some students pass; some fail. Regardless of the levels of student comprehension, the teacher then presses on to the next concept, and so on.

The problems resulting from such an approach are obvious: many students don't understand the basic concepts and are forever behind those who do. There are no provisions to ensure all students gain the necessary knowledge to move on. Hence, there are failures and, in some cases, students are being held back. Other students, who grasp the information quickly, are forced to wait until the concept has been tested before they can resume learning. In this scenario—played out in schools across the country—the curriculum invariably gets in the way of learning.

In this book, we have proposed a very different approach to learning. In our model, students start with an understanding of the competencies they are expected to achieve during a time period. This list of competencies is determined by the teacher with input from stakeholders and students. The competencies must be continuously reviewed and upgraded as students learn more and achieve more through the CQI learning approach. This means that even though the outcomes may be listed, they must be fluid enough that students who go beyond what is expected are not penalized or put into a "holding" pattern, but can continue to move forward.

This method of teaching comes at a time when education is being pressed to interconnect with the business community. Robert Gavin, the chief executive officer of Motorola Corp., recently suggested to a group of educators that they start thinking about how they can pack 50 percent more into each class they teach. He said that this was the kind of thinking that Motorola had to do in order to be competitive and stay in business. Furthermore, this continues to be the challenge of business—to do more in less time with less money and to continue to improve the product to satisfy customers while anticipating their future needs.

That is also education's challenge. Ironically, many college and university educators do not feel the sense of urgency affecting business because of the belief that higher education will always remain a mainstay in America. The tragedy of this kind of thinking is that there is no real understanding of how education (as a system) interacts with business or the systems that comprise our communities. Yet, the principle of continuous improvement is a way of life in companies that expect to stay in business. For those businesses that ignore the customers, their suppliers, and their competition, success (if any) will be fleeting.

For Americans to compete in a world market, we must ingrain CQI into our business practices. As Deming realized, such an approach must begin in the schools, the training grounds for our future business leaders. It is a fact that we *must* change the way we do business in higher education: We can no longer sit back and pretend that we are doing a good job or that our students are competitive in the global economy. We must listen to our external customers.

Do we know what they are saying? Yes, we do. Business leaders are speaking out all the time. Can we incorporate their needs into a curriculum. Yes, we can. We have. The following article was taken from the May 1995 issue of *The Chronicle of CQI*. It shows how the voice of the customer can be included in building a curriculum when CQI tools and techniques are used. In the article that follows, the authors report on building a curriculum to meet the need of their customers (the employers) who will hire their products (nursing graduates). Among other tools, they used a **Pareto Diagram** and **Quality Function Deployment** (QFD)

∆∆∆∆∆∆∆∆∆

Quality Approaches for Curriculum Redesign Using a CQI Framework
by *Mary Jo Boyer* and *Carol Lillis*

We set out to do the difficult—redesign a nursing curriculum at Delaware County (Pa.) Community College that was not only responsive to a constantly changing health-care environment, but also addressed accreditation standards and student expectations. Most educators would agree that curriculum revisions is a lengthy and difficult process. Then we made the process almost impossible by instituting on quality accountability from the customer's perspective.

But it worked. By relying on such TQM tools as **affinity diagrams,** a **Pareto chart** (see below), and a customer window, we modified the **Quality Function Deployment** (QFD) matrix for use in education and clearly illustrated the linkage between customer needs and curricular-design requirements. At the same time, we developed a process built on a collaborative-leadership style to create an environment of empowerment. In effect, customers in the system took ownership of the change process.

Instead of generating insurmountable problems, we discovered that a customer orientation provided focus and direction, was more cost-effective and less time-consuming, and resulted in a supportive and interactive learning environment.

The **QFD** matrix (see below) provided a voice to customers as we attempted to determine important attributes of our new curriculum. It graphically displayed relationships between curricular content and methods of instructional delivery. This approach helped us concentrate on process and design rather than specific faculty areas of concern. Use of this matrix and CQI techniques resulted in: (a) increased student, graduate, and employer satisfaction; (b) enhanced faculty accountability; and (c) improved system efficiency.

In addition, an increased awareness of student needs encouraged faculty to be more innovative in the classroom by using collaborative learning techniques to promote active learning.

Figure 11.0: A Pareto Diagram showing customer suggestions for curricular redesign.

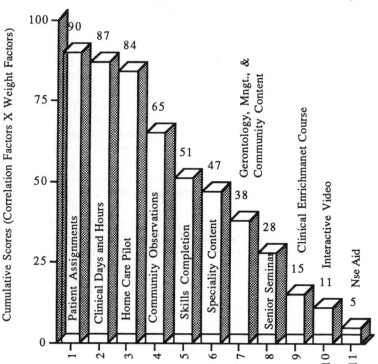

Customer Suggestions for Curricular Redesign

Activities to Implement New Curriculum

Figure 11.1: House of Quality for Curriculum Development

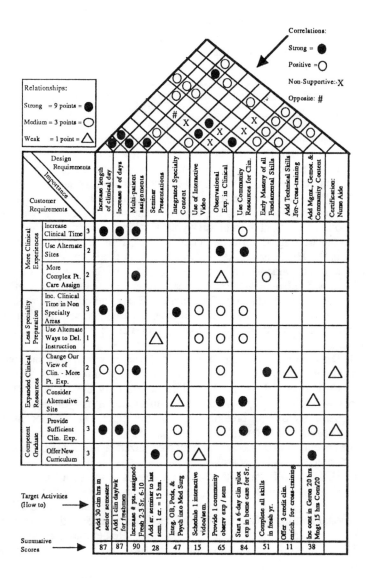

QUALITY FUNCTION DEPLOYMENT (QFD)

How are you going to incorporate the needs of your suppliers into your curriculum? Here is a technique that has worked successfully in classrooms around the country: use **Quality Function Deployment** (QFD) and build yourself a **House of Quality** (Cornesky, 1993).

Quality Function Deployment was first applied in a Mitsubishi Industries in 1972 and is a flexible but disciplined planning and implementation procedure in which the customer's wants and needs are deployed throughout your course. **QFD** will provide a supporting system for making sure that the customer's wants and needs are sought after and heard and then incorporated into your teaching procedures.

By using the **QFD** and the **House of Quality** (HOQ) tool, you can greatly reduce misunderstandings about the objectives and expected terminal competencies of the course and how they apply to meeting the needs of each student. **QFD** can also provide you with a structured way of measuring personal performances in meeting the wants and needs of the students, even to the point of being able to modify your teaching style in the middle of a class to meet the needs of a particular student. Remember, however, that **QFD** and the **HOQ** are remarkably flexible, so they can be adapted and molded to meet a wide variety of needs of both teacher and the student.

QFD will also serve you by permitting you to establish a quality improvement team of students. By using the **HOQ** and other CQI tools, the team can arrive at a consensus early in the class schedule of what should be modified in the presentation of the material for a better understanding by the students.

QFD recognizes that there are several layers in which customer wants and needs are transformed. These layers are often linked by a series of matrices. There will be many occasions where only one or at most two matrices will provide you with all of the information that you will need to accomplish a significant breakthrough in your class. On other occasions, you may be required to complete four to six matrices.

We have modified three commonly recognized layers of **QFD** for use in the classroom setting. They are:

1. Effective Planning: the wants and needs of the students and other customers are translated into competencies or design specifications of your course (See Figure 11.2 below). On most occasions, especially in professional and technical courses, the needs and wants of the **employers** also have to be included as those of "customers." Remember, the building of the **HOQ is flexible**, and it should be constructed to meet your needs and the needs of your customers.

2. Effective Design : the course competencies or design specifications are translated into instructional techniques.

3. Process Planning: the instructional techniques are translated into processes that will eventually improve the teaching and learning systems.

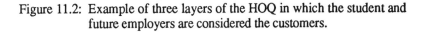

Figure 11.2: Example of three layers of the HOQ in which the student and future employers are considered the customers.

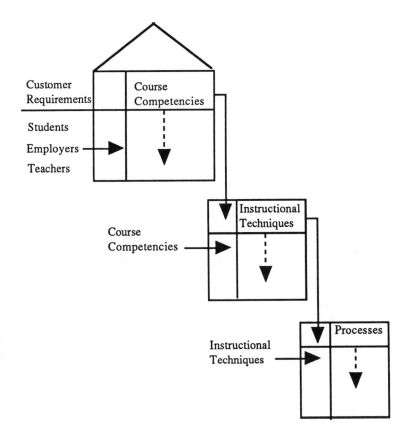

Each "house" reflects a single goal with a detailed "process" for achieving that goal. For example, for a journalism class, the "customers"— a panel of newspaper managing editors—report that members think graduates of your program should know the Associate Press style. You create a house to reflect that goal and include the steps—classroom presentation, examples, research, etc.—by which that goal will be met. Sometimes, you need one or more houses when one process will lead to another.

HOQ is nothing more than a set of matrices that address the wants and needs of your students and other customers and detail how your course will supply the services necessary to meet their needs. The matrices will show where relationships exist and may reveal the strength and compatibility of the relationships. A completed HOQ will also enable you to identify the needs and wants of the customer that are not being met or are poorly met by your course. This will permit you to effectively develop a strategic plan for continuously improving your course.

The design not only insures that the voice of the customer is built into the process, but that your educational approach is designed around need. Your students will leave your class with the skills required for the next level. The work then becomes important to them, not just something to learn and forget.

The minimum requirement for implementing QFD in your course is your commitment. Of course, it is much better if your students buy into the CQI process. They will if you take the time to explain its importance.

EXPANDING THE VISION

Let's take what we have learned and look to the future. You must focus on the vision of the future. Create your vision of the optimal learning environment. What does it look like, sound like? What kinds of activities are going on? How are students organized? Imagine your utopia in an educational setting. To do this, it will be necessary to eliminate all your biases about people, the community, the school, the world. Open yourself to the possibilities of having *all* your students achieve far beyond your wildest imagination. Include in your vision of excellence those students who have been difficult for you, those with disabilities, and those who are different. This is a learning environment that is totally without fear, where students help each other, where the teacher is the leader, mentor, and facilitator and learner right along with the students.

How can you change the vision from the traditional to the new—towards CQI learning? We recommend strongly that students be allowed to co-create these learning experiences. Teachers can and should start the process by creating the first one or two experiences, but beyond that students can play a major role in determining their own learning experiences.

With students as co-creators of learning experiences, teachers spend less time creating lectures. The course goals and competencies are created together as the semester progresses. If everyone knows what is expected, why do teachers have to be rigid in determining how these competencies will be achieved? If students are allowed to help in creating the learning experiences, they will be motivated to accomplish them. In the traditional view, teachers are responsible for planning and creating everything that happens in their course. The problem is that either only those students who are eager to please the teachers or who are blessed with some internal discipline that keeps them focused will buy into your assignments.

We suggest that even those students you typically thinks of as being fully challenged are only about half challenged and that we have absolutely no idea how far they could advance if given the opportunity to co-create their own learning experiences. The majority who seem unmotivated or disinterested in school will never do any better than they currently do unless something dramatic changes in the system to make a learning environment that works for them. Do not sell these students short. They are motivated to learn!

One of the most frequent complaints students have about school is that most course content lacks relevance to the real world. If students don't know how something can benefit them, they most likely will not fully invest in learning it. They might do the "work," but few will retain it other than in their short-term memory, and if asked the following year to build on previously learned concepts, they will have no recollection of learning it at all. This is frustrating for teachers who have worked so hard only to discover that their students go to the next class where the next instructor complains that the students weren't taught the necessary prerequisites for success in their course.

Imagine taking an entirely different approach to the teaching and learning processes. Imagine asking the students how they want to learn the desired outcomes and for input into how much time they need to learn. Imagine creating a **systematic diagram** together that shows specific tasks and the order each should be done, along with a time table and an indication of who's responsible. This is the way to engage students and relieve yourself of the burden of daily lectures. Of course, you'll have to guide this process, but allow the students as much freedom as possible.

You must believe that you can assist all students to learn even the most complex concepts in your course, provided you find ways to create an experience that they perceive as fun, interesting, and intriguing, and always related to their world.

When creating a learning experience, do it with the end in mind. What would you like the students to know, demonstrate, or create at the end of this experience? Point out the competencies that are included in this experience. Discuss the ways they will demonstrate they've achieved each of these outcomes. Then, they will know your expectations.

Each day you'll want students to give you a minute of their time for fast feedback. This is the way you'll keep updated on how each student is progressing, where their frustrations are, and how you can help. If you don't have the opportunity to talk with each student during the day, the daily written fast feedback can give you very valuable information.

Of course, you've set a time limit for this activity, and students have created a **systematic diagram** for themselves or a **flow chart** with key process points fixed so you can assess how they are doing.

NEW ACTIVITIES FROM THE OLD

When the first learning experience (particular competencies) is over, you should debrief your students so you can get a clear picture of what worked for them and what didn't. Have students review the competencies for the term and see how they can build upon the previously learned ones. Then brainstorm with students how they want to build onto this experience. Allow everyone time to share their ideas and move towards building consensus. The product they end up with may be very different, but the learning experience can be the same for all.

Imagine your students building upon this first learning experience by wanting to do something to make the school a better place to learn. In a college setting, they might research opportunities in student aide, financial services, admissions, computer center, library, and/or housing, or there may be some pressing concern that interests them. Build a consensus among students as to what direction they would like the learning experience to take and write the purpose (mission) on the board. Next, ask students what they'd consider quality factors. This will be the basis for evaluation or the expectations upon which their projects will be assessed. Next, ask students what they would say if they were to describe the "best" way to accomplish the project. In other words, you will want students to define their expectations. If they don't come up with all the pertinent quality factors, then you, as a partner in the class, can add yours.

Prior to asking students to commence, review the expected terminal course competencies and see which one(s) will be accomplished by completing the learning experience. Have students again go through and circle those that apply, and place a small check mark at the level at which the class agrees each competency must be achieved.

With your students, create a **flow chart** of the process that will be used for this learning experience. Students will then have a picture of how the learning experience will unfold and what the process check points will be. You can add a time line and identify the person responsible on any **flow chart** simply by creating a **deployment flow chart** and adding dates.

With this method students have information that gives them a clear picture of expectations, responsibilities, check points, and results. Everyone knows what is expected, and everyone knows what criteria will be used to assess the final product. This takes away excuses, but more importantly allows students the freedom to work without fear of a breakdown in the process. Enthusiasm will run high when the learning environment and learning experiences are established collaboratively, with students identifying their products.

THE FINAL PRODUCT

We've been schooled to believe that an assignment means that everyone does the same thing. In quality classrooms there is plenty of room for creativity and invention. Many students may be creating new and different products from other students, though the competency is the same for all. Remember the importance of the constancy of purpose and think about how to optimize the learning experiences for all students. Some students may view the product visually, others will want to write, while still others will want to use a different approach. With time, all students can expand their approach to learning by experiencing it in many forms.

Through a process of teaching students how to create learning experiences that are fun and real-world oriented and then applying CQI tools for planning and studying the results, students can and do become fully engaged in their own learning. These students are enthusiastic and energetic learners, eager to stretch the limits of their knowledge and hence their world.

In classrooms where quality improvement is a way of life, students eagerly work past the last day of school.

ΛΛΛΛΛΛΛΛ

The following is a check sheet to help you implement the CQI Action technique into the classroom.

FACILITATING SYSTEM

Step 1:   You are demonstrating leadership.
- √   Develop a definition of a quality classroom.
- √   Walk-the-Talk about quality.
- √   Understand Deming's system of Profound Knowledge.
- √   Use a variety of teaching styles.
- √   Have a CQI program for yourself and your students.

Step 2:   The mission, goals, and operational definitions of your course are absolutely clear.
- √   Establish a course mission statement.
- √   Develop quality goals for the course.
- √   Co-create mission statement, quality goals and operational definitions with the students.
- √   Align course mission and goals with those of the institution (program/major).

Step 3:   Most work is pertinent and flows from the students through teams.
- √   Break down barriers on day one by refining the course mission statement with the students.
- √   Have students co-create learning experiences.
- √   Stress the importance of teamwork in problem solving and decision making.
- √   Define quality and what it means.
- √   Create interdisciplinary learning activities.

FACILITATING/LEARNING SYSTEM

Step 4:   The course content is connected to the surrounding community and the real world.
- √   Demonstrate the connectedness between work and the real world.
- √   Ask the students to analyze the learning assignments.
- √   Begin CQI tool and team training for the students.
- √   Implement student suggestions on how best to improve the learning system.

LEARNING SYSTEM

Step 5: The student is treated as a "worker," but s/he is also considered a valuable team member of the "research and development" department.

√ Re-examine the role of students: Discuss quality systems with students and why they are viewed as both primary customers and workers within the educational system.

√ Give the students an historical overview about the quality movement and discussed examples.

√ Discuss the PDCA cycle and root causes of problems.

√ Discuss the importance of "trust" in a quality classroom.

Step 6: Peer teaching, small group work, and team work are emphasized.

√ Engage the students in activities that emphasized teaming and making learning fun.

√ You and your students understand why you are studying a particular aspect of your course.

√ Engage students to work independently away from the team, but encourage them to report the results to their peers.

√ Provide guidelines and opportunities for students to assess each others' work.

√ Encourage each student to ask you for an assessment and recommendations for improvement.

√ Emphasize the systems approach and regularly asked the students how we can reduce fear.

√ Provide students with the opportunity for peer tutoring.

√ Elaborate upon the types of quality teams.

√ Introduce the students to additional CQI tools and techniques.

LEARNING/IMPROVEMENT SYSTEM

Step 7: Students should have aesthetic experiences.

√ Encourage students to use their imagination daily.

√ Discuss the importance of art, music, nature, relaxation techniques, meditation, diet, and exercise with one or more students.

√ Discuss news headlines and/or controversial topics with one or more students.

√ Gather specific data to evaluate and improve creative experiences.

IMPROVEMENT SYSTEM

Step 8: Classroom processes include reflection.
- √ Develop instant feedback form with students in order to measure classroom processes.
- √ Distribute instant feedback forms in order to examine classroom processes.
- √ Reflect on my mission, goals, and classroom processes.
- √ Set time aside for students to reflect on the relevance of course work to real world issues and encouraged them to discuss their perceptions.
- √ Develop self-assessment and goal-setting instruments with students.

Step 9: The teaching and learning systems are constantly evaluated.
- √ Use a modified Malcolm Baldrige National Quality Award Criteria to judge the effectiveness of your classroom processes.
- √ Refine your professional work plan and based it on the mission and goals of my department and school.
- √ Discuss your professional work plan with your supervisor.
- √ Constantly interview and survey students as to the effectiveness of the teaching/learning system.
- √ Teach students additional CQI tools, including the use of portfolios for self-assessment.

Step 10: New activities constantly evolve from the old.
- √ Present the competencies that the students are expected to achieve during the semester.
- √ Reaffirm that all classroom processes are student-focused.
- √ Constantly revise your vision of the optimal learning environment.
- √ Co-create learning experiences with the students.
- √ Integrate the learning experiences and demonstrate how they relate to the real world.
- √ Facilitate new activities that arise from the old.

PAYMENT SYSTEM

Chapter 12:   Audience Beyond The Teacher

Congratulations, you have almost reached the end of your CQI journey. Your students are learning at a pace you never imagined was possible. You have discovered a wide array of techniques and exercises to help them learn. They are evaluating your work; you are encouraging colleagues to join you. Now what? In the last phase of this long trek, you need to help your students carry their newfound knowledge beyond your classroom. Here's how to reward them as you provide an audience beyond the teacher.

WHAT'S IN IT FOR ME?
Upon completing the chapter you will be able to:
- Discuss the "future" with your students
- Understand why it is important to encourage students to share their classroom experiences with others
- Encourage students to keep portfolios of their learning
- Implement mechanisms to have students extend their learning experiences into the community.

THERE MUST BE A BETTER WAY
In the past, educators have created assignments that students "do for them." That is to say, the teacher creates the assignments based on the scope and sequence of the course in the curriculum, and students complete the assignments and turn them in to the teacher who grades and returns them to the student. The cycle goes from teacher to student to teacher to student.

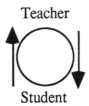

Teacher

Student

   In this model, the student performs work for the teacher and solely for the teacher. Seldom is there any intrinsic reward or pride in workmanship, other than the grade. It is an illusion to imagine that students complete their work in traditional classrooms for anyone but the teacher, although occasionally, a student will be motivated by wanting to please parents or through some other force. Some students do learn and complete complex tasks because they see the inherent virtue in doing it or because they know this is but one step along a long road towards some far-off career goal. It is a wonder that so many students complete their work, especially when considering how irrelevant so many assignments are.

In the above model, the teacher is the final customer. In other words, the teacher has to be "satisfied" if the student is to be rewarded with a grade. The classroom becomes "teacher-centered," rather than "student-centered."

In quality classrooms, however, students are responsible for co-creating the learning experiences required to demonstrate the mastery of competencies. By engaging in this exercise, students create experiences that have meaning to them.

What motivates human behavior is not producing for others, but producing or creating something for ourselves. When students have break-through learning, they experience an exhilaration that extends far beyond the satisfaction of performing a task simply because they have been told to do so.

Pride in workmanship comes from performing feats and solving "puzzles" that are a stretch beyond our current limitations. It comes from the good feelings about being able to do something for oneself.

Humans are naturally curious, and in courses where experiences for exploration are encouraged, the students become better problem-solvers and engage in higher-level thinking skills. In courses where rote memorization and learning by regurgitating facts is a way of life, less critical thinking, less creativity, and less curiosity are achieved. These students may have learned to memorize and remember long enough to give back answers on a test, but they've learned nothing about how to collect many sources of information, to generate a hypothesis or create new knowledge from previously learned material. In the rote classroom, students "learn" because someone directs them. In the CQI classroom, natural curiosity and invention make learning a joy. The resulting product is a source of great pride to the student, her/his parents, peers, and others.

As an example, consider this scenario with some college professors who wanted to establish a "Learning Community" for at-risk students who were entering as freshmen. During the previous spring, the professors agreed that they would work together with students to eliminate all busywork and combine assignments in **World Geography**, **English Composition**, and **Economics**. The three professors agreed that they would team teach each class from 9 a.m. to noon on Monday, Wednesday, and Friday. The 60 students would receive nine semester hours of credit, three for each of the courses. They would be advised by these professors and would receive special help on Tuesdays and Thursdays, as requested. The professors agreed to show the inter-relationships between the world economy and world geography. The essay exams would be corrected for the English Composition portion of the credit. Students and teachers together could co-create the experiences. Since this was new for the professors (also for the students), they were somewhat concerned about how this would happen, but were determined to forge ahead. Since students and professors were already organized into teams (with administrative approval), it provided an organizational pattern that could work.

In the fall, professors gathered and asked the students for suggestions about what interested them and explained that the plan was to build educational experiences around their interests. With some guidance, the students were able to list a wide range of topics. Next, the professors led the group in a discussion of "how do you want to learn about these things." This naturally led to "what will the product of our education be ... or how will we demonstrate that we've learned."

The sixty students were placed into 10 teams ranging in size from 3 to 10. Each team conducted research on a variety of topics, such as the role of trade routes and regional religions, beliefs, and economy. No less that 58 of these "at-risk" students completed the competencies of the Learning Community with grades of A's or B's. The students and professors became very excited about the possibilities of performing this type of experiment with other courses.

In the spring, the students went on to other classes—the traditional type. Unfortunately, approximately 40 of the students soon dropped out of college. That should not be a surprise. Once students experience CQI classrooms, they find other approaches boring and quickly become disenchanted with school.

Other Learning Community possibilities exist between courses in English, speech, art, history, sociology, science, computer science, and mathematics. Teachers can work together and provide common learning experiences that allow students to prepare one or more significant pieces of research that can be assessed by teachers of each discipline for style and content.

STUDENTS' HOPES AND DREAMS

At all levels of education, you should invite others into your course regularly. Allow students to share with their peers what they are working on. They should be able to explain how any learning experience relates to the required competencies. If they are going to go beyond the required competencies to attain much higher levels of learning, that, too, should be noted. Empower students to speak to a variety of people, since students assume a lead role in the learning experience. This expands students' abilities to communicate with older adults as well as enables them to demonstrate pride in workmanship. The focus of any course must remain on the students, since they are the reason for schools.

Portfolios also provide a means of demonstrating growth in knowledge and capabilities. Students determine what belongs in their portfolios based on the **Operational Definitions** agreed upon by the class and their own sense of "best" work. Since students are selecting their best work for the portfolio, it follows that they are in the best position to relate this information to parents, peers, other teachers and potential employers.

Other ways to demonstrate student growth is by producing videos of them in action. Students truly enjoy seeing the results of their progress. A videotape also provides valuable feedback to the student(s). Teams of students can critique their own teamwork and their results. Individual students can do a self-assessment of progress and be taught to look for the quality factors. Teams and individuals can even be taught to critique each other's work and thereby provide valuable feedback. In the end, the results of any videotaped experience can extend far beyond the particular learning experience that has just been completed.

VOLUNTEER OR SERVICE LEARNING
While it is important for students to experience pride in creating educational products that extend beyond the classroom, it is also important for students to give back to their community and thus gain a sense of oneness with their community. Some schools, especially community colleges and universities, have implemented a volunteer project as a requirement for graduation. We believe that service work or volunteerism can and probably should become a part of everyone's educational experiences each academic year (beginning in elementary school).

The experiences that students co-create can easily include volunteerism. Also, intergenerational volunteer experiences can help provide a connection to other adults that is often missing in the lives of many youth.

A FINAL NOTE
Professor Peter Haugh of Western Washington University in Bellingham, Washington wrote the following about how he recognizes his **Student Advisory Committee** (SAC): *At the end of the course, I use several techniques to reinforce the importance of the SAC. During one of the last classes, I present Distinguish Service Awards to each SAC participant, and then I take the members to lunch. These events highlight the importance of the SACs and are passed on by word of mouth to future students.* Isn't this a great idea?

Some educators believe that January 29, 1904 is the most important date in the history of education. This is the day that the letterman's club was started at the University of Chicago. Ever since, students have been recognized more for their achievements in sports and other extracurricular activities (band, debate, theater, etc.) than they are for their academic achievements.

There are awards programs, of course, but it's safe to say they do not carry the same prestige or achieve the same recognition as sports' awards. Besides, they are too limited. They acknowledge only winners of special prizes or contests. Perhaps we should give "letters" to all students who have excelled in course work.

Once we begin to acknowledge and honor students who succeed academically, we will create an audience beyond the teacher for the achievements every individual student as well as for the team in which they worked. If students can have pride in their football letters, surely we can instill the same pride for academic achievements.

∆∆∆∆∆∆∆∆

The following is a check sheet to help you implement the CQI Action technique into the classroom.

FACILITATING SYSTEM

Step 1:   You are demonstrating leadership.
- √ Develop a definition of a quality classroom.
- √ Walk-the-Talk about quality.
- √ Understand Deming's system of Profound Knowledge.
- √ Use a variety of teaching styles.
- √ Have a CQI program for yourself and your students.

Step 2:   The mission, goals, and operational definitions of your course are absolutely clear.
- √ Establish a course mission statement.
- √ Develop quality goals for the course.
- √ Co-create mission statement, quality goals and operational definitions with the students.
- √ Align course mission and goals with those of the institution (program/major).

Step 3:   Most work is pertinent and flows from the students through teams.
- √ Break down barriers on day one by refining the course mission statement with the students.
- √ Have students co-create learning experiences.
- √ Stress the importance of teamwork in problem solving and decision making.
- √ Define quality and what it means.
- √ Create interdisciplinary learning activities.

FACILITATING/LEARNING SYSTEM

Step 4:   The course content is connected to the surrounding community and the real world.
- √ Demonstrate the connectedness between work and the real world.
- √ Ask the students to analyze the learning assignments.
- √ Begin CQI tool and team training for the students.
- √ Implement student suggestions on how best to improve the learning system.

LEARNING SYSTEM

Step 5: The student is treated as a "worker," but s/he is also considered a valuable team member of the "research and development" department.

√ Re-examine the role of students: Discuss quality systems with students and why they are viewed as both primary customers and workers within the educational system.

√ Give the students an historical overview about the quality movement and discussed examples.

√ Discuss the PDCA cycle and root causes of problems.

√ Discuss the importance of "trust" in a quality classroom.

Step 6: Peer teaching, small group work, and team work are emphasized.

√ Engage the students in activities that emphasized teaming and making learning fun.

√ You and your students understand why you are studying a particular aspect of your course.

√ Engage students to work independently away from the team, but encourage them to report the results to their peers.

√ Provide guidelines and opportunities for students to assess each others' work.

√ Encourage each student to ask you for an assessment and recommendations for improvement.

√ Emphasize the systems approach and regularly asked the students how we can reduce fear.

√ Provide students with the opportunity for peer tutoring.

√ Elaborate upon the types of quality teams.

√ Introduce the students to additional CQI tools and techniques.

LEARNING/IMPROVEMENT SYSTEM

Step 7: Students should have aesthetic experiences.

√ Encourage students to use their imagination daily.

√ Discuss the importance of art, music, nature, relaxation techniques, meditation, diet, and exercise with one or more students.

√ Discuss news headlines and/or controversial topics with one or more students.

√ Gather specific data to evaluate and improve creative experiences.

IMPROVEMENT SYSTEM

Step 8:   Classroom processes include reflection.

- √ Develop instant feedback form with students in order to measure classroom processes.
- √ Distribute instant feedback forms in order to examine classroom processes.
- √ Reflect on my mission, goals, and classroom processes.
- √ Set time aside for students to reflect on the relevance of course work to real world issues and encouraged them to discuss their perceptions.
- √ Develop self-assessment and goal-setting instruments with students.

Step 9:   The teaching and learning systems are constantly evaluated.

- √ Use a modified Malcolm Baldrige National Quality Award Criteria to judge the effectiveness of your classroom processes.
- √ Refine your professional work plan and based it on the mission and goals of my department and school.
- √ Discuss your professional work plan with your supervisor.
- √ Constantly interview and survey students as to the effectiveness of the teaching/learning system.
- √ Teach students additional CQI tools, including the use of portfolios for self-assessment.

Step 10: New activities constantly evolve from the old.

- √ Present the competencies that the students are expected to achieve during the semester.
- √ Reaffirm that all classroom processes are student-focused.
- √ Constantly revise your vision of the optimal learning environment.
- √ Co-create learning experiences with the students.
- √ Integrate the learning experiences and demonstrate how they relate to the real world.
- √ Facilitate new activities that arise from the old.

PAYMENT (REWARD) SYSTEM

Step 11: There is an audience beyond the teacher.

- √ Encourage students to "dream" about what they want to do in the future.
- √ Allow students to invite others into the classroom and to share with them what they are working on.
- √ Encourage students to share their portfolios with parents, other teachers, other faculty, and peers.
- √ Extend learning experiences into the community.

References

Barker, Joel . *Future Edge: Discovering the New Paradigms of Success.* New York, NY: Wm. Morrow & Co., Inc., 1992.

Batemen, G. and H. Roberts, 1993. Personal communication.

Baxter, Kay et. al. *Total Quality: A Teacher's Handbook.* Georgia Department of Education, 1994.

Baugher, K. *LEARN: The Student Quality Team Process for Improving Teaching and Learning.* Birmingham, AL: Samford University, 1992.

Bemowski, K. "Restoring the Pillars of Higher Education," *Quality Progress* (October 1991).

Byrnes, Margaret A., Robert A.Cornesky, and Lawrence W. Byrnes, *The Quality Teacher: Implementing Total Quality Management in the Classroom.* Port Orange, FL: Cornesky & Associates, Inc. 1992.

Byrnes, Margaret and Robert A. Cornesky. *Quality Fusion: Turning Total Quality Management Into Classroom Practice.* Port Orange, FL: Cornesky & Associates Press, 1994.

Cornesky, R.A., Ron Baker, Cathy Cavanaugh, William Etling, Michael Lukert, Sam McCool, Brian McKay, An-Sik Min, Charlotte Paul, Paul Thomas, David Wagner, and John Darling. *Using Deming to Improve Quality in Colleges and Universities,* Madison, WI: Magna Publications, Inc., 1989.

Cornesky, R.A., Sam McCool, Larry Byrnes, and Robert Weber. *Implementing Total Quality Management in Institutions of Higher Education.* Madison, WI: Magna Publications, Inc., 1991.

Cornesky, R.A. and Sam McCool. *Total Quality Improvement Guide for Institutions of Higher Education.* Madison, WI: Magna Publications, Inc., 1992.

Cornesky, R.A. *The Quality Professor: Implementing Total Quality Management in the College Classroom.* Madison, WI: Magna Publications, Inc., 1993.

Covey, Stephen R. *The 7 Habits of Highly Effective People.* New York, NY: Simon & Schuster, 1989.

Crosby, Philip B. *Quality Without Tears: The Art of Hassle-Free Management.* New York, NY: McGraw-Hill Book Co., 1984.

References

Cross, K.P., and T.A. Angelo, *Classroom Assessment Techniques: A Handbook for College Teachers* (2nd. ed.). San Francisco: Jossey Bass, 1993.

Deming, W. Edwards. *Out of the Crisis*. Cambridge, MA: Productivity Press or Washington, DC: The George Washington University, MIT-CAES, 1982.

Glasser, William. *The Quality School* . New York, NY: Harper & Row. 1990.

Glasser, William. *The Quality School Teacher*. New York, NY: Harper Collins Publishers, Inc. 1993.

Harris, J.W. and J.M. Baggett, (Eds.) *Quality Quest in the Academic Process*. Birmingham, AL: Samford University, 1992.

Hau, I. *Teaching Quality Improvement by Quality Improvement in Teaching*. Center for Quality and Productivity Improvement, University of Wisconsin, Report No. 59. 20., 1991.

Imai, Masaaki. *Kaizen: The Key to Japan's Competitive Success*, New York: Random House, 1986

Levering, Robert. *A Great Place to Work*. New York: Random House, Inc., 1988.

Manz, Charles C., and Henry P. Sims, Jr. *Super-Leadership*. New York: The Berkley Publishing Group, 1990.

Teeter, D.J. and G.G. Lozier, (Eds.). *Pursuit of Quality in Higher Education: Case Studies in Total Quality Management*. New Directions for Institutional Research, 78, San Francisco: Jossey-Bass, 1993.

Waterman, Robert H. *Adhocracy: The Power to Change*. Knoxville, TN: Whittle Direct Books, 1990.

Wigginton, Eliot. *Sometimes a Shining Moment: The Foxfire Experience*. New York, NY: Doubleday, 1985.

APPENDIX

TABLE OF CONTENTS

INTRODUCTION

Throughout this book, we have referred to a variety of CQI tools and techniques. This section will provide detailed information on each of the tools, so you can use them in your classroom.

By using the tools and techniques of Continuous Quality Improvement (CQI), you will be able to help you and your students focus on the classroom processes

When you properly implement the **CQI** system, the tools and techniques will encourage your students to participate in their education. The students will become involved in peer teaching, small group work, and team work as they constantly reflect upon the classroom processes. With your help, they will be able to develop self-assessment and goal-setting instruments.

By properly using the CQI tools and techniques, you will be able to constantly evaluate the facilitating system and the learning system. You will easily be able to:

1. Develop new classroom activities from the old
2. Show that your classroom processes are student-focused
3. Constantly revise your vision of the optimal learning environment
4. Co-create learning experiences with your students
5. Extend the learning experiences into the community.

Each tool is listed in alphabetical order. Along with the procedure on how to use a tool, we have included one or more specific examples from various grade levels.

As you will see, some of the tools require data analysis and statistics. Not all of us are comfortable with such mathematical requirements. We highly recommend you use a computer with certain software programs. For example, **TopDown**™ **Flowcharter** is excellent not only for flowcharting, but also for many other CQI tools such as the Affinity Diagram, Cause and Effect Diagram, Relations Diagram, the Systematic Diagram and the Scenario Builder. It can be purchased from Kaetron Software Corp., 25211 Grogans Mill Road, Suite 260, The Woodlands, Texas 77380; PH: (713) 298-1500; fax: (713) 298-2520. Two very good programs for producing Histograms, Pareto Diagrams, Run Charts, Scatter Diagrams and Control Charts are: **DeltaGraph**™**Pro 3.5** [DeltaPoint, Inc., 2 Harris Court, Suite B-1, Monterey, CA 93940; PH: (408) 648-4000; fax: (408) 648-4020]; and **Cricket Graph III** [Computer Associates International, 1 Computer Associates Plaza, Islandia, NY 11788-9820; PH: (516) 342-5224; fax: (516) 342-5734].

AFFINITY DIAGRAM

The **Affinity Diagram** was invented by Kawakita Jiro and is used as a planning tool, because it is a creative procedure that tries to organize the issues concerning a process or a problem without quantification.

An **Affinity Diagram** is especially useful in clarifying a problem or issue that is difficult to understand, or a problem or issue that appears to be enormous and in disarray. One benefit of using the **Affinity Diagram** at the very beginning of a CQI process is that it helps build consensus among the team members studying the problem.

An **Affinity Diagram** is rarely used alone. However, when used with the Scenario Builder, and/or with a Relations Diagram, and/or with the Nominal Group Process, it can help an action team and/or team identify the major root causes of a problem or issue. When the major root causes of a problem or issue are identified, the group can direct its efforts more efficiently.

Procedure
1. Statement of the Problem

Under the direction of a team leader, members of a team should arrive at a statement of the problem or issue being addressed. For example, Mr. Jones' tenth-grade social studies classes wanted to include a community service project as part of the curriculum. A team consisting of students, Mr. Jones and two parents agreed to work on the situation. The question they asked was: What are the obstacles to including a community service project requirement in Mr. Jones' tenth-grade social studies classes?

2. Recording the Perceptions

Working alone, each person writes his/her comment on sticky note paper or on an index card after announcing his/her idea to the group. The purpose of announcing the perception is to permit others to piggyback with related ideas. Only a single idea should be entered on any note paper/index card. This proceeds until all of the people have exhausted their perceptions. Remember, as in any brainstorming session, there is no verbal exchange between the members. All of the notes are placed on the wall or in the center of a large conference table.

Let's assume the following perceptions were generated and posted.

> The school board won't permit it.

> Students lack transportation

> Class periods are too short.

> The principal won't support it.

> The superintendent won't support it.

> There is no need.

> Other teachers won't support the idea and cooperate in flexible scheduling.

> The liability of having students out of the building is too great.

> The community doesn't want students out of school unsupervised (too difficult to supervise).

> Community service isn't perceived to be a school function.

> Parents don't want students out of school.

> Students lack commitment.

3. Group Similar and/or Related Perceptions

The members of the group place similar cards (or sticky notes) into related groups. These are said to have an "affinity" for each other. It is important that the members of the team do this without criticism. The notes (or cards) can be moved any number of times. It is not uncommon to have ten related groups, although you may have a few as three.

The grouping that resulted from the aforementioned example are shown below.

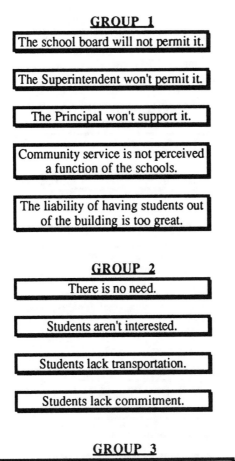

GROUP 1

The school board will not permit it.

The Superintendent won't permit it.

The Principal won't support it.

Community service is not perceived a function of the schools.

The liability of having students out of the building is too great.

GROUP 2

There is no need.

Students aren't interested.

Students lack transportation.

Students lack commitment.

GROUP 3

Parents don't want students out of school.

GROUP 4

Impossible to supervise.

Parents don't want students out of school.

Other teachers won't support the idea and cooperate in flexible scheduling.

Class periods are too short.

4. Assign a Name to Each Group with a Header Designation

The team leader should read all of the cards in each group, and the members should agree to a name that can be assigned to each of the groups. The team leader then writes a header card for each group. If there is a miscellaneous group, the team should exam each perception and, if possible, place each note or card into one of the groups. If not, it is acceptable to have a group named "miscellaneous." In the above example, the four header groups are shown below.

GROUP 1: THE ADMINISTRATION

| The school board will not permit it. |

| The Superintendent won't permit it. |

| The Principal won't support it. |

| Community service is not perceived a function of the schools. |

| The liability of having students out of the building is too great. |

GROUP 2: THE STUDENTS

| There is no need. |

| Students aren't interested. |

| Students lack transportation. |

| Students lack commitment. |

GROUP 3: THE PARENTS

| Parents don't want students out of school. |

GROUP 4: THE TEACHERS

| Impossible to supervise. |

| Parents don't want students out of school. |

| Other teachers won't support the idea and cooperate in flexible scheduling. |

| Class periods are too short. |

5. Draw the Affinity Diagram

The team members should tape the cards/sticky notes in each group either onto a board or a large flip chart. With the header cards at the top, the leader should draw borders around each group. In the figure below, the completed **Affinity Diagram** is shown for the above example.

6. Discuss Each Group

The team members should discuss each of the groups and how it relates to the situation. An **Affinity Diagram** will not solve any problems but will result in a better understanding of the issues and/or processes making up the situation. That, in turn, permits the group to focus on each concern through the use of other tools.

In order to arrive at deeper understandings of each of the root causes, the team may want to use a Relations Diagram for each of the groups. Depending upon the problem or issue, the Scenario Builder, Systematic Diagram, and/or Cause and Effect Diagram may be of value.

AFFINITY DIAGRAM
OBSTACLES TO ESTABLISHING A COMMUNITY
SERVICE PROJECT REQUIREMENT

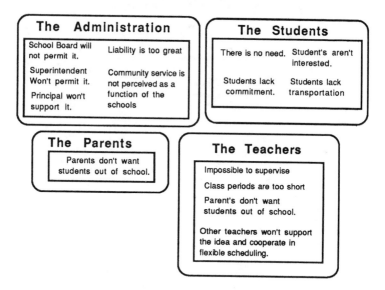

Note

An **Affinity Diagram** is a way of collecting, identifying, and organizing a large number of ideas in a short time. It is used when a team needs a method for analyzing an issue. It encourages everyone to contribute, to interact, and to build consensus. Once you have built an **Affinity Diagram**, you can move onto the next step of analyzing the concerns and developing solutions for them.

Here are some possible topics that might be approached through **Affinity Diagrams**:
1. Possible middle school topics
   > What are the benefits of quality work?
   > How does subject A relate to subject B?
   > What are the components of quality writing?
   > What are the obstacles to good reading habits?
2. Possible high school topics
   > Why are the communication skills important?
   > What are the skills that employers want?
   > What characteristics are colleges looking for?

CAUSE AND EFFECT DIAGRAM

The **Cause and Effect Diagram** was developed by Kaoru Ishikawa in 1943. It is also referred to as a "fishbone" diagram since it looks like a fish skeleton, or as an "Ishikawa diagram" after its inventor.

A **Cause and Effect Diagram** (CED) is extremely useful for obtaining information about the root causes of a specific problem. It can be used in brain storming sessions within a task force, committee or action team, or as a method to get input from an entire class, school, or district since the **CED** can be posted at various sites.

A **CED** is rarely used alone. However, when used with a Relations Diagram, an Affinity Diagram, and/or a Nominal Group Process, it can help expose the root causes of a problem in many different ways.

Procedure
1. <u>Statement of the Problem</u>

A specific, identified problem contributing to a non-quality result is identified. It is placed on the far right hand side of an overhead, paper, flip chart or other type of paper.

2. <u>Recording the Perceptions</u>

After the backbone and the box with the either the identified problem or the effect is drawn, add the primary causal category boxes (people, equipment, materials and procedures environment) and draw arrows to the backbone. This is the beginning of the **CED**. Some institutions have reusable 3' x 2' boards with the skeleton and primary causal categories painted on permanently. They have Highland ™ note pads attached, so that written remarks could be added by those participating in the analysis.

Remember, the **CED** categories **do not** have to consist of just those mentioned above nor do you have to use these categories. For example, if a teacher is trying to encourage the students to analyze the causes of misbehaving in class, the categories might end up being the home environment, peer pressure, classroom environment, the teacher and the students.

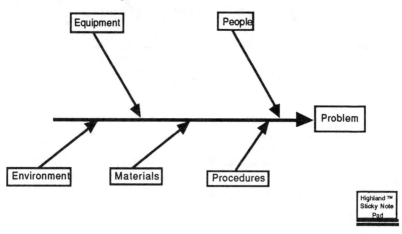

The **Causes** and **Sub Causes** are written on the sticky note pads and are placed in one of the primary causal categories.

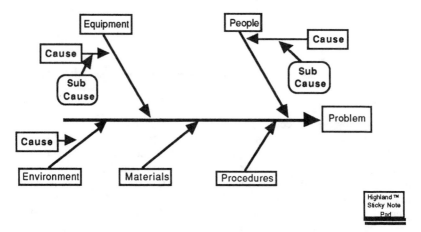

In some instances, additional levels can and should be added to **Sub Causes**.

3. Complete the Diagram

Shown below is a **CED** reflecting the perceptions of Mr. Lake's students as to why they are doing poorly in chemistry.

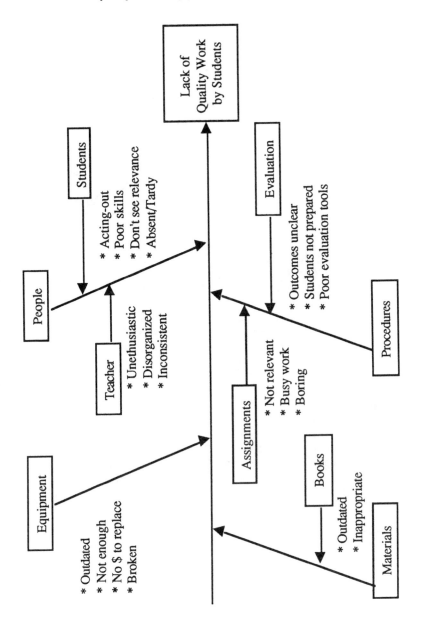

4.   Record and Discuss the Results

The results are then recorded and discussed to determine the root causes of the undesired effect or problem. Remember: the purpose is to generate ideas as to the probable causes of the problem and to get everyone involved in submitting suggestions. Therefore, criticism of any idea or comment should not be tolerated by the group. Instead, participants should be encouraged to build upon the causes and sub causes posted by others.

5.   Other Suggestions

If a major root cause for a problem is identified, it could become a likely candidate for a fishbone problem.

Note

The **Cause and Effect Diagram** is helpful in determining possible causes of specific problems. It is a way of identifying, organizing, and analyzing the causes of a condition. It encourages everyone to share ideas and makes it easy to visualize the causes and effects of a problem identified by a team. It encourages everyone to contribute, to interact and to build consensus.

1.   Possible elementary school topics
   > Why don't students get to school on time?
   > Why do students misbehave in class?
   > What were the causes of the civil war?
2.   Possible middle school topics
   > What are the inhibitors of quality work?
   > What are the components to good writing?
   > What are the obstacles to good reading habits?
3.   Possible high school topics
   > Why are laboratory reports not completed?
   > Why do students act out?
   > What are the causes of poor grades?

Other examples of **Cause and Effect Diagrams** follow. The first is from a second-grade class, the second is from a ninth-grade social studies class, and the third is from a fifth-grade class. (Source: Byrnes and Cornesky, 1994.)

Example 1: **CED** from a second grade class of why students don't get to school on time.

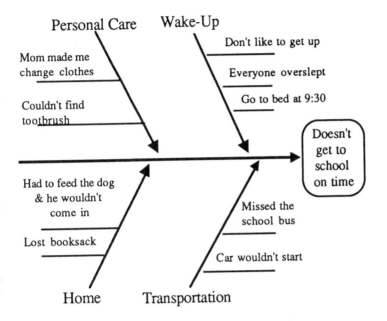

Imagine the lively discussion that could be generated from these comments on this **Cause and Effect Diagram.**

If you have a sense that students are not responding enthusiastically to an assignment that you have poured your heart and soul into, then use a CED and ask the students to analyze the problem for you.

Here is an example of how one high school social studies teacher approached this problem. Candace Allen, a ninth-grade social studies teacher from Centennial High School (grades 9-12, total student body approximately 1,200, school district population of 18,000: approximately 51 percent Hispanic, 48 percent white, and 1 percent African-American and Asian) in Pueblo, Colorado, reported that over 45 percent of all students were failing. Mrs. Allen had approximately 32 students per class; about half Hispanic and half white with abilities that covered the spectrum. She tried everything, including giving them a learning-styles inventory. Ms. Allen is considered one of the finest teachers in Pueblo and was both puzzled and concerned by the results she was getting. She was concerned about the high failure rate (which had remained fairly constant for the past 10 years) even though she continuously tried to make the course more interesting and the assignments more fun. She concluded that indeed it was the case that there are just too many students out there who don't care and are unmotivated.

Ms. Allen had prepared a world geography assignment that she thought the students would love. They were to work in small groups, research one of the Eastern European countries, and answer a series of questions regarding its people, customs, topography, trade, and government. Each group was to present a written response to the questions and an oral report summarizing what they'd learned. Phase two of the project was to create a new government (a utopian government for that country) and project what would happen in the future to it. At first, the students were excited, but, after about three days, their interest waned. That is when Mrs. Allen decided to use a **Cause and Effect Diagram** (she called it a Stinky Fish Diagram) with her class. The following **CED** lead to a positive resolution.

Example 2: **Cause and Effect Diagram** from Mrs. Allen's ninth-grade social study class.

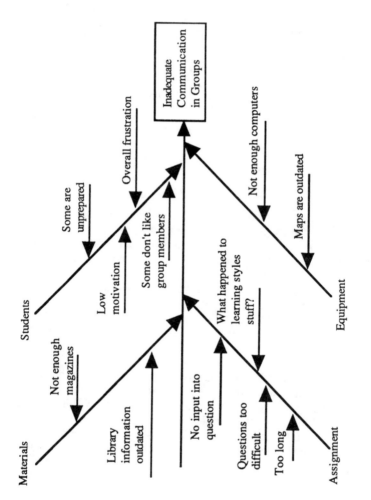

Example 3: **Cause and Effect Diagram** from a fifth-grade class.

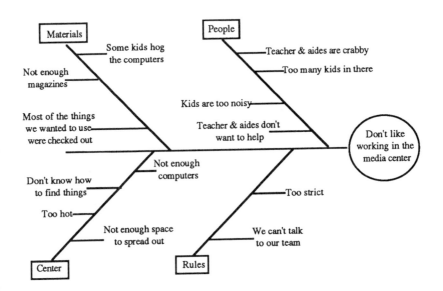

This example is unique—it uses the "fishbone" diagram to get a class to analyze a story. (Source: Baxter et. al., 1994).

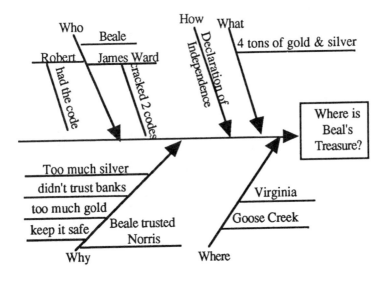

CONTROL CHARTS

Control Charts are used to test the stability of a system. They measure the number or proportion of nonconforming items. They all have a common centerline which represents a process average and additional lines that display upper and lower control limits to provide information on the variation. They are used to identify either "common" or "special" causes of variation and to prevent over- or under-control of the processes within a system.

The charts are drawn by gathering samples, called subgroups, from a process, product, or service characteristic. Control limits are based on the variation that occurs within the subgroups. The centerline of the chart is taken to be the estimated mean of the sampling distribution while the upper control limit (UCL) is the mean plus three times the estimated standard error and the lower control limit (LCL) is the estimated mean minus three times the estimated standard error.

We will describe two control charts in detail—the **np-chart** and the **p-chart**. Both charts are **attribute** (characteristic) charts in that the characteristic under study gives an yes/no, good/bad, pass/fail, or present/absent answer. The **np-chart** is used to plot the **number** of nonconformances and the subgroup size is constant. The **p-chart** is used plot the **proportion** of nonconformances and the subgroup size is either **constant** or **variable**.

Two additional charts, the **c-chart** and the **u-chart**, will also be described briefly. They are used when the characteristic under study is too complex for a simple answer. Finally, we will describe the **mean and range chart,** which can be used to measure the performance of the entire class over a period of time.

np-Chart

A **np-chart**, an attributes control chart, is used when the stability of a system is to be measured and when the characteristic under study has a definite yes/no answer, the subgroups are of equal size, the sampling time is consistent, and the data is plotted in the order it was taken.

1. Select the Data to be Analyzed

We have assumed that a task force or the individual studying a system has collected the attribute (counts) data. In the case study below, the number of incomplete homework assignments in Miss Wright's basic math classes for six weeks (30 days) was examined. Miss Wright had a total of 60 students in her math classes and she gave a homework problem after every class period. The homework problem was to be turned in at the beginning of the following class period.

2. Record the Data

Record the data in the order which it was collected.

Day #	Day	# Students Sample Size	Homework Assignments Not Completed	Proportion
1	M	60	3	0.05
2	T	60	6	0.10
3	W	60	14	0.23
4	H	60	12	0.20
5	F	60	15	0.25
6	M	60	2	0.03
7	T	60	6	0.10
8	W	60	14	0.23
9	H	60	17	0.28
10	F	60	16	0.26
11	M	60	1	0.01
12	T	60	8	0.13
13	W	60	11	0.18
14	H	60	18	0.30
15	F	60	20	0.33
16	M	60	5	0.08
17	T	60	6	0.10
18	W	60	25	0.41
19	H	60	12	0.20
20	F	60	26	0.43
21	M	60	6	0.10
22	T	60	21	0.35
23	W	60	18	0.30
24	H	60	17	0.28
25	F	60	17	0.28
26	M	60	11	0.18
27	T	60	26	0.43
28	W	60	27	0.45
29	H	60	29	0.48
30	F	60	33	0.55
Totals		1,800	442	0.25

3. Do the Calculations

The **Average**, the **Upper Control Limit** (UCL) , and the **Lower Control Limit** (LCL) have to be calculated in order to determine the stability of the "system." Note, however, that a minimum of 25 to 30 subgroups are required to calculate the control limits.

3.1 **The average =**   total number / number of subgroups
$$= \quad \Sigma np + 30$$
$$= \quad 3 + 6 + 14 + 12 + ... + 33 + 30$$
$$= \quad 442 + 30$$
$$= \quad 14.73$$

This number (14.73) should be recorded with the space labeled "Avg" in the control chart.

3.2 **The Upper Control Limit** (UCL) is calculated using the formula:

$$UCL = \text{Average} + 3\sqrt{\text{Average}\,(1 - [\text{Average} \div n])}$$

$$= \quad 14.73 + 3\sqrt{14.73\,(1 - [14.73 \div 60])}$$

$$= \quad 14.73 + 3\sqrt{14.73\,(1 - 0.2455)}$$

$$= \quad 14.73 + 3\sqrt{14.73 \times 0.7545}$$

$$= \quad 14.73 + 3\sqrt{11.1138}$$

$$= \quad 14.73 + 3\,(3.333)$$

$$= \quad 14.73 + 10.00$$

$$UCL = \quad 24.73$$

This number (24.73) should be recorded with the space labeled "UCL" in the control chart.

3.3 **The Lower Control Limit** (LCL) is calculated using the formula:

$$LCL = Average - 3 \sqrt{Average (1 - [Average \div n])}$$

$$= 14.73 - 3 \sqrt{14.73 (1 - [14.73 \div 60])}$$

$$= 14.73 - 3 \sqrt{14.73 (0.7545)}$$

$$= 14.73 - 3 \sqrt{11.1138}$$

$$= 14.73 - 3 (3.333)$$

$$= 14.73 - 10.00$$

$$LCL = 4.73$$

This number (4.73) should be recorded with the space labeled "LCL" in the control chart.

4. Draw the Chart

The first thing one has to do is to scale the chart. Begin by determining the largest number in your data and compare this with the UCL number. In our example the largest number is 33 and the UCL number is 24.73.

A rule of thumb is to count the lines on your chart paper and multiply it by 0.66. The chart paper in our example is shown below. It has 30 lines, therefore, 30 x 0.66 = 19.8, or ≈ 20.

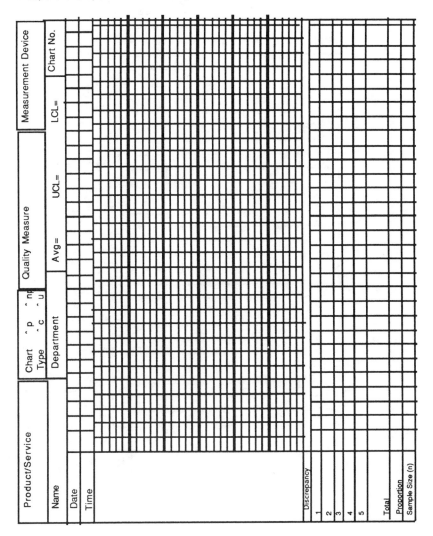

Divide the largest number in your example by 20 to obtain your increment value: 33 + 20 = 1.65. Always rounding the figure upwards, every line in this case will represent 2.

The lines are usually numbered from the bottom up. The bottom line is 0 and every line will represent two incomplete homework assignments. (In other cases it may be necessary to label the lines with other multiples such as 5, 10, 25 etc.) The attributes control chart completely labeled with our example is shown below.

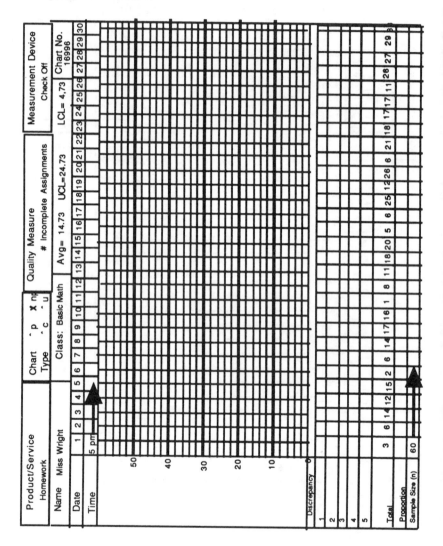

Now draw the center line and the control limits then plot the values and connect the points. The completed chart is shown below.

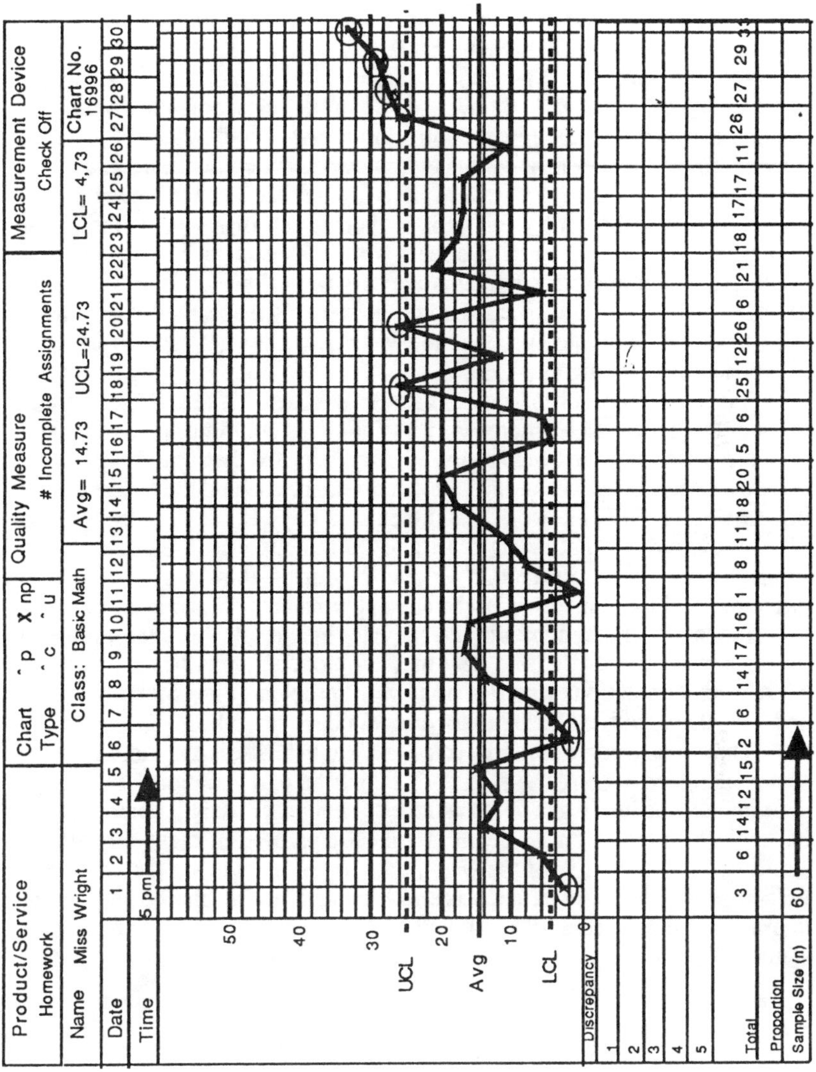

5. Analyze the Chart

All control charts are analyzed using basic rules:

> Look for points above or below the control limits.
> Look for a run of seven or more points above or below the average (center line).
> Look for a run of seven or more points either going up or down.
> Look for cyclical patterns.

In our example the "homework" system in Miss Wright's class appears to be unstable. On days 1, 6 and 11 the number of incomplete homework assignments is below the lower control limit line. On days 18, 20, 27, 28, 29, and 30 the number of incomplete homework assignments are above the upper control limit line. However, there are neither a run of seven points above or below the center line, nor is there a run of seven points either going up or going down. A cyclical pattern appears to be present: the number of incomplete assignments appears to be lowest on Monday and Tuesday and highest towards the end of the week. Perhaps, the students have time to do the assignments over the weekends, but get too involved in school activities during the week.

The above system has "special causes" as a defect and improvement in the number of completed homework assignments could not be undertaken until these special causes were analyzed, addressed and the system stabilized.

After Miss Wright examined the circumstances behind the apparent lack of completing the home work assignments on days 18, 20, 27, 28, 29, and 30, she discovered that on days 18 and 20 the basketball team made the finals for the state tournament; likewise, during the days 27—30, the basketball team was involved in the actual tournament. Apparently, many of the students were caught up in the excitement of the championship tournament and that might be why they did not complete their homework. Miss Wright's solution: give five homework problems after Monday's class and have them returned by the following Monday. It worked!

When first using np-charts you may want to assess the stability of a system and then analyze the factors that contribute to variations. However, after improvements are generated and the system under study is determined to be stable, you may want to begin to collect data in a different way and to stratify your data by day of the week, time, location and redo the np-charts. Of course recalculations of new control limits will eventually be needed but this should be delayed until enough data are gathered to make the new chart statistically valid.

p-Chart

A p-Chart is used when one wants to plot the **proportion** of nonconformances and the subgroup size is either **constant** or **variable**. Like the np-chart, the p-chart is an attribute control chart that studies a characteristic that has an either/or, pass/fail/, yes/no answer. For example:

> A teacher may want to plot the proportion of students failing his/her class over the term.
> A teacher may want to plot the proportion of students not completing homework assignments over the semester.

> A principal may want to plot the proportion of graduating seniors who have a SAT score above 1000 over a period of time.

The p-chart, like any control chart, helps determine "special" and/or "common" cause variations in a system so that proper action can be taken for improvement without exerting over- or under-control. It is used by teams to help determine the stability of a system and to monitor the improvement of the system after action is taken.

1. Select the Data to be Analyzed

In the case study below we will examine the proportion of students that failed "Introduction to Accounting" per term over a 7.5 year period. Since number of students who took the course varied over the seven year period, the sample size is variable. As a result the p-chart had to be used.

2. <u>Record the Data</u>

k #	Term-Yr	n Subgroup Size	np Number of Failures	np + n Proportion
1	1-84	100	15	0.150
2	2-84	100	6	0.060
3	3-84	100	11	0.110
4	4-84	100	4	0.040
5	1-85	94	9	0.096
6	2-85	94	7	0.074
7	3-85	94	4	0.043
8	4-85	94	8	0.085
9	1-86	91	3	0.033
10	2-86	91	2	0.022
11	3-86	91	1	0.011
12	4-86	91	10	0.109
13	1-87	91	7	0.077
14	2-87	91	25	0.275
15	3-87	91	5	0.055
16	4-87	79	3	0.038
17	1-88	79	8	0.101
18	2-88	79	4	0.051
19	3-88	79	2	0.025
20	4-88	79	5	0.063
21	1-89	79	5	0.063
22	2-89	72	7	0.097
23	3-89	72	9	0.125
24	4-89	72	1	0.014
25	1-90	72	3	0.042
26	2-90	72	12	0.167
27	3-90	72	9	0.125
28	4-90	72	3	0.042
29	1-91	72	6	0.083
30	2-91	72	9	0.125
	Totals	2,535	203	0.0801

3. <u>Do the Calculations</u>

   3.1   The **Proportion** for each subgroup has to be calculated. As shown in the table above, this is accomplished by dividing total number (np) by the subgroup size (n). In our first entry above, 15 (number of failures during the first term of 1984) is divided by the 100 (sample size). Carry the calculations out to three places.

   3.2   The **Average Proportion** is calculated by taking the total number in the sample row (2,535) and dividing it by the total number in the subgroup row (203).

Average Proportion   ($\overline{p}$) = total number / number of subgroups

$$= \quad \Sigma np + \Sigma n$$
$$= \quad 203 \; + 2,535$$
$$= \quad 0.0801$$

This number (.0801) should be recorded with the space labeled "Avg" in the control chart.

   3.3   The **Average Subgroup Size** ($\overline{n}$) is calculated by dividing the total number of the subgroup size (2,535) by the number of the subgroups taken (k).

Average Subgroup Size   ($\overline{n}$) $= \quad \Sigma n \div k$
$$= \quad 2,535 \div 30$$
$$= \quad 84.5$$

   3.4   Make certain that none of the subgroup size varies more than ± 25% of Average Subgroup Size (84.5). This is done by multiplying 84.5 by 1.25 for the number greater than 25%; and 84.5 by 0.75 for the number less than 25%.

     >25%   =   84.5   x   1.25   =   105.6
     <25%   =   84.5   x   0.75   =   63.4

Since none of our sample sizes (n) were higher than 105.6 or less than 63.4, separate calculations for the control limits do not have to be done. If, however, you have subgroup sizes 25% above or below 84.5, you will have to calculate separate UCL's and LCL's on **EACH** of the points by substituting the appropriate number (n) in the formula shown below. These points with their separate UCL and LCL are plotted on the same graph. (Refer to the example in the u-chart at the end of this section.)

3.5 Do the calculations for the **Control Limits.**

$$UCL = \bar{p} + 3 \sqrt{\frac{\bar{p}(1-\bar{p})}{\bar{n}}}$$

$$= 0.0801 + 3 \sqrt{\frac{0.0801\ (1 - 0.0801)}{84.5}}$$

$$= 0.0801 + 3 \sqrt{\frac{0.0801\ (0.9199)}{84.5}}$$

$$= 0.0801 + 3 \sqrt{\frac{0.0737}{84.5}}$$

$$= 0.0801 + 3\ (0.02953)$$

$$UCL = 0.1687$$

Now calculate the lower control limit:

$$LCL = \bar{p} - 3 \sqrt{\frac{\bar{p}(1-\bar{p})}{\bar{n}}}$$

$$= 0.0801 - 0.0886$$

$$LCL = 0$$

4. Draw the Chart

The scaling and plotting are done in exactly the same manner as in the np chart. The largest proportion of failures in our example is 0.275 and 66% of the number of lines in our graph is 20, therefore, each line has to be $0.275 \div 20 = 0.014$, and since adjusting is always done upwards, each line represents 0.020.

The completed chart is shown below.

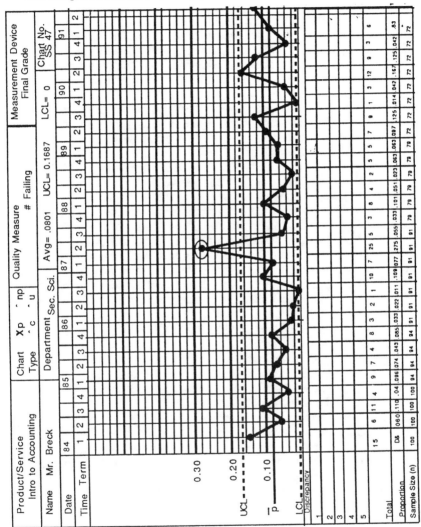

5. Analyze the Chart

All control charts are analyzed using basic rules:

> Look for points above or below the control limits.
> Look for a run of seven or more points above or below the average (center line).
> Look for a run of seven or more points either going up or down.
> Look for cyclical patterns.

In our example the system appears to be unstable since one of the points lay outside the UCL—the second term of 1987. During that time, the number of failures was above the upper control limit line. However, there are no run of seven points above or below the center line, nor is there a run of seven points either going up or going down, nor are there any cyclical patterns.

The above system appears to have "special cause" as a defect, and implementing TQI processes to improve the number of students who would pass could not be undertaken until these special causes were analyzed, addressed and the system stabilized.

After the teacher examined what occurred during that time, he informed us that the local textile plant announced massive layoffs and that it would be phasing out its operations in that area over the next several years. As a result, many students were more concerned about having to relocate and losing their friends than their final grades. A check of the high school records indicated that an unusually high rate of failing grades were given in the entire school that particular term. When this special cause is removed, the system could be considered to be stable. Mr. Breck may begin to add changes in order to increase the passing rate. Remember, however, new control limits have to be calculated when changes are made on the system.

C- AND U- CONTROL CHARTS

There are two other control charts, both of which can be useful in the academic setting. They are the **c-chart** and the **u-chart**. Like the np-chart and the p-chart, the **c-chart** and the **u-chart** are used to test the stability of the system and both are attribute control charts.

The **c-chart** and the **u-chart** measure the number of nonconforming items. The **c-chart** is used when the number of nonconformities are measured, and the subgroup size is the constant, while the **u-chart** is used when the number of nonconformities are measured and the subgroup size is either constant or variable.

Since the preparation of the **c-chart** and the **u-chart** are very similar to the np-chart and the p-chart described previously, we will present briefly when they may be appropriately used as well as the related formulae.

c-Chart

A **c-chart** is used when the stability of a system is to be measured and when the characteristic under study is too complex for either a simple yes/no, or a positive/negative answer. In other words, the data may have a number of discrepancies per subgroup. An example might include the type of errors while composing a letter in a word-processing class. The errors might include: 1) format, 2) grammar, 3) punctuation, 4) spacing, 5) date, and 6) spelling. (If you wanted to calculate the number of mistakes in composing a letter regardless of the type, you would use the np-chart; if you desired to calculate the proportion of nonconformances regardless of the type of mistake, you would use the p-chart.)

As with the other control charts, one should 1) select the data to be analyzed, 2) record the data, 3) do the calculations, 4) draw the chart, and 5) analyze the chart.

1. <u>Select the Data to be Analyzed</u>

Before using any control chart, it is essential that the operational definition of the nonconforming characteristics be carefully identified in order to insure consistency in the collection process. In our example, a teacher and the students identified four major problems in the five sections of the word-processing classes: 1) format, 2) grammar, 3) punctuation, and 4) spacing. These were perceived to be the major problems of the students not being able to produce an error-free letter the first time. They decided to randomly sample two letters at the end of the five classes for five straight days.

2. Record the Data

The data are recorded as shown in the table and in the completed **c-chart** below.

The date, class period, type and number of mistakes, and the total number of mistakes in Mrs. Herbst's word-processing classes.

Type of Mistake

Date	Class Period (k=25)	Format	Grammar	Punctuation	Spacing	Total
Jan. 7	1	2	0	1	1	4
	2	2	3	2	1	8
	3	1	1	2	2	6
	4	1	0	1	0	2
	5	0	0	0	0	0
Jan. 8	1	3	1	2	0	6
	2	1	0	0	1	2
	3	3	3	0	2	8
	4	0	0	0	0	0
	5	1	1	1	1	4
Jan. 9	1	2	1	1	0	4
	2	2	1	2	1	6
	3	0	0	0	0	0
	4	1	1	1	1	4
	5	3	2	2	1	8
Jan. 10	1	0	0	0	0	0
	2	3	1	1	1	6
	3	1	1	1	1	4
	4	3	3	2	0	8
	5	0	0	0	2	2
Jan. 11	1	3	1	1	1	6
	2	0	0	0	0	0
	3	2	0	0	0	2
	4	2	1	0	1	4
	5	0	1	1	0	2
	Totals	36	22	21	17	96

3. Do the Calculations

    3.1   The **Average Number** is calculated according to the formula:

$$\bar{c} = \text{total number} \div \text{number of subgroups}$$
$$= C1 + C2 + C3 + ... + Ck \div k$$
$$= 4 + 8 + 6 + ... + 2 \div 25$$
$$= 96 \div 25$$
$$= 3.8$$

This number is placed in the placed marked "Avg."

    3.2   The **Control Limits** are calculated according to the formulae:

$$UCLc = \bar{c} + 3\sqrt{\bar{c}}$$
$$= 3.8 + 3\sqrt{3.8}$$
$$= 3.8 + 5.8$$
$$UCLc = 9.6$$

$$LCLc = \bar{c} - 3\sqrt{\bar{c}}$$
$$= 3.8 - 3\sqrt{3.8}$$
$$= 3.8 - 5.8$$
$$= -2$$
$$LCLc \approx 0$$

4. Draw the Chart

Do the scaling as described previously. In this case the largest c number is 8 and the UCLc is 9.6. Therefore, take the 9.6 value and multiply it by 0.66 of the number of lines on your graph. In our case, the number of lines is 30 ,and 0.66 of 30 is ≈ 20. Each line, in our case, has an incremental value of 9.6 ÷ 20 = 0.48. Adjusting upward, we have an incremental value of 0.5.

The completed **c-control chart** is shown below.

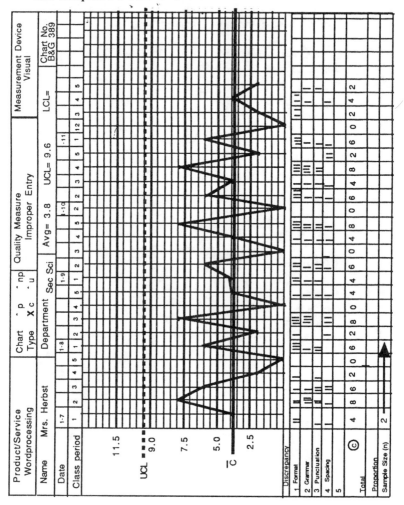

5. Analyze the Chart

The above chart does not demonstrate any special cause variations. Therefore, the variability in the system appears to be due to common causes which can be reduced by improving the processes within the system. Both the teacher and the students in all five classes were happy to hear that they did not have to consider any special causes and that they could now begin to work as a team to improve the learning experiences for all!

u-Chart

A **u-chart** is used when the stability of a system is to be measured and when the characteristic under study is too complex for either a simple yes/no, or positive/negative answer. In other words, the data may have a number of discrepancies per subgroup. An example might include laboratory reports that are incorrectly completed because of errors in filling out one of many entries.(If you want to calculate the number of incorrectly completed reports regardless of which information item was incorrectly completed, you would use the np-chart; if you want to calculate the proportion of nonconformances regardless of which information item was incorrectly completed, you would use the p-chart.) However, unlike the c-chart mentioned above, the **u-chart** can be used with either a **constant** or **variable** subgroup size. If the subgroup sizes vary more than 25 percent, as demonstrated in our example below, individual control limits have to be calculated.

As with the other control charts, one should 1) select the data to be analyzed, 2) record the data, 3) do the calculations, 4) draw the chart, and 5) analyze the chart.

1. Select the Data to be Analyzed

Before using any control chart, it is essential that the operational definition of the nonconforming characteristics be carefully identified in order to insure consistency in the collection process. In the example below, a high school chemistry teacher, working with her students, identified five principal discrepancies that resulted in incorrect laboratory reports being submitted. For this study we simply designated them "type 1" through "type 5." The discrepancies are scored in the same manner as shown for the c-chart above. Redoing the reports was not only a major cause of extra work, but not submitting the reports in a timely fashion led to unhappy customers—students, teacher, and parents. A group of students, several parents, and the teacher formed a team to examine the root causes and decide what could be done to improve the quality of the initial submission of the reports. They decided to examine a random number of reports for 25 straight school days.

2. Record the Data

The data are recorded as shown in the completed **u-chart** below.

3. <u>Do the Calculations</u>

    3.1   The **Average Number per Unit** is calculated according to the formula:

$$\overline{u} = \Sigma c \div \Sigma n$$
$$= 192 \div 103$$
$$= 1.86$$

        This value is placed in the placed maker "Avg."

    3.2   The **Average Subgroup Size** is calculated according to the formula:

$$\overline{n} = \Sigma n \div k$$
$$= 103 \div 25$$
$$= 4.12$$

    3.3   The **Subgroup Size Limits** are calculated:

        >25% = 4.12 x 1.25 = 5.15
        <25% = 4.12 x 0.75 = 3.09

        Therefore, any proportion number in any subgroup that is less than 3.19 or greater than 5.15 will have to have its UCL and LCL's calculated separately. In our example shown below, please refer to subgroups #1, #7, #8, #11, #15, #16, #17, and #20.

    3.4   The **Proportions** (u) for each subgroup are calculated according to the formula:

        u = number in subgroup (c) + subgroup size (n)

These figures are added to the chart as shown.

3.5   The **Control Limits** are calculated according to the formulae:

$$UCLu = \bar{u} + 3\sqrt{\bar{u} \div \bar{n}}$$

$$= 1.86 + 3\sqrt{1.86 \div 4.12}$$

$$= 1.86 + 3\sqrt{0.4514}$$

$$= 1.86 + 3(0.6719)$$

$$= 1.86 + 2.02$$
$$= 3.88$$

$$LCLu = \bar{u} - 3\sqrt{\bar{u} \div \bar{n}}$$

$$= 1.86 - 2.02$$
$$= -0.16$$
$$\approx 0$$

3.6   The control limits for these subgroups that vary ± 25 percent are calculated separately. In our case, this includes #1, #7, #8, #11, #15, #16, #17, and #20.
For subgroups #1, #7, #15, and #17:

$$UCLu = 1.86 + 3 \quad u \div n$$
$$= 1.86 + 3 \quad 1.86 \div 3 = 4.22$$

$$LCLu = 1.86 - 3 \quad u \div n$$
$$= 1.86 - 3 \quad 1.86 \div 3 \approx 0$$

For subgroups #8 and #16:

$$UCLu = 1.86 + 3\sqrt{\bar{u} \div n}$$

$$= 1.86 + 3\sqrt{1.86 \div 2} = 4.75$$

$$LCLu = 1.86 - 3\sqrt{\bar{u} \div n}$$

$$= 1.86 - 3\sqrt{1.86 \div 2} \approx 0$$

For subgroups #11 and #20:

$$UCLu = 1.86 + 3\sqrt{\bar{u} \div n}$$

$$= 1.86 + 3\sqrt{1.86 \div 7} = 3.41$$

$$LCLu = 1.86 - 3\sqrt{\bar{u} \div n}$$

$$= 1.86 - 3\sqrt{1.86 \div 7} = 0.32$$

4. Draw the Chart

Do the scaling as described previously. In this case, the largest proportion (u) is 8 and the UCL is 1.86. Therefore, take the 8 value and multiply it by 0.66 of the number of lines on your graph. In our case, the number of lines is 30, and 0.66 of 30 is ≈ 20, therefore, 8 + 20 = 0.4 or ≈ 0.5. Adjusting upward is done so that the dark lines have numbers whose multiples are easy to work with—1, 2, 5, 10 etc. The completed chart is shown below:

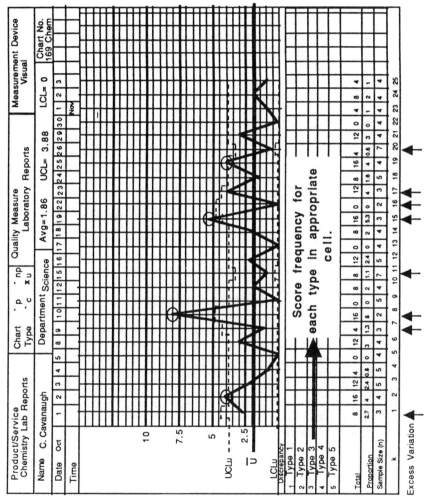

5.   Analyze the Chart
     The above chart indicates that the laboratory reporting system is not in control. On October 2, 10, 19 and 25, the number of errors exceeded the UCL which indicates special cause variation. The team can begin to examine the reasons as to the variations.

OTHER CONTROL CHARTS

These **Individual-Moving Range** (X-MR) and the **Mean and Range** charts have been contributed by Dr. Larry Sharp, president and principal consultant, Six Sigma Enterprises, 2110 Vickers Drive, Suite 100, Colorado Springs, CO 80918; PH: (719) 598-8393.

The Individual-Moving Range (X-MR) Chart

The **X-MR Chart** (referred to as an Individual-Moving Range Chart) is a special type of control chart used to test the stability of a process which generates continuous data **from an individual measurement** rather than from a small sample of measurements. As such, the **X-MR Chart** is an ideal tool for classroom use because it permits the teacher to monitor a wide variety of student characteristics (or for students to monitor their own progress as they keep a portfolio). Rather than wait till mid-term or final exams to signal problems, both student and teacher can use daily performance, aided by the interpretive power of the **Individual-Moving Range Chart** to signal when a student's performance is out of control. With the availability of a variety of recently released DOS, Windows and Macintosh-based SPC programs, the teacher can easily set up a control chart for each student (or have students format their own).
     In this example, a teacher of statistics administers daily quizzes in her Introduction to Statistics class. The inherent nature of the material requires students to have a firm grasp of each day's material so later material will not produce debilitating anxiety which so often characterizes student reaction to statistical material. With just a hour or so of instruction at the beginning of the term, each student can be taught to format the **Individual-Moving Range Chart** and the simple calculations to begin plotting daily performance against the control limits. Within the first five class periods, both student and teacher now have a tool to unambiguously signal deficits in mastering the sequential nature of the material. As is the case with all continuous improvement strategies, the object is to detect unsatisfactory performance earlier in the process cycle, then act to remove the causes.
     While the **Individual-Moving Range Chart** is offered as a tool for individual measurements (n=1), the power of the chart flows from the fact that each value is compared against each subsequent value (in fact, creating a subgroup of 2, n=2). What is important of course is the **change in performance** over time. The magnitude of these changes indicates what is happening during the process of learning the material. Shown below is

the performance for a typical student over the first 10 lessons on the daily, 20-point quizzes.

STUDENT PERFORMANCE

Subject	Quiz Score =X	Moving Range = MR
Measurement	14	n/a
Frequency Dist	16	2
% Ranks	15	1
Graphs of f Dist	18	3
Stat Notation	13	5
Central Tend.	12	1
Dispersion	10	2
Standard Scores	11	1
Normal Dist	9	2
Intro Correlation	10	1
Average	12.8	2

Procedure

As is the case with all control charts, average values are determined, control limits established based on +/- 3 standard deviations from the process average, points are plotted and the points examined for signals of an out of control process.

The **Individual-Moving Range Chart** has two sections: a Moving Range Control Chart and an Individual Values Control Chart. To create the Moving Range Chart:

1. Calculate the Average Moving Range.

$$\overline{MR} = \Sigma MR \div (n-1)$$
$$= 18 + 9$$
$$= 2$$

2. At a value of 2 on the Y axis of the Moving Range Chart, draw a horizontal line. This represents the average moving range or the Center Line (CL).

3. Calculate the Upper Control Limit (UCL) for the Moving Range Chart:

$$UCL = 3.26 \times \overline{MR}$$

(Note: 3.26 is always used as the multiplier for R for the **Individual Moving Range Chart**)

$$UCL = 3.26 \times 2 = 6.52$$

4. At a value of 6.52 on the Y axis of the **Moving Range Chart,** draw a horizontal line. This represents the upper control limit (UCL).

5. The lower control limit (LCL) for the **Moving Range Chart** will always be 0 (differences cannot be smaller than 0).

6. Interpret the **Moving Range Chart** before you calculate the values for and plot the Individual Values chart.

You are looking for differences (changes from quiz score to quiz score) which exceed the 3 standard deviation control limit and thus signal a "special cause" of variation. If the changes (differences) arise from an increase in scores, the student's performance is significantly improving. Ask the student to reflect on what was different about study habits, teacher presentation etc. so that those factors can be replicated. If the changes (differences) arise from a decrease in scores, this is a clear signal of a "special cause" factor which resulted in a decrement in performance. The student and teacher should examine study habits, notes, teacher presentation as before to determine the cause of the decrease.

To create the **Individual Values Chart:**

1. Calculate the average quiz score from the individual quiz scores:

Average = sum of data points ÷ no. of subgroups

$$\overline{X} = \Sigma X \div N$$

$$= \frac{128}{10} = 12.8$$

2. At a value of 12.8 on the Y axis of the **Individual Values Chart,** draw a horizontal line. This represents the Individual Values Average and is the Center Line (CL).

3. Calculate the upper control limit (UCL) for the **Individual Values Chart.**

UCL = Average Quiz Score + (2.66 x the Average Range)

UCL = 12.8 + (2.66 x 2) = 12.8 + 5.32
     = 18.12

(Note: 2.66 will always be the multiplier of the **Individual Values Chart** for calculating the upper and lower control limits)

4. At a value of 18.12 on the Y axis of the **Individual Values Chart,** draw a horizontal line and label it UCL.

5. Calculate the lower control limit (LCL) for the **Individual Values Chart.**

LCL = Average Quiz Score - (2.66 x   Average Range)

LCL = 12.8 - (2.66 x 2)
     = 12.8 - 5.32
     = 7.48

6. At a value of 7.48 on the Y axis of the **Individual Values Chart,** draw a horizontal line and label it LCL.

7. Plot the quiz scores on the chart.

8. Interpret the set of charts.

As noted, the differences in ranges are examined before you invest the time to calculate the values for the **Individual Values Chart.** This is so because the Average Range (R) is used to determine the control limits for the **Individual Values Chart.** If one or more ranges is out of control, the reasons for the lack of control must be detected, understood and replicated if positive or eliminated if negative, before the **Individual Values Chart** has meaning. Once the **change** in student performance from quiz to quiz is understood (i.e. in control), then both teacher and student can use the values displayed on the **Individual Values Chart** to reliably track the student's performance.

Data from this exercise show that, while the Moving Ranges are in control, the student's performance on the 4th topic, "Graphs of frequency distributions" was particularly exemplary and culminated a rising trend beginning with the first quiz. Following that, however, the next six quizzes display a significant downward trend beginning with the material on "Statistical Notation." While neither the Range Data nor the Individual Values data exceed control limits, this downward trend highlights an additional rule for interpretation of control charts: "Six successive points either increasing or decreasing signals an out-of-control process" even though the 3 standard deviation limits have not been exceeded. The downward trend may be the result of the failure to present/grasp the material regarding "Statistical Notation" or perhaps an external environmental factor must be investigated by both student and teacher.

Once the first 5 to 10 data points are plotted, the student and teacher need only examine succeeding differences between quiz scores by referring to where that value of the difference falls on the **Moving Range Chart**. New control limits do not need to be calculated once the **Moving Range Chart** signals an in-control process.

When both Ranges and Individual Values signal an in-control process, the teacher and student can monitor learning on a quiz-to-quiz basis, confident that the charts will reliably signal the status of the learning process for succeeding quiz performances.

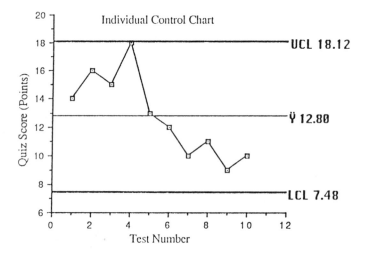

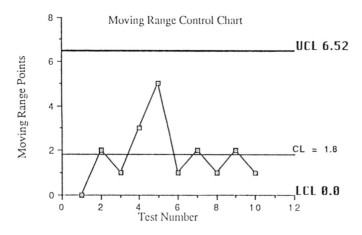

The Mean and Range Chart

While administrative applications of most control charts are relatively easy to discern, especially the attributes control charts, classroom applications are more difficult to find. This is particularly true for the **Mean and Range Chart**, which depends on the availability of relatively homogeneous subgroups of equal size. Thoughtful reflection by a faculty member, however, will reveal opportunities for the **Mean and Range Chart**.

For example, the teacher could track the teaching/learning process by charting the individual student performance on daily quizzes over time by using the **Individual Mean and Range Chart** as described above. Or, as we shall demonstrate, the performance of the entire class can be followed by using the **Mean and Range Chart**.

In this application, the subgroup is made up of all student scores for a quiz on a given day. Means and ranges are determined over time. The teacher then examines the chart for evidence that overall class performance is improving. In this case s(he) is looking for evidence that the process is not stable. Evidence which would suggest this would be an upward trend in the mean class scores over time. Notice that in this case, a stable, in control process would signal that nothing special is happening to the class mean scores. If this were the case, class mean scores would randomly fluctuate around a relatively stable mean with no discernible trend. This would be evidence that neither the teaching strategy nor the students' attention to the material is producing any change in class mean.

Use of a class-wide **Mean and Range Chart** is particularly helpful if the teacher has adopted a cooperative learning strategy in which the class as a team is rewarded for improved performance, and each student has a vital interest in other student's success. Shown below are the data from a small seminar section with five students and their scores on daily quizzes over 10 class periods.

Class #	Score 1	Score 2	Score 3	Score 4	Score 5	Mean	Range
1	6	5	7	6	4	5.6	3
2	5	7	6	6	7	6.4	2
3	7	6	6	7	7	6.6	1
4	6	7	8	7	6	6.8	2
5	7	7	6	7	7	6.8	1
6	7	8	6	8	8	7.4	2
7	7	8	8	7	8	7.6	1
8	8	9	7	8	7	7.8	2
9	8	7	9	9	8	8.2	2
10	8	9	9	9	8	8.6	1

PROCEDURE
1. Add the values for each row.
2. Find the average or mean for each row. (Sum the values in each row and divide by 5)
3. Calculate the overall mean. Sum the row means and divide by 10 (5.6 + 6.4 + 6.6 +......+7.8 + 8.2 + 8.6) = 71.8/10 = 7.18= $\overline{\overline{X}}$ which is the overall process mean.
4. Note the largest and smallest values in each row.
5. Determine the range for each row by subtracting the smallest value from the largest value. This is the range for each subgroup.
6. Find the Average Range ($\overline{R}$) by summing the 10 sub-group ranges and divide by 10 (3 + 2 + 1 + ...2 + 2 + 1) = 17. R bar = 17/10 = 1.7.

Calculate the Upper and Lower Control Limits for the Range Chart first.

This is typically done before the control limits for the **Means Chart** are calculated since the range chart analyzes variability *within* subgroups and it is this variability which is used to calculate the limits for the subgroup means chart. We expect variability *within* subgroups to be due only to inherent, common cause or random variability. We are interested in that variability which appears *across sub-groups* because it is that variability which tells us if the teaching/learning process is systematically changing.

1. Upper control limit for Ranges UCL_R = D4 x $\overline{R}$. (D4 varies as a function of sample size; for a sub-groups of size 5 it is 2.114. This value

comes from external sources and it is related to the standard deviation. Consult any statistical process control text for values of D4 for other sample sizes.)

2. $UCL_R = 2.114 \times 1.7$
3. $UCL_R = 3.6$
4. Draw a horizontal line across the Range Chart at the value of $\overline{R} = 1.7$ and label it $\overline{R}$.
5. Draw a horizontal line across the Range Chart at the Value 3.6 and label it UCL_R.
6. Since the sample size is less than 6, draw a horizontal line across the Range Chart at the 0 value on the Y axis and label it LCL_R.
7. Plot each of the subgroup ranges on the range chart.

Interpret the Range Chart

Points outside the control limits would indicate the ranges are not in statistical control. In this application, this would mean that there are systematic differences between students. If this were the case, the teacher would consult the students whose ranges were beyond the UCL_R and try to generalize their learning strategies to the other students, especially those whose ranges might be closer to the LCL_R. In a similar fashion, the teacher would want to consult these latter students to determine the special cause of their lower performance.

Since the Range Chart reflects a process "in control," we can proceed to calculate the Means Chart Control Limits.

Calculate the Upper and Lower Control Limits for the Means Chart.

1. $UCL_X = \overline{\overline{X}} + (A2 \times R \text{ bar})$. (A2 varies as a function of sample size; for a sub-group of 5 (number of students), it is 0.577. This value comes from external sources and is related to the standard deviation. Consult any statistical process control text for other values of A2.)
2. $UCL_X = 7.18 + (0.577 \times 1.7)$
3. $UCL_X = 7.18 + 0.98$
4. $UCL_X = 8.16$
5. Draw a horizontal line across the Means Chart at the value 8.16 on the Y axis and label it UCL_X.
   The Lower Control Limit for the Means Chart (LCL_X) is simply the process mean ($\overline{\overline{X}}$) minus the quantity ($A2 \times \overline{R}$).
6. $LCL_X = 7.18 - (0.577 \times 1.7)$
7. $LCL_X = 7.18 - 0.98$.
8. $LCL_X = 6.2$

Notice how narrow are the control limits—6.2 to 8.16. This is because the sub-group ranges have very little variation. We want this to be the case so that we maximize the likelihood of detecting a subgroup average exceeding these limits, thus indicating a change in process, hopefully on the high end.

9. Draw a horizontal line across the Means Chart at the value 6.2 on the Y axis and label it LCL$_X$.

10. Draw a horizontal line across the means chart at the value of the process mean ($\overline{\overline{X}}$) = 7.18 and label it $\overline{\overline{X}}$.

11. Plot each of the sub-group means on the Means Chart.

Interpret the Means Chart

While this data is hypothetical and specifically chosen to demonstrate the use of the **Mean and Range Control Chart**, the graph clearly shows the upward trend in mean scores over time. With addition of control limits, you can now assert with a high degree of confidence that the process demonstrates a non-chance increase in mean scores. That is, the mean values vary (systematically upward) due to factors other than chance and this variation can be attributed to the teaching/learning process and the continuous improvement strategies which the teacher has implemented. For example, if the teacher facilitated cooperative learning as a classroom strategy for this class section, but retained competitive learning in another section of the same class, s(he) would be able to compare the effects of the differing strategies by constructing a **Mean and Range Chart** for the second section.

It is important to emphasize that the purpose of the **Mean Range Control Chart** is to *detect a process not in statistical control* by demonstrating the influence of special causes of variation, such as cooperative learning.

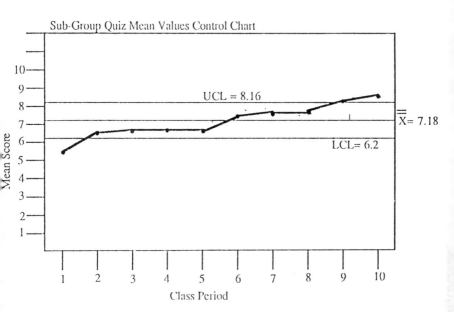

Sub-Group Quiz Mean Values Control Chart

FLOW CHART

Although flow charting is one of the most useful tools in continuous quality improvement (CQI), it is probably the most under utilized in education. Flow charting is a way in which one can get a snapshot of each process within a system. As a result, a **flow chart** can demonstrate where nonvalue-added work is performed. Of course, nonvalue-added work increases the cost of doing business. In the case of education, this cost can be substantial.

When a **flow chart** is drawn and redundant processes are identified, a task force can easily generate a different **flow chart** showing how the processes within the system should be done. It is essential that when a **flow chart** of a system is drawn that everyone working within the system be involved in drawing it. There are many different types of **flow charts**, but we will describe two which we found to be useful in the academic units, namely, the **Deployment Flow Chart** and the **Process Flow Chart**.

As with any universal visual tool, flow charting has standardized symbols. One very functional and simple set of standards were described by Myron Tribus (1989). They are shown as follows:

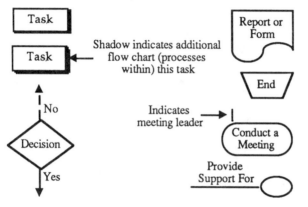

A more comprehensive set of symbols was approved by the American National Standards Institute (ANSI). These are used in the recommended flowcharting software package: **TopDown™ Flowcharter.** It can be purchased from Kaetron Software Corp., 25211 Grogans Mill Road, Suite

260, The Woodlands, Texas 77380; Phone: (713) 298-1500; fax: (713) 298-2520. They are:

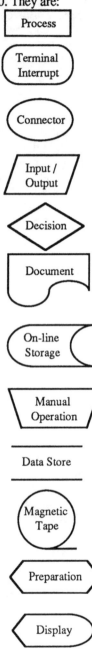

Process
Represents any kind of processing function

Terminal Interrupt
Represents a terminal point such as start, stop, halt, delay

Connector
Represents an exit to or an entry from another part of the flowchart

Input / Output
Represents an input/output (I/O) function

Decision
Represents a decision operation

Document
Represents an I/O function in which the medium is a document

On-line Storage
Represents an I/O function using any type of on-line storage

Manual Operation
Represents any off-line process geared to the speed of a human being without using mechanical aid

Data Store
Represents data stored for later use by a process

Magnetic Tape
Represents an I/O function in which the medium is magnetic tape.

Preparation
Represents the modification of an instruction or group of instructions which change the program itself

Display
Represents an I/O function in which the information is displayed for human use at the time of processing

Don't get too concerned about the use of "symbols" when you begin to flowchart. In the lower grade levels, in fact, you can use either a variety of visual graphics that usually come as part of flowcharting programs, or you can design your own with the students. For example, in TopDown™, there are a few examples symbols that you may find useful. Remember, it's the process of flowcharting that is important.

Deployment Flow Chart

Procedure

1. <u>Definition of the System</u>

Each system consists of a series of processes. However, it is not always clear where one system ends and another begins, since many systems involve more than one process. Therefore, the team should agree as to the starting and ending points members wish to study.

2. <u>Drawing the Deployment Flow Chart</u>

A **Deployment Flow Chart** is useful when you want to show the inter-relationships between the people and the tasks they actually perform to generate either a service or a product within a system.

Team members should actually walk through each step in the system they are studying. As they do, they should ask each person performing a task what is actually involved. Copious notes should be taken along with sketches. Only after this is done should the members draw a **Deployment Flow Chart**.

It should be mentioned that flow charts should not be drawn only when there are problems within a system. Instead, charts should be drawn for every task and process within all systems in order to root out nonvalue-added work. In addition, if there are any changes within a system, its flow chart should be updated immediately for all to see.

The first thing that should be done in preparing the **Deployment Flow Chart** is to enter the "people" coordinates horizontally. The boxes can contain either the particular person or his/her position or the particular department/unit that is performing a task. In the example below, we will follow an actual **Deployment Flow Chart** of an assignment in a social studies class.

Next the actual tasks and/or major steps are listed:

1. Prepare Assignment (Teacher)

2. Determine Options (Teacher and Group)

3. Analyze Options and Select Preferred (Group)

4. Approve Group Option (Teacher)

5. Research Assignment (Individual Students)

6. Compile Research (Group)

7. Outline Research Paper and Submit for
   Approval (Group)

8. Approve Outline (Teacher)

9. Write Subsections or Implement
   Project (Individual Students)

10. Approve Subsections (Group)

11. Combine Paper or Project Results
    (Group)

12. Approve Combined Effort (Group)

13. Submit Final Results (Group)

14. Approved? (Teacher)

15. Evaluate (Teacher and Group)

CQI Tools and Techniques

Using the symbols described above, draw the flow chart.

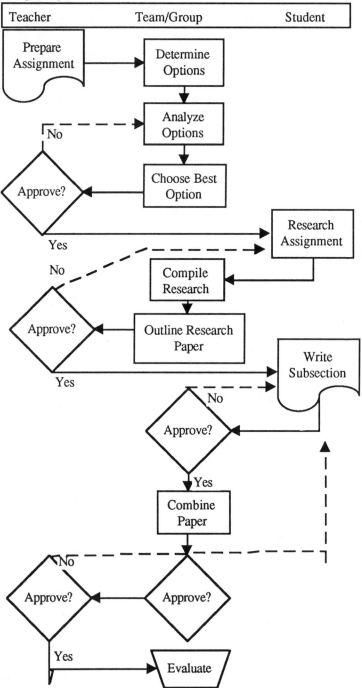

| Teacher | Team/Group | Student |

3. <u>Record and Discuss the Results</u>

Because the horizontal lines represent a customer-supplier relationship, the flow chart reveals the nature of the interactions. Examine the lines and try to determine if there is any nonvalue-added work that can be reduced or eliminated. If there appears to be a breakdown in the system where someone is not supplying his customer with quality work, try to examine the reason(s) why. Are there barriers or decision-making delays that slow the flow?

A team, after examining the system, recommended the following revision, which reduced the inspection time and empowered groups of students to make decisions about work quality. As a result, the students worked harder, assignments were completed faster and results were excellent.

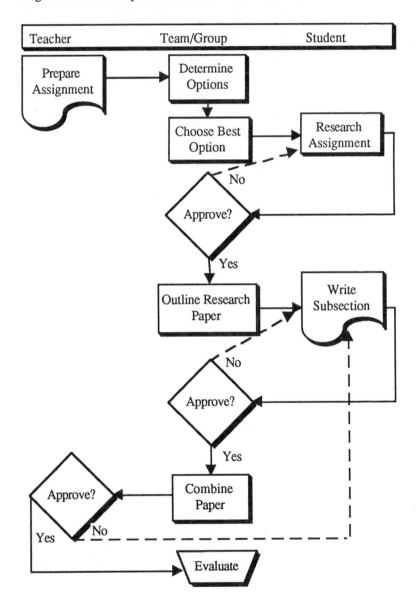

Process Flow Chart

Procedure

1. Statement of the Problem

The **Process Flow Chart** simply shows the major steps within a system and does not attempt to demonstrate the interrelationships between the people doing the tasks. As with any flow chart, the task force should agree to the starting and ending points of the system they wish to study.

2. Drawing the Process Flow Chart

The members of a team should walk through each step in the system they are studying. As they do, they should ask the people performing each task what is actually involved. Copious notes should be taken along with sketches. Only after this is done should the members draw a **Process Flow Chart.**

The first thing that should be done in preparing chart is to list the major steps in the system. Then using standardized symbols like those shown below you should draw the flow chart.

Using the example in the previous **Deployment Flow Chart,** you may have listed the major steps as follows:

1. Prepare assignment ☐

2. Determine options ☐

3. Choose best option ☐

4. Research assignment ☐

5. Outline paper ☐

6. Write subsections ☐

7. Prepare final paper ☐

8. Submit results ☐

9. Get approval ◇

10. Evaluate ⬜

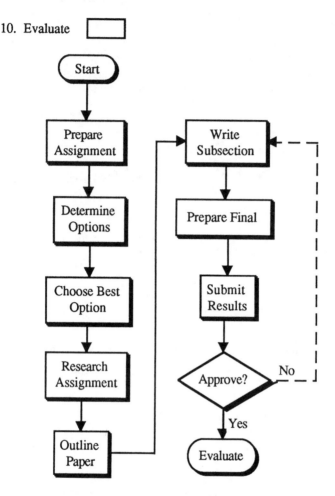

3. Record and Discuss the Results

By studying the flow chart, team members may be able to recommend ways to reduce redundant steps and improve the processes of the system.

Notes

The following are examples of actual **Flow Charts** showing the teaching/learning system of several different teachers. The first two **Flow Charts** show the processes in Mr. Waldon's approach to teaching vocabulary to ninth-grade students before and after learning about the positive affect of teaming (Source: Byrnes, Cornesky, and Byrnes. 1992). The last **Flow Chart** shows the processes of Tony Horning, a math teacher at Azelea Elementary, St. Petersburg, Florida. Mr. Horning's procedures have integrated a plan-do-study-act (PDSA) cycle—this encourages students to take an active role in examining the quality of their own work.

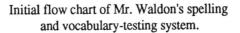

Initial flow chart of Mr. Waldon's spelling
and vocabulary-testing system.

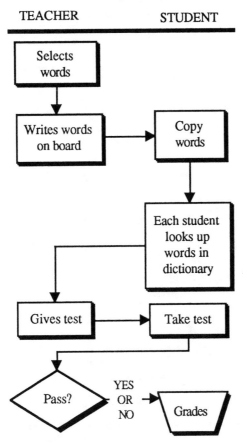

Revised flow chart of Mr. Waldon's spelling and vocabulary-testing system.

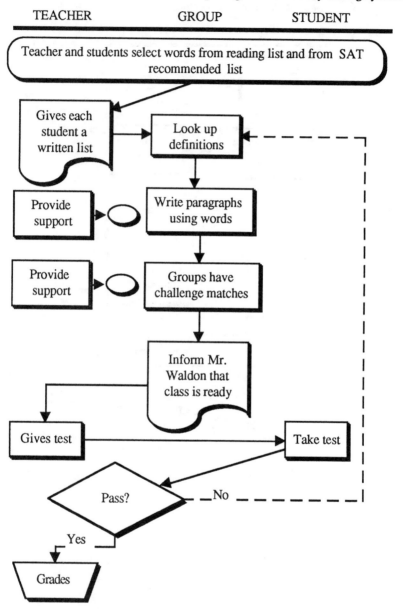

Below is a flow chart from Mr. Tony Horning, a fifth grade teacher at Azalea Elementary School in St. Petersburg, Florida. Note that his classroom procedures have an integrated plan-do-study-act (PDSA) cycle built into the learning process—this encourages students to take an active role in examining the quality of their own work.

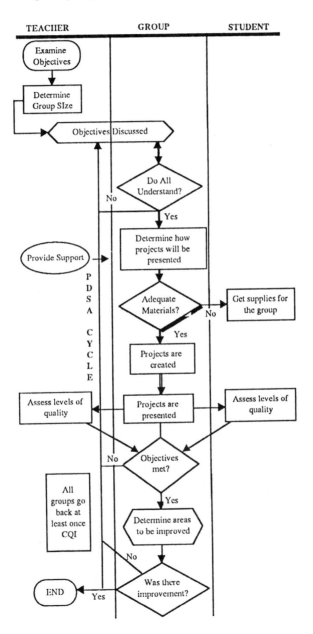

FORCE FIELD ANALYSIS

The **Force Field Analysis** tool was the product of federally funded research to change the meat-buying habits of American housewives during World War II and was invented by Prof. Kurt Lewin of the University of Iowa.

Force Field Analysis helps a task force identify the perceived driving and restraining forces affecting a recommended change. Then, by increasing the forces driving the change or by decreasing the forces inhibiting the change, or both, a task force can bring about a successful change.

The **Force Field Analysis** is much more useful when used with other CQI tools—the nominal group process, affinity diagram, and/or scenario builder—especially if the recommended change is counter to the "tradition" of the classroom. Like the nominal group process, affinity diagram, and/or scenario builder, the **Force Field Analysis** involves the use of proper brainstorming procedures: a facilitator is selected, team members have an equal opportunity to express their ideas without criticism, and participants are encouraged to built on the ideas of others.

Procedure

1. Statement of the Problem

Under the direction of the team leader (or the facilitator) the members of the task force should arrive at a statement of the precise desired change that will be made to management. To arrive at this statement it may be necessary to use other CQI tools such as the nominal group process (NGP) and the affinity diagram as previously explained.

For example, Dr. Moore teaches World Geography in a traditional university. Since she had heard from a professor in another school that "Learning Community" concepts represented an effective teaching technique, she wanted her class to participate in one of the Learning Community Models. She realized there were some potential problems and established a task force to analyze the feasibility of such a change.

2. <u>Recording the Suggestions</u>

    After brainstorming on the driving and restraining forces much like the procedure for the NGP, the task force, consisting of including herself, prior students, the other professors that would be involved in the collaborative teaching situation, and the dean recorded the following perceived driving and restraining forces.

FORCE FIELD ANALYSIS Recommended Change: Infuse Learning Community Concepts into Classroom	
Driving Forces (+)	**Restraining Forces (–)**
	Alters the curriculum
Students respond enthusiastically to this approach	Professor isn't knowledgeable about Learning Communities
	Requires the professor to think about the curriculum differently and plan alternative activities
Interrelates many aspects of the curriculum	Professor lacks the skill to create instructional materials for all learning community courses
	No incentive for professors to try new ideas in their classes
Accommodates many different learning styles	School lacks resources for professors to create materials

3. Discuss and Prioritize the Driving and Restraining Forces

We recommend that the person who generated the idea give his/her rationale as to why s/he felt it was important. Then an open discussion should be conducted on each point, and, if possible, certain points could be combined under a single heading if the task force agrees.

After discussion and grouping of the driving and restraining forces, the task force should assign a value of relative importance to each point. The values could be determined much like the way we recommended in the nominal group process (NGP) where either a rank value or total points could be determined using a n-1 numbering system. (For example, in the restraining forces there are 6 separate items listed. Therefore, the group may wish to use the NGP technique and assign #5 to the most important perceived restraining force, #4 for the second most important, etc.)

In this case, the task force decided to use the NGP and the final ranking value, *i.e.*, #1 was considered the most significant driving/restraining force, #2 the second most important, etc. These values are placed along side of the comments and are shown below.

FORCE FIELD ANALYSIS	
Recommended Change: Infuse Learning Community Concepts into Classroom	
Driving Forces (+)	**Restraining Forces (−)**
	Alters the curriculum (-5)
Students respond enthusiastically to this approach (+1)	Professor isn't knowledgeable about Learning Communities (-1)
	Requires the professor to think about the curriculum differently and plan alternative activities (-4)
Interrelates many aspects of the curriculum (+3)	Professor lacks the skill to create instructional materials for all Learning Community courses (-6)
	No incentive for professors to try new ideas in their classes (-2)
Accommodates many different learning styles (+2)	School lacks resources for professors to create materials (-3)

4. <u>Recommending Steps to be Taken</u>

After the driving and restraining forces are recorded, discussed, and prioritized the task force should begin to recommend steps that should be taken in order to effect the desired change. This should be done on the bottom of the form as shown below.

FORCE FIELD ANALYSIS
Recommended Change: Infuse Learning Community Concepts into Classroom

Driving Forces (+)	Restraining Forces (−)
	Alters the curriculum (-5)
Students respond enthusiastically to this approach (+1)	Professor isn't knowledgeable about Learning Communities (-1)
	Requires the professor to think about the curriculum differently and plan alternative activities (-4)
Interrelates many aspects of the curriculum (+3)	Professor lacks the skill to create instructional materials for all Learning Community courses (-6)
	No incentive for professors to try new ideas in their classes (-2)
Accommodates many different learning styles (+2)	School lacks resources for professors to create materials (-3)

RECOMMENDED ACTIONS:
1. The dean should provide funding for the professors to attend a workshop on Learning Communities. (This would address the #1, #4, #5, and #6 ranked restraining forces and the #2 and #3 ranked driving forces.)
2. This professor should be encouraged to implement Learning Communities and present her plans and outcomes before the entire department faculty. (This would address the #2 and #5 restraining forces and all driving forces.)
3. Professors who agree to share their Learning Community plans will receive money from the Innovation Committee for creating additional instructional materials. (This would address the #2, #3 and #6 restraining forces and #1 and #3 driving forces.)
4. This professor can become a lead instructor within the department, training colleagues in the use of Learning Community concepts. (This would address restraining forces #2,#4, #5, #6.)

Note

The **Force Field Analysis** can be used as part of a total class effort to improve the overall quality of your class. In addition, it can be used as a tool for individual students to reflect on habits that can lead to success.

The example below is taken from *Quality Fusion* (1994). It shows a **Force Field Analysis** completed by a high school student as part of his CQI journey.

Completed Force Field Analysis for High School Student.

FORCE FIELD ANALYSIS	
Name: Rick	Week of: November 9-13
Class: Algebra 2	Period: 6th
Goal: To finish my homework each night.	
Driving Forces	Restraining Forces
1. Stay eligible for football team 2. Drive the car to school 3. Get a college scholarship 4. Keep parents off my back	1. Talk to girlfriend on phone 2. Too tired after football practice 3. Don't always understand the homework problems 4. Not interested—don't always see a need for it
ACTION PLAN: 1. Set timer—limit phone calls to 30 minutes once per night 2. Speak to teacher and ask for clarification of problems 3. Eat a snack for more energy after football practice 4. Do Algebra 2 homework from 7-7:45 PM each night before calling girlfriend	

Source: Byrnes and Cornesky, 1994.

HISTOGRAM

The **Histogram** is a depiction of data on a bar graph which represents how often that group of data occurs. One of the main purposes of using a **Histogram** is to predict improvements in a system. The system must be stable, however, or the **Histogram** cannot be used to make predictions. If the system is unstable, the **Histogram** might take different shapes at different times. Therefore, the Histogram is often used with a Control Chart.

A team studying a system may gather statistical data about the system and then draw a **Histogram** to help members assess the current situation. Then, in order to test the resulting evidence, the team may change one or more processes within a system and, after gathering additional statistical data and redrawing another **Histogram**, check to see if the modifications improved the system.

The **Histogram** is also used to analyze the variation within a system. You must have a set of either related attributes or variables. Although we will describe how a **Histogram** is prepared and how the shape of the **Histogram** may vary, we will not do the actual calculation of the statistics. Instead, we refer the reader to any elementary statistics book for the actual calculations.

In the example that follows, we have selected a case study from a seventh-grade science class where Mrs. Appleton wanted to have her students analyze their study habits and the relationship to their success rate in science. The class participated in discussions and agreed on possible factors affecting their school success and study habits. Each student agreed to monitor the amount of time s/he spent talking on the telephone for one month. They also agreed to keep track of the grades they received in science class during the month. At the end of the first month, a team of students combined all data. Class members spent a total of 95,250 minutes on the telephone. That represented 3,175 minutes per student for the month, or an average of 53 minutes per day for 30 days. The total number of minutes spent studying for the same period of time was 31,399. This meant that each student spent an average of 17 minutes studying science per day.

The team recorded the data and made a Frequency Distribution chart. This was posted, and the students then discussed ways to improve their grades. At the end of the first month, the class agreed to cut the amount of talking on the telephone in half and use that time to study science. As before, each student again kept track of time spent on the telephone and all science grades. The class wanted to see if making a small alteration in daily habits would dramatically affect science grades.

Procedure
1. Select the Data to be Analyzed

We have assumed that the team or the individual studying a system has collected either the attribute data or the variable data. In our case study, the students kept tract of both telephone time and grades received.

2. Record the Data

A frequency table is constructed similar to those shown below.

Frequency Distribution

Distribution of grades for Mrs. Appleton's seventh-grade science class for November 1991.
(Before reducing the time spent on the telephone.)

Grade	Absolute Frequency	Relative Frequency %	Relative Cumulative %
A	01	3.33	3.33
B	03	10.00	13.33
C	06	20.00	33.33
D	12	40.00	73.33
F	08	26.66	100
Total	30	100	

Frequency Distribution

Distribution of grades of the students from Mrs. Appleton's science class for December 1991 (After reducing the time spent on the telephone in half.)

Grade	Absolute Frequency	Relative Frequency %	Relative Cumulative %
A	6	20.00	20.00
B	9	30.00	50.00
C	13	43.33	93.33
D	2	6.66	100
F	0		
Total	30	100	

3. Draw the Histogram

Draw the x-axis (horizontal) and the y-axis (vertical). They should be of approximately of equal length and of sufficient size to best display your data. Then draw a bar for each "Grade" with the corresponding "Frequency" for which it occurred.

The **histograms** showing the distribution of grades of the students from Mrs. Appleton's science class from November 1991 (before the self-imposed telephone restrictions) and from (after the self-imposed telephone restrictions) December 1991 are shown below.

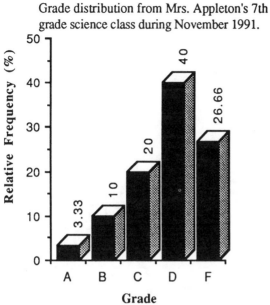

Grade distribution from Mrs. Appleton's 7th grade science class during November 1991.

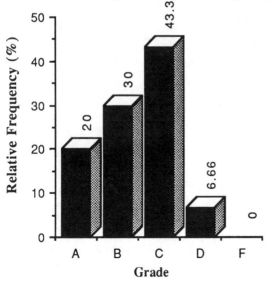

Grade distribution in Mrs. Appleton's 7th grade science class in December 1991.
(After altering the time spent on the phone.)

4. Analyze the Shape of the Histogram(s)

Histograms have six common shapes, namely 1) symmetrical, 2) skewed right, 3) skewed left, 4) uniform, 5) random, and 6) bimodal. These are shown below.

The Common Shapes of Histograms

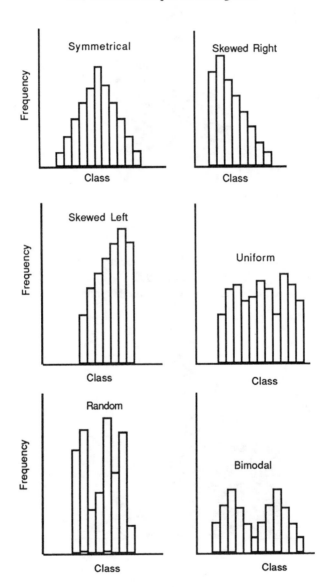

The symmetrical figure, called a bell-shaped curve, usually represents a "normal" distribution and indicates that the system under investigation is probably under control. Ideally, the mean (average), mode, and median of the class data are equal and that 99.73 percent of total area under the curve is plus or minus 3 standard deviations.

Histograms can also trail off either to the right or left. Whereas the skewing to the right is known as a positive skew, the trailing to the left is known as a negative skew. These can occur when the data has values greater than zero, as in our case study.

The uniform and random distributions can indicate that the system under investigation is out of control. By the same token, a uniform distribution may be the result of not having sufficient units in your data, while the random distribution may result if you have multiple sources of variation in the system under study. In either case, these distributions usually provide little information.

The bimodal **Histogram** may indicate that the system under study is the result of several sources of data.

The first **Histogram** in our case study of Mrs. Appleton's science class is skewed left.

The skewed left is "negatively skewed"—it has a larger number of instances occurring with lower grades (C—F) and a few in the higher grades (A—B). As mentioned above, this skewed distribution occurs when data within a system has a possible zero point, and all the data collected has a value larger than zero.

The second **Histogram** is also skewed to the left, although class grades did improve. In this case, you could make the case that the majority of students in Mrs. Appleton's class were able to achieve a grade better than "C" (93.3 percent) after making a slight change in their study habits.

After analyzing the data, students in this class decided to embark on a continuous improvement project to see how each could improve his/her performance in all classes. Next, they agreed to monitor the amount of time spent watching television while tracking their grades. The graphic data was a powerful tool indeed!

NOMINAL GROUP PROCESS

This technique is a structured process which helps the group identify and rank the major problems or issues that need addressing. This technique is also good for identifying the major strengths of a department/unit/institution. The technique gives each participant an equal voice, a key element of the group process.

The example below is taken from Mr. Jones' Social Science class. The session was called by the teacher because of his concerns of a lack of quality in his classroom. Students, a representative number of parents and Mr. Jones participated in the process and were to arrive at a consensus as to the perceived problems and/or weaknesses that inhibited quality.

For the **Nominal Group Process** (NGP), we recommend that each group have a facilitator who is not part of the team/unit. The facilitator may have to encourage some members of the team who are reluctant to participate; likewise, the facilitator may have to restrain members who normally tend to control such processes. All members need to feel comfortable with the process and comfortable in participating. Each facilitator will require a stopwatch during the workshop.

Each group should consist of 5 to 10 persons. Since large classes will have several groups, it is possible, although unlikely, that each group may perceive different problems/weaknesses. If this should happen, the facilitator may have to review the results and plan another session for the entire unit before the final ranking can be assigned.

Procedure

1. Introduction to the Process (5 Minutes)

The facilitator provides instructions regarding the process but does not influence the group's decision. The facilitator keeps the group working within the time limits.

The facilitator tells participants that the NGP allows them to explore areas systematically and to arrive at a consensus. The process consists of developing a list and ranking perceived problems. The results of the ranking are discussed, and the perceived problems which are the most important to the group are identified.

2. Presentation of the Question (15 Minutes)

The facilitator should direct the question to be considered by the group. For example, the facilitator, as in this case, might be instructed to ask the group: "What do you consider to be the major problem of your unit that is affecting quality?"

The facilitator should ask each participant to write short and specific 3-to-5 word answers for each perceived problem on **Form A** (see below). The facilitator should request that each member complete Form A silently and independently, reminding the participants that they have 5 minutes for this task. At the end of 5 minutes, if several members have not finished, the facilitator should state that s/he will allow 2 additional minutes. If most members have already finished, the facilitator should not allow the extra time.

FORM A

Listing of Perceived Problems

What do you think are the major problems in your unit that inhibit quality? Please use the form below and write out short but specific answers.

Item #	Perceived Problem
1	
2	
3	
4	
5	

3. Development of a Master List (20 Minutes)

While the group is developing its list of perceived problems, the facilitator should use an overhead projector to project **chart I.**

At the end of the time allotted for listing the perceived problems of the unit, the facilitator should ask the participants to stop writing. Then in a round-robin fashion, the facilitator will ask each to read aloud one of the perceived problems on his/her list. The facilitator will tell the participants that if they come to a problem on their list that has been given, they need not repeat it. If one item is phrased differently from another but appears to be the same, the facilitator will ask the group members to indicate by a show of hands if they think the items are the same. If a majority of the group feel the items are the same, the perceived problem will not be listed again; otherwise, both items will be listed. It may be necessary during this time for the facilitator to ask the participants not to speak out of turn. There should be **no discussion** of the list at this point. For a period of time, the participants should not be influenced (to avoid coercion) by the opinions or remarks of others. This must be adhered to early in the process. Otherwise, those less assertive members will not raise problems which they alone might perceive: for instance, that another member likes to control department meetings. As each perceived problem is given, the facilitator will record the item on the **chart I.** The facilitator must **not** suggest categories or combinations. The items should be numbered and recorded as presented by the participants without editing, unless the item is too long, in which case the facilitator may try to shorten the phrasing of the perceived problem without changing the meaning. If at the end of 20 minutes, some group members' have items that have not been presented, the facilitator will ask each member to give the one **most important** perceived problem remaining on his/her list.

A sample of some of the initial results of the perceived problems that resulted from the NGP in Mr. Jones' Social Science class are shown below.

Chart I

Perceived Problems that Inhibit Quality in Mr. Jones' Social Science Class.

Item #	Perceived Problem	Initial Value	Final Value	Final Rank
1	Class size too large			
2	Textbooks are out of date			
3	Classroom is in disrepair			
4	Students are tardy			
5	Too many students are absent			
6	Too many interruptions (announcements, etc.)			
7	Class periods are too short			
8	Teacher is unenthusiastic			
9	Teacher hasn't kept up new techniques & information			
10	Class activities are too routine (boring)			
11	Coercive, punitive discipline policy			
12	Students don't complete homework assignments			
13	Mr. Jones coaches football & uses class time to work out new plays			
14	Tests are too hard			

4. Master List Item Clarification (15 Minutes)

The facilitator should point to each perceived problem on the master list and read the item aloud. The facilitator should ask if each item is understood. If an item is unclear, the facilitator should ask the individual who generated the item to clarify it. The facilitator should **not** attempt to either condense the list nor permit the group to discuss the relative importance of the perceived problems at this point. Remember, the purpose of this step is **clarification.**

5. Initial Ranking of the Items (15 Minutes)

The facilitator should distribute **Form B** (see below) to each member of the group and should request that each member select and rank the **five (5)** most important perceived problems of the unit. The most important perceived problem should be assigned a #5; the next most important item should be assigned a #4; and so forth with the #1 being assigned for the least important. The participants then record their rankings on **Form B.** The facilitator then should collect the forms and tally the results on the master list giving each item an initial score.

Form B
Initial Ranking of Perceived Problems

Please refer to the master list (Chart I) that describes the perceived problems and indicate in the table below what you think are the five major problems.

Item Number from the Master List	Initial Subjective Ranking Value
	#5 (Most Important)
	#4
	#3
	#2
	#1 (Least Important)

Using the listings from our aforementioned example in Chart I, the members of the team in Mr. Jones' class assigned the following values to the listed perceived problems.

Chart I
Perceived Problems that Inhibit Quality in Mr. Jones' Social Science Class.

Item #	Perceived Problem	Initial Value	Final Value	Final Rank
1	Class size too large	7		
2	Textbooks are out of date	23		
3	Classroom is in disrepair	17		
4	Students are tardy	40		
5	Too many students are absent	20		
6	Too many interruptions (announcements, etc.)	1		
7	Class periods are too short	3		
8	Teacher is unenthusiastic	29		
9	Teacher hasn't kept up new techniques & information	31		
10	Class activities are too routine (boring)	45		
11	Coercive, punitive discipline policy	8		
12	Students don't complete homework assignments	30		
13	Mr. Jones coaches football & uses class time to work out new plays	27		
14	Tests are too hard	35		

6. Discussion of Initial Ranking (30 Minutes)

The facilitator should ask the participants to discuss the results of the ranking. The participants may wish to **elaborate, defend,** and to **dispute** the rankings. They may not add items. Items may be discussed even if they did not receive a high score. The members should be reminded that this is their opportunity to express opinions and to persuade others. The facilitator should attempt to keep the discussion orderly and to prevent anyone from dominating.

At this point, similar items may be combined into a single category. In the above example, a total of 14 separate items was eventually reduced to nine. These are shown below.

Class size too large	Too many interruptions
Textbooks are out of date	Class periods are too short
Classroom is in disrepair	Teacher is unenthusiastic
Students are tardy	
Coercive, punitive discipline policy	
Students don't complete homework assignments	

7. <u>Break (20 Minutes)</u>

The facilitator should encourage the participants to take a break . Some members may want to take the discussion into the hallway.

8. <u>Final Listing and Ranking of Items (15 Minutes)</u>

After the items have been discussed, the facilitator should distribute a copy of **Form C** (see below) to all group members. The facilitator should request each member to rank the top five choices as before: assign #5 to the one item they consider the most important; #4 to the second most important; etc. At the end of the allocated time, the facilitator should record the final values to each item on the master list.

Form C
Final Ranking of Perceived Problems
Please refer to the revised master list (Chart I) that describes the grouped perceived problems and indicate in the table below what you think are the five major problems.

Item Number from the Master List	Initial Subjective Ranking Value
	#5 (Most Important)
	#4
	#3
	#2
	#1 (Least Important)

The results of the Master List should be recorded and typed on **Form D** (see below). When this was done in Mr. Jones' class mentioned above, the following data were obtained.

Form D

Summary and Rank of the Perceived Problems that Inhibit Quality in Mr. Jones' Social Science Class

Item #	Perceived Problem	Initial Value	Final Value	Final Rank
1	Class size too large	7	0	9
2	Textbooks are out of date	23	17	5
3	Classroom is in disrepair	17	2	7
4	Students are tardy	40	29	4
5	Too many students are absent	20	0	
6	Too many interruptions (announcements, etc.)	1	32	3
7	Class periods are too short	3	5	6
8	Teacher is unenthusiastic	29	97	2
9	Teacher hasn't kept up new techniques & information	31	0	
10	Class activities are too routine (boring)	45	0	
11	Coercive, punitive discipline policy	8	1	8
12	Students don't complete homework assignments	30	110	1
13	Mr. Jones coaches football & uses class time to work out new plays	27	0	
14	Tests are too hard	35	0	

The results allowed the class to begin to address the real causes for the lack of quality.

Below are the various charts and forms you will need to conduct the NGP in your class.

Chart I
Perceived Problems that Inhibit Quality in our Class

Item #	Perceived Problem	Initial Value	Final Value	Final Rank
1				
2				
3				
4				
5				
6				
7				
8				
9				
10				
11				
12				
13				
n				

FORM A
Listing of Perceived Problems.
What do you think are the major problems in this class that inhibits quality?
Please use the form below and write out short but specific answers.

Item #	Perceived Problem
1	
2	
3	
4	
5	

Form B
Initial Ranking of Perceived Problems.
Please refer to the master list (Chart I) that describes the perceived problems
and indicate in the table below what you think are the five major problems.

Item Number from the Master List	Initial Subjective Ranking Value
	#5 (Most Important)
	#4
	#3
	#2
	#1 (Least Important)

Form C
Final Ranking of Perceived Problems
Please refer to the revised master list (Chart I) that describes the grouped
perceived problems and indicate in the table below what you think are the
five major problems.

Item Number from the Master List	Initial Subjective Ranking Value
	#5 (Most Important)
	#4
	#3
	#2
	#1 (Least Important)

Form D
Summary and Rank of the Perceived Problems that Inhibit Quality.

Item #	Perceived Problem	Initial Value	Final Value	Final Rank
1				
2				
3				
4				
5				
6				
7				
8				
9				
10				
11				
12				
13				
n				

OPERATIONAL DEFINITION

An **Operational Definition** is a very precise statement of what is expected from process objectives. It is probable that most of the troubles within the classroom are the result of operational definitions which are imprecise or undefined. An operational definition is a prerequisite for collecting data, and it must be clearly understood by everyone—the members of the team, teachers, students, etc.

Major problems arise in everyday events within schools because of unclear or undefined operational definitions. For example, students may want a clear definition of how their grades are going to be determined, including such simple and basic items as to what are they expected to know when they complete a course, how are they to be tested, and what are the classroom rules.

Operational definitions are used for **every** process that you are trying to be improved. It is not necessarily right or wrong, but it must be **accepted by all members working on the system or process.** In addition, if the conditions change as you are examining the process, the operational definition may change.

Procedure:

1. Statement of the Problem

Before any characteristic of a system or process is examined, the actual problem or issue has to be clearly defined. This is best done in form of a question such as, "How can I increase the success rate of students identifying major bones in the body and giving examples of three types of joints."

2. Identify the Criterion to be Applied to the Object or the Group

The criterion to be measured is the success rate of third-grade students identifying the major bones of the body and giving examples of three types of joints.

3. Identify the Test

The actual testing method must be precisely described including the evaluation procedure. In this example, a student must identify 10 major bones of the body from numbered bones on a skeleton. In addition, they must name and give an example of three types of joints. (The students have previously been taught all major bones and joint types. They have participated in a variety of exercises using differing instructional modes to learn. There have been group activities utilizing the skeleton to experiment with types of joints.) Students have the option to leave their seats and to examine the skeleton closely as well as to test out joint theories.

4. Describe the Decision Process

The decision process is what permits you to confirm or deny success. In this example, students will assess each other's answers using a scoresheet each group has developed and checked against a master sheet.

Note

After you have established your Classroom Mission Statement, you will have to list the Quality Factors or Goals and the **Operational Definitions**—the things that are necessary to demonstrate that the students have achieved the Quality Factors. To help clarify this point, we have developed the following tool. A chart like this should be completed for each un t of study.

CQI Guide
CQI Team Leader: Date:
Mission Statement:
Quality Factors (What are the goals?)
Operational Definitions (What is necessary to achieve the Quality Factors?)

We suggest that when establishing the quality factors and the operational definitions, you get the students involved. You may want to begin by seeding the lists with one or two obvious particulars and then allow the students to come up with others. You'll need to guide them through this, particularly when first starting the CQI process. If the students don't think of all the fundamentals, you should add to the lists by stating that you are a part of the group, too. Once this tool is fully developed and understood by all, post the **Operational Definitions** along with the quality factors and mission statement.

PARETO DIAGRAM

The **Pareto Diagram** is a CQI tool that is used to identify the few significant factors that contribute to a problem and to separate them from the insignificant ones. It is based on the work of Vilfredo Pareto, an Italian economist (1848-1923) and was made popular by Joseph Juran in the 1940's. However, it was Alan Lakelin who came up with the 80/20 rule of the Pareto Diagram. The rule says that about 80 percent of the problem comes from about 20 percent of the causes.

The Pareto Diagram is a simple bar chart with the bars being arranged in descending order from left to right. Although many people consider it a problem-solving tool, it is really best for guiding a team to the problem areas that should be addressed first.

In the example below, we have selected a case study from a high school auto shop where requests for repairs (known as "work orders") were not being completed in a timely fashion. Many of the repairs were not accomplished simply because the work order form was not completed correctly. The students and shop teacher identified six categories which attributed to the majority of errors: 1) unclear requests, 2) absence of the principal's signature, 3) method of payment for parts not indicated, 4) date on which the work was to be performed was absent, 5) location of automobile not specified, and 6) work order request misfiled. The shop teacher appointed a team and asked the members to collect and analyze the data. As part of their study, they used the Pareto Diagram which is shown below.

Procedure

1. Select Categories to be Analyzed

The members of the team should seek to identify data that they need to address a particular problem—such as time, location, number of defects, number of errors—and to place them into a category. The number of categories should be kept to 10 or less.

2. Specify the Time period in Which the Data will be Collected

Obviously, the time period that is selected will vary according to the system under study. It may be hours in the measuring the time it takes accounting to cut a check or years in case of testing an improvement theory. However, the time selection should be constant for all diagrams that are being compared.

In the above example, the shop teacher chose to compare the six categories across the past academic year.

3. Record the Data

A table is constructed with a category column and a frequency column, as shown below.

Category	# of Violations
Unclear requests	130
Principal's signature absent	74
Method of payment absent	46
Date to perform absent	40
Location of auto not identified	38
Work order misfiled	32
Total	360

The frequency table is constructed which shows the category, frequency, relative percent, cumulative frequency, and cumulative percent.

Category	Number Occurrences	Relative %	Cumulative Frequency	Cumulative %
Unclear request	130	36.1	130	36.1
No Principal's signature	74	19.7	204	55.8
Method of payment absent	46	12.8	250	68.6
Date to perform absent	40	11.1	290	79.7
Location of auto not identified	38	10.6	328	90.3
Work order misfiled	32	8.9	360	99.2
Total	360	99.2%		

4. Draw the Graph

Draw the x-axis (horizontal). It should be long enough to best display your graph, and it may vary from several inches to 6 or 7 inches. The width of each bar should be equal. In the case study we are examining, the x-axis of 3.6 inches was selected, and the scaling factor of 0.60 inch was selected to represent each of the categories.

Draw two vertical lines (y-axis) of equal length as shown below. They should be as long as the x-axis, if not longer. Again, they should be long enough to best display your graph.

Label and scale the axes. In this case study, the x-axis will represent the categories being compared, the y-axis on the left will represent the number of occurrences, and the right y-axis will represent cumulative percent.

After the graph is drawn, plot the cumulative frequencies and draw a line connecting the marks (**x**) as shown below.

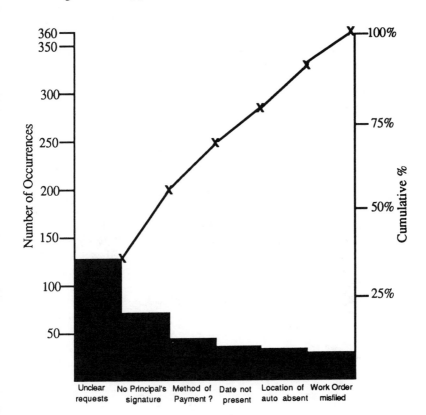

237

5.   Analyze the Diagram

It is not unusual for 80 percent of the problem to be caused by a few categories, and the Pareto Diagram will easily demonstrate this. In the above example, more that 55 percent of the occurrences were due to the first two categories.

You must be careful when using this powerful tool. It is true the Pareto diagram can point out chunks of data that can be used by a team to analyze causes and then direct efforts towards a few categories; however, some data cannot be categorized easily. Other data, without further analysis, may be misleading if the information is too general. The above data could be misinterpreted if the shop teacher simply concentrated on the first two categories.

Note

As with teachers, students need to debrief as well. The format should be determined based on the type of learning experience the students just completed. Debriefing may start as an individual or team effort and then progress to the entire class. It can be formal—having students complete a questionnaire—or informal by having discussion follow some sort of format. In either case, results should be recorded and analyzed for making decisions about future projects, learning experiences, team selection, materials, etc.

With informal debriefings, we recommend a student be selected (providing leadership opportunities to all students) to lead the discussion based on a format such as the following:

Typical interview questions that a student quality-improvement representative might ask of the class.

- The thing I liked best about this learning experience was:
- The thing that I didn't like was:
- The best thing about my group was:
- The thing I'd like to change about my group was:
- These kinds of learning experiences are:
- The thing(s) I learned from this is/are:

Have a student write all responses on the board. Students can then engage in creation of a **Pareto Chart** to determine the most critical problem(s). This information can be used to set parameters for the next learning experience. For example, in response to the question *The thing I didn't like about this learning experience was...* Mrs. MacElroy's fifth-grade class gave the following responses:

Number of Responses	Issue
11	working in the media center
3	the media teacher was crabby
9	not enough access to computers
6	books were outdated
1	not enough time to do research

Pareto Chart from Student Debriefing Exercise

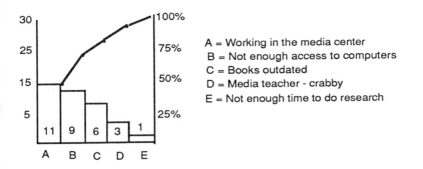

A = Working in the media center
B = Not enough access to computers
C = Books outdated
D = Media teacher - crabby
E = Not enough time to do research

You can easily see that 14 of 30 students (nearly 50 percent) indicated some problems with the media center directly. Three students felt that the media specialist was crabby, but eleven other students indicated they did not like working in the media center. At this point, there is not enough information to clearly understand the problems students were having with the media center. However, there is ample evidence that points to getting more information about the cause of their problems with the media center. Example from Byrnes and Cornesky (1994)

SELF-ASSESSMENT RATING OF THE TEACHING AND LEARNING SYSTEMS IN YOUR COURSE

The following self-assessment tool has been designed to facilitate the measurement of quality teaching and learning systems. It is not proposed as a mandatory set of guidelines without possibility of modification.

The goal is to encourage **self-assessment** of your classroom procedures and outcomes. The tool should enable faculty and academic departments to grapple with the strong external requirement in all classrooms to demonstrate quality in teaching and learning. Separate tools have been designed for evaluating the effectiveness of the Academic Support Systems and the Administrative Support Systems.

To use this tool, you must be familiar with its vocabulary.

- A <u>syllabus</u> is a written declaration of course expectations, schedule and instruction.
- A <u>systematic approach</u> is a set of activities considered from the point of assignment to evaluation.
- A <u>procedure</u> or <u>process</u> is an operational activity that can be observed. It is a subset of a systematic approach.
- A <u>strategy</u> is an operational design to be implemented or attempted. It is not an established procedure or process.

In considering performance on each criterion that follows, consider the weights shown below:

- 10 points =   This statement is **ALWAYS** true in my course and is being implemented in **ALL** portions of my teaching and learning systems.
- 9 points =   This statement applies to **VIRTUALLY ALL** (90 percent) of my teaching and learning systems.
- 8 points =   **MOST MAJOR** portions of my teaching and learning systems meet this standard.
- 7 points =   This statement is applicable to **MAJOR** elements (70 percent) of my teaching and learning systems.
- 6 points =   This statement is applicable to **SOME** elements of my teaching and learning systems.
- 5 points =   This statement is applicable to a **FEW** portions of my teaching and learning systems.
- 4 points =   This statement has **VERY LITTLE** relationship to the procedures, processes, and systems used in my teaching and learning systems.
- 3 points =   This statement is **NOT TRUE** for my teaching and learning systems, but I am planning to implement this approach or strategy within a year.
- 2 points =   This statement is **NOT TRUE** for my teaching and learning systems, but I am planning to learn more about ways to bring quality-producing initiatives, strategies and systematic approaches into my courses.

- 1 point = This statement is **NOT TRUE** for my teaching and learning systems, and I have no intention of learning how I might improve my learning and teaching environments.

You are now ready to evaluate the teaching and learning systems in your course. As you complete this survey, enter a value (from 1 to 10) that best matches your situation at the right of every question. Your Quality Index will be calculated at the end of this survey.

Remember, however, the point of this self-evaluation is **NOT** the score. The goal of the activity is to help you to evaluate ways for improving the quality of the learning environment for your students. Be prepared to use the tool as a guide for your continuous quality improvement (CQI) efforts.

Category 1.0: Leadership

This category examines teachers' personal leadership and involvement in sustaining a student focus, clear goals, high expectations and developing a leadership system that promotes performance excellence. Also examined is how objectives and expectations are integrated into the teaching and learning systems.

1.1   You personally and visibly establish a clear, course mission statement, clear course objectives and operational definitions on how the course objectives will be demonstrated and how they will result in a student-focused, learning system. ____

1.2   You personally and visibly developed strategies, systems, and processes for achieving excellence in your course. ____

1.3   You have done a thorough job of ensuring that your course syllabus reinforces a learning system that encourages initiative, self-directed responsibility, collaborative learning and continuous improvement. ____

1.4   You enhance the operational definitions of the course, so your students can achieve the course competencies and reach their performance goals. ____

1.5   You use a systematic approach to evaluate and improve the effectiveness of the leadership system for both yourself and your students. ____

1.6   Your course syllabus, schedule, and methods communicate clearly and regularly the expectation that all classroom processes exist to help all students develop to their fullest potential. ____

1.7   You have a process or procedure for regularly analyzing individual and team performances, and you can determine how to use the results to improve academic performance. ____

1.8   You serve as a role model for your students by protecting public health, safety and the environment. ____

1.9   You conduct research and systematic planning to anticipate problems associated with meeting course objectives and to correct problems before they occur. ____

Category 2.0: Information and Analysis

This category examines the management and effective use of data and information to support the overall mission-related performance of the course.

2.1   Both you and your students co-create measurements derived from and supportive of the mission of the course and learning-assignment strategies. ____

2.2   You have a process for tracking the reliability and access to data that are used for measuring both student and instructor performance. ____

2.3   You have a data-collection system for your course that includes input from students, future employers and the instructor next in line. ____

2.4   In the past few years, you have evaluated and made major improvements in how you assess students, collect data on the needs of your customers and report the data. ____

2.5   You developed a method of selecting and using comparative information and data to help improve overall classroom performance. In addition, you evaluated and improved the scope, sources, and uses of the comparative data. ____

2.6   Key course decisions and future course modifications are made after an analysis of the data and after identification of trends, projections and opportunities for improvement. ____

2.7   You understand thoroughly the correlation between different types of assessments and student performance. ____

Category 3.0: Strategic and Operational Planning

This category examines how you set strategic directions and how you determine key plan requirements. Also examined is how the course requirements are translated into an effective performance system, with a primary focus on student performance.

3.1 You do a thorough analysis of student needs and expectations. You examine key internal and external factors affecting improvement of student performance, and you use this information to develop annual improvement plans for your course. ____

3.2 In the last several years, you have evaluated and improved both the strategic planning and the plan deployment for your course, including plan-completion time and deployment time. ____

3.3 You have developed long- and short-term action plans for: 1) each of the major performance-improvement course goals, 2) the students, and 3) yourself. ____

3.4 You have developed specific projections or forecasts that indicate how student, your own and overall course performances will compare with past performances. ____

3.5 You benchmark courses where the performance of the students are projected or are known to be superior. ____

Category 4.0: Human Resource Development and Management

This category examines how you and your students' development are aligned with the performance objectives of your course. Also examined are your efforts to build and maintain a climate conducive to performance excellence and full participation, as well as to personal and student growth.

4.1 You have a human resource development plan in your course to get students involved in continuous quality improvement training, empowerment and recognition. ____

4.2 You have identified specific goals and strategies for improving human resource systems, including career-development help for your students. ____

4.3 You have implemented innovative approaches to course design to ensure effective communications and cooperation, so groups/teams in your class can work together to meet individual student and course requirements. ____

4.4 Your assessment and recognition approaches promote high performance in areas related to meeting student- and course-performance goals. ____

4.5 You have a systematic plan for keeping your colleagues and incoming students aware of your quality expectations. ____

4.6 You routinely conduct workshops for your colleagues and students that address quality-performance requirements and performance-assessment methods—such as the use of CQI tools and techniques. ____

4.7 You have many different approaches for rewarding students. ____

4.8 Your students feel well recognized for their accomplishments. ____

4.9 You have a structured student-development program that is based on a thorough analysis of the needs of all your students. ____

4.10 Your student-development plans are derived from an analysis of course competencies that are needed to meet key performance-improvement goals. ____

4.11 You have a systematic and effective strategy to promote the "in-your-daily-life" reinforcement of skills learned in your course. ____

4.12 You use systematic methods to assess the effectiveness of student development and, as a result of your assessments, you can demonstrate quality improvements in student development. ____

4.13 You have a well-defined and multi-faceted strategy in place for providing information on the special services available to your students, such as counseling, recreational programs, day-care, drug/alcohol treatment and mentoring. ____

4.14 You have a wide variety of methods to measure and to improve both student and stakeholder satisfaction. ____

Category 5.0: Educational and Business Process Management
This category examines the key aspects of process management in your course, including a learning-focused education design, educational delivery and personal services you offer.

5.1 You design new course competencies based on a thorough analysis of student needs and identified improvement criteria. ____

5.2 You modify your course (or design new courses) based on the appropriate linkages between the curricula and the needs of all stakeholders. ____

5.3   You have a measurement plan in your course that identifies what is to be assessed, how and when assessments are to be conducted, and how the results will be used.____

5.4   You have a plan in your course that stresses early intervention when learning is not progressing adequately. ____

5.5   You have a plan to ensure that any new competencies in your course focus on active learning. ____

5.6   You anticipate and prepare for individual student differences in the learning rates and styles. ____

5.7   You use assessments that measures the intellectual growth of students when you design course competencies. ____

5.8   You consider faculty/student feedback when you modify your course.____

5.9   Your course competencies are evaluated and improved by data from stakeholders and by benchmarking best practices. ____

5.10   You use assessment results, peer evaluations, research on learning and teaching assessments, and information from industries, governing bodies and technology when you update the objectives of your course.____

5.11   Through oral and written surveys from students, families, and faculty, you select key educational support services that are designed to meet the needs of your students.____

5.12   You have clearly defined competencies for your course, and you have clearly communicated these competencies to your suppliers—those who teach and grade the students who enter your class. ____

5.13   If any supplier gives you a defective product (a student who has not mastered the agreed-upon competencies), you immediately contact the supplier and give him/her the data to take preventive measures on behalf of future students. ____

5.14   Using various techniques, you evaluate key course operations to achieve better performance from your students, including feedback from your customers, benchmarking, process analysis and supplier improvement. ____

Category 6.0: School Performance Results

This category examines student performance and improvement, including improvement in the education climate of your course, services offered by you and by students in your course, and improvement performance of your classroom operations. Also examined are performance levels relative to comparable courses and/or selected instructors.

6.1 Student performance results reflect the improvement objectives of your course. _____

6.2 You base course performance results on various assessment methods._____

6.3 Performance data in your course is achieved through holistic appraisals of students._____

6.4 By key measurements, you have demonstrated constant improvement in the performance of students during the past three or more years._____

6.5 You can show that there was constant improvement in the performance of students in all other classes after they have taken your course. _____

6.6 The student-improvement results in your course equal or exceed results generated by comparable courses and/or student populations._____

6.7 You have key measurements to demonstrate that the learning climate in your course shows improvement. _____

6.8 Key measurements of your course's learning climate equal or exceed learning climates in other, comparable courses. _____

6.9 Key measurements of knowledge transfer to your students show continuous improvement. _____

6.10 Key measures of knowledge transfer to the students show continuous improvement in your course, and they equal or exceed the knowledge transferred during other comparable courses and/or with other student populations. _____

6.11 Key measurements of the "business" operations of your course— student credit hours generated, percentage of students who are retained, percentage of students receiving higher grades, stakeholder satisfaction with graduates, and so forth—constantly show improvement. _____

6.12 Key measurements of the "business" operations of your course constantly show improvement, and they equal or exceed business-related data generated by other, comparable courses and/or student populations. ____

Category 7.0: Student Focus and Student and Stakeholder Satisfaction

This category examines how you determine student and stakeholder needs and expectations. Also examined are levels and trends in key measurements of student and stakeholder satisfaction as well as satisfaction relative to comparable schools.

7.1 You frequently use multiple methods to determine student needs and expectations before offering a course. ____

7.2 You continually evaluate your methods used to identify students' needs. ____

7.3 You personally monitor the availability and effectiveness of the support services —mentoring, learning resource center, tutoring center, and so forth—to judge the influence they have on student satisfaction and on active learning in your classroom.____

7.4 In your course, you have a system for tracking formal and informal complaints as well as a process for timely resolution of any complaints. ____

7.5 You have data about every student who enters your course as to needs and expectations, and to the support services required to master course competencies.____

7.6 During the past two years, you have made improvements in data collection regarding why any student enters your course. ____

7.7 During the past two years, you have made improvements on how you collect data about the support services that your students will need to master course competencies. ____

7.8 You have ongoing research to project future student needs, expectations and key competencies from your course. ____

7.9 You have a well-defined process in place for using the data gathered about future student needs, expectations, and key competencies from your course. ____

7.10 You frequently use multiple methods to determine the needs and requirements of all stakeholders, not only as they apply to the mission statement of your course, but also as they apply to the mission statement of your school. ____

7.11 In recent years, you have instituted a number of improvements in the approaches you use to build a positive, fear-free climate in your classroom as well in the approaches you use to build positive relationships with other stakeholders. ____

7.12 You have a student- and stakeholder-satisfaction measurement system in place that provides you with reliable information about student and stakeholder satisfaction regarding the teaching and learning systems in your course. ____

7.13 You constantly evaluate your methods for implementing suggestions from your students and stakeholders. As a result of this input, you have made a number of improvements in the teaching and learning systems in your course. ____

7.14 You have data from the past several years to indicate that student and stakeholder satisfaction has followed a continually improving pattern.____

7.15 You have data from the past several years to indicate that measures of student and stakeholder dissatisfaction have shown a continually decreasing trend. ____

7.16 You have data to show that the levels and trends in all facets of student and stakeholder satisfaction with your course compare favorably to levels and trends generated at other, comparable courses and schools. ____

QUALITY INDEX

Score your self-assessment as follows:

1) Add up the points in Categories 1, 2, 3, 4, 6 and items 7.1, 7.2, 7.3, 7.4, 7.5, 7.6, and 7.7.
2) Add up the points in Category 5 and items 7.8, 7.9, 7.10, 7.11, 7.12, 7.13, 7.14, 7.15, and 7.16 and multiply by 2.
3) Add the points in items 1 and 2 above and determine your total score.

or

Transfer your scores from the previous pages and conduct the calculations below.

Category 1.0:   Leadership

      1.1 _____
      1.2 _____
      1.3 _____
      1.4 _____
      1.5 _____
      1.6 _____
      1.7 _____
      1.8 _____
      1.9 _____
      Total _____   Category 1.0 Total _____

Category 2.0: Information and Analysis

      2.1 _____
      2.2 _____
      2.3 _____
      2.4 _____
      2.5 _____
      2.6 _____
      2.7 _____
      2.8 _____
      Total _____   Category 2.0 Total _____

Category 3.0: Strategic and Operational Planning

      3.1 _____
      3.2 _____
      3.3 _____
      3.4 _____
      3.5 _____
      Total _____   Category 3.0 Total _____

Category 4.0: Human Resource Development and Management

    4.1   _____

    4.2   _____

    4.3   _____

    4.4   _____

    4.5   _____

    4.6   _____

    4.7   _____

    4.8   _____

    4.9   _____

    4.10 ____

    4.11 ____

    4.12 _____

    4.13 _____

    4.14 _____

    Total _____   Category 4.0 Total_____

Category 5.0: Educational and Business Process Management

    5.1   _____

    5.2   _____

    5.3   _____

    5.4   _____

    5.5   _____

    5.6   _____

    5.7   _____

    5.8   _____

    5.9   _____

    5.10 ____

    5.11 ____

    5.12 _____

    5.13 _____

    5.14 _____

    Sub-total ____ x 2 = Total_____ Category 5.0 Total_____

CQI Tools and Techniques

Category 6.0: School Performance Results

6.1 _____
6.2 _____
6.3 _____
6.4 _____
6.5 _____
6.6 _____
6.7 _____
6.8 _____
6.9 _____
6.10 _____
6.11 _____
6.12 _____
6.13 _____
6.14 _____
Total _____   Category 6.0 Total _____

Category 7.0: Student Focus and Student and Stakeholder Satisfaction

7.1 _____
7.2 _____
7.3 _____
7.4 _____
7.5 _____
7.6 _____
7.7 _____
        Sub-total (I)_____

7.8 _____
7.9 _____
7.10 _____
7.11 _____
7.12 _____
7.13 _____
7.14 _____
7.15 _____
7.16 _____
        Sub-total (II)_____ x 2 = _____
        Sub-total (I)_____ + Sub-total (II) _____ =
                                        Category 7.0 Total_____

QUALITY INDEX = SUM OF THE SEVEN CATEGORIES____

We suggest the following interpretation:

751—1,000 points: **Quality Teacher.** You should be benchmarked, and you should help other teachers.

600—750 points: **Progressive Teacher.** You should work on the teaching, learning, continuous quality improvement (CQI), and reward systems of your course to attain Quality Teacher status within one to three years. Most likely you need to re-examine your performance in Category 2.0, Information and Analysis, and Category 5.0, Educational and Business Process Management.

400—599 points: **Traditional Teacher.** You probably need work on all aspects of the teaching, learning, continuous quality improvement (CQI), and reward systems of your course. With proper support and training, you could attain the Progressive Teacher status within two years and the Quality Teacher Status within five or six years.

300—399 points: **Struggling Teacher.** You probably have some good systems in place and most likely 30 percent of your students can learn from your teaching style. However, you have a lot of work to do to refine your classroom systems and processes before you can deploy a variety of teaching and learning approaches in your courses. Most likely you will have difficulty obtaining tenure in an institution that values teaching.

299 or less points: **Inadequate Teacher.** You have a lot of work to do to make your classroom climate a friendly and fun place to learn. Most likely students avoid your classes. You will probably not obtain tenure in an institution that values teaching. However, with a lot of work and training in CQI tools and techniques and collaborative learning, you can change your classroom culture. If you want to be an effective teacher, don't give up.

QUALITY TEACHING INDEX

This Quality Teaching Index tool has not been tested thoroughly on teachers, and its validity has not been ascertained. This tool, based on the 1995 Malcolm Baldrige National Quality Award Education Pilot criteria, was adapted from the business model developed by M.G. Brown, "Measuring Up Against The 1995 Baldrige Criteria," *Journal for Quality & Participation*, December 1994, and from a survey instrument developed by Carol Sager of Sager Educational Enterprises, publisher of *Critical Linkages II* newsletter. Other Quality Index Rating Profile tools have been tested on the older versions of the Baldrige criteria and have been validated (Cornesky, R., *The Quality Professor: Implementing TQM in the Classroom* , Madison, WI: Magna Publications, 1993, and Margaret Byrnes, Cornesky, R. and Byrnes, L., *The Quality Teacher*, Port Orange, FL: Cornesky & Associates, Inc., 1992).

RELATIONS DIAGRAM

The **Relations Diagram** is used as a planning tool. When combined with either the Scenario Builder and/or the Affinity Diagram, the **Relations Diagram** is a powerful tool to arrive at root causes and effects of a process or a problem.

It helps a team examine a complex problem over an extended period of time and can constantly update and modify the necessary actions that might result from observed changes in the "system" under study.

Procedure
1. Statement of the Problem

Although it is possible to use the **Relations Diagram** by identifying a problem/issue and then stating it in a brief and specific manner, it is much more efficient to have examined a complex problem/issue with other tools before using it. For example, we recommend that your team first utilize one of the other tools such as the Nominal Group Process and/or the Affinity Diagram to arrive at a consensus about the process/issue under investigation, then analyze the findings further with the **Relations Diagram**.

In this example, a high school drama class was attempting to establish a set design and construction shop. The students determined that a team was the best way to achieve their goal. Their school district could not underwrite such a project, but the class was positive that the added capability such a shop would provide was worth the effort. After doing an analysis with an Affinity Diagram, the team posted the following header cards to the question "What are the issues associated with us establishing a set design and construction shop?"

Their answers included:
1. Get the support of parents.
2. Get the support of local business.
3. Demonstrate a need to the principal.
4. Get the support of the student body.
5. Develop and design a plan for the design & construction shop.
6. Prepare informational materials and programs
7. Develop and carry out a fund raising campaign.
8. Organize a volunteer effort to collect equipment and materials.

In order to examine the root cause and effects of issue, they next did a **Relations Diagram**. This is shown below.

2. Recording the Perceptions

Place the header cards from the Affinity Diagram in a circular pattern around the problem/issue being examined as shown below. This can be done using an overhead projector, but a large sheet of flip chart paper is usually better.

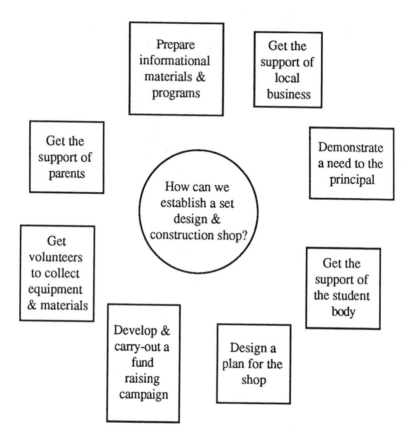

3. Demonstrate Interrelationships

You should ask if there is a "cause-and-effect" between the header groups. If a relationship exists, draw a line to connect the headers. An arrow is placed from the header that is a cause of something having an effect on the other header.

In the example below, the team decided that it was necessary to gain the support of the principal before going ahead with their plans. As a result, they drew arrows away from the cause and towards the header that it would affect or have influence over.

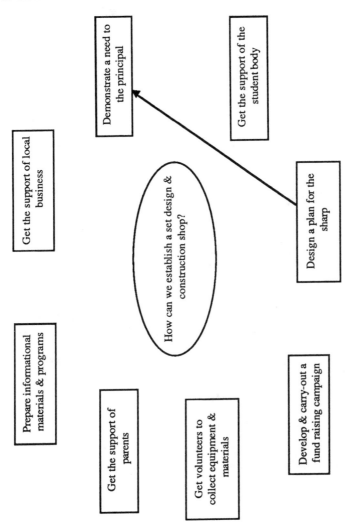

The inter-relations are continually examined until all headers are compared to each other. When this was done with the aforementioned example, the following diagram was finally constructed.

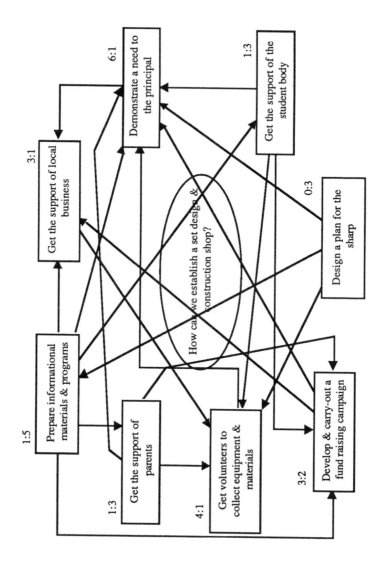

4. Analyze the Interrelationships

Count the number of arrows that are directed towards each header and the number that leave. Express this as #Towards and #From. Write the numbers next to their respective headers as shown above.

The **root causes** are those headers that have the greatest number of arrows going **FROM**; the **root effects** are those headers having the greatest number of arrows going **TOWARDS**. In the above example, the two root causes suggest that the team should design and draw plans for the shop and develop informational materials and programs prior to going to the principal for his approval and support.

RUN CHART

A **Run Chart,** also called a tier chart, is a line graph of data where the observed values can be either measurements (variables) or counts (attributes). The data is plotted on the vertical axis while the time is plotted on the horizontal axis.

One of main benefits of a **Run Chart** is to examine the functioning of any system over time. Similar data plotted together in a histogram may not reveal an important trend in the system that might require corrective action.

A **Run Chart** is constructed from data that is collected as the system is in operation and is often used by a team as the initial tool in gathering information about the system under study. Usually, more than 25 points are required for a valid run chart.

A **Run Chart** is a simple CQI tool and can be used with a wide variety of data. It is good for a single snapshot or for tracking trends. Various units within the school could make excellent use of run charts by posting good and poor trends for all to see and analyze. (Note: these charts should never be used as a threat or employees will refuse to offer their suggestions for improving the system.) Depending upon the data the time factor can be seconds, minutes, hours, days, weeks, or years. Depending upon the data, it may be possible to add the statistical upper-control limits (UCL) and lower-control limits (LCL), and make the **Run Chart** a "Control Chart."

Procedure
1. Select the Data to be Analyzed

    We have assumed that a team or an individual studying a system has collected either the attribute (counts) data or the variables (measurements) data. In the case study below, Mrs. Salmon was interested in discovering the average amount of time her students needed to achieve mastery for each unit of study. She wanted to examine her assignments and teaching styles for each unit and was going to focus on those units where the students were having the most difficulty with mastery.

2. Record the Data

Record the data in the order which it was collected.

Average time (in days) to achieve mastery per unit

Class period	Unit 1	Unit 2	Unit 3	Unit 4	Unit 5	Unit 6
#1 (8-8:50 AM)	13	15	14	16	15	14
#2 (9-9:50 AM)	14	13	14	13	13	14
#3 (10-10:50 AM)	13	14	16	15	15	14
#4 (11-11:50 AM)	19	23	20	18	21	16
#5 (12-12:50 PM)	16	16	17	17	16	14
#6 (1-1:50 PM)	14	16	16	15	15	14

3. Draw the Graph

First, you must scale the chart. This will vary depending upon the type of data collected—variables or attributes.

In scaling for the variables data, you start by finding the largest and smallest values in the data. In our case, the largest was 23 and the smallest was 13. The difference between these is determined by subtracting (23-13=10). Then, a rule of thumb is to divide the difference (10) by 66 percent of the number of lines on your graph paper. The chart paper used in our case study is shown below. It has 30 lines: 66 percent (30 x 0.66) equals 19.8, or approximately 20. Therefore, 10 + 20 is 0.5. By rounding to the higher number, each line will have an incremental value of 1.0.

Next, the lines should be numbered from the middle of the chart. Since our values range from 13 to 23 minutes, the value which is one half is 5 minutes. Since the center number is 5 minutes + 13 minutes or 18 minutes, we can set the center line at either 15 minutes or 20 minutes and assign an incremental value of one minute to the other lines.

Scaling for attributes data is identical to that of the variables scaling except the first line of the chart is assigned a value of zero and the increment values are added from the bottom up.

The data points are plotted on the graph paper as shown in and the points are connected with straight lines.

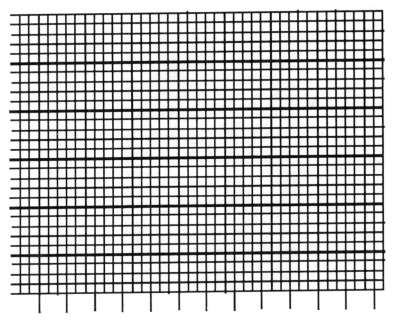

It should be mentioned that almost any chart paper can be used to plot the data of run charts and that the process of scaling would be the same.

The chart should be carefully labeled so that the results can be clearly understood by all members of the task force. An example of a completed run chart is shown below.

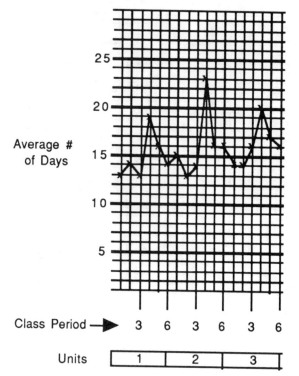

Average #
of Days

Class Period ➤   3   6   3   6   3   6

Units   1   2   3

4.   Analyze the Chart

You should look for runs of 7 or more points showing increases or decreases as well as for other patterns.

In our case, a pattern was discovered: students in "Period 4" took significantly longer to achieve mastery than students in all the other classes. Period 4 is just before lunch. Students may be tired, or hungry and distracted from their studies. (It could also be that Mrs. Salmon is tired and hungry and is not providing the necessary leadership.) She also discovered that the second period class averaged only 13.5 days to complete mastery in all the units. Her task now is to match this data with her teaching styles for the fourth and second periods. Based on that information, she will examine the learning styles of her students prior to making any adjustments in the class. Mrs. Salmon also will engage the students in the continuous improvement project, utilizing one or more of the other tools.

Note

A **Run Chart** can be used in the classroom to measure on-time performance, grading, classroom disruptions, time on task, charting of personal goals, proficiency in mastering a competency, etc. **Run Charts** are simple to construct, easy to read and can be used to encourage continuous improvement.

By using a simple computer graphing program, **Run Charts** can not only be informative, but they can be fun to make and analyze as well. For example, the following **Run Chart** data was taken from Baxter et. al. (1994) and plotted by Cricket Graph™.

The number of times food items are chosen by students over a two week period.

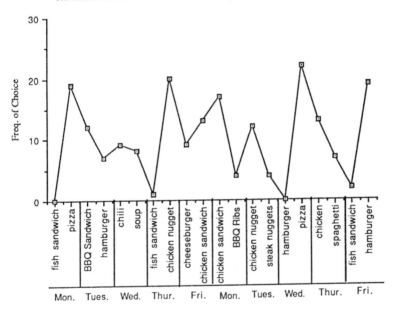

SCATTER DIAGRAM

Scatter Diagrams are used to test the possible interrelationships of two factors. If a relationship appears to exist, the factors are said to be correlated. However, a cause-and-effect relationship can be verified only with the use of control charts.

1. Select the Data to be Analyzed
    In the following case study, a teacher wanted to test whether the grades of students in a fourth grade mathematics unit were related to the time they watched television. As part of their CQI contract, parents were asked to record the amount of time in minutes that their child spent watching TV over a week and to submit this log to the teacher. At the end of the report period, the teacher plotted the results.

2. Record the Data

Student ID Number	Hours per Week Viewing TV	Math Grade in %
001	<1.0	96
002	2.5	98
003	14.0	60
004	21.0	72
005	21.0	56
006	2.5	88
007	3.0	83
008	7.0	86
009	8.0	71
010	3.0	91
011	3.0	86
012	18.0	60
013	21.0	56
014	<1.0	93
015	10.0	75
016	9.0	76
017	10.0	77
018	2.5	92
019	6.0	70
020	7.5	73
021	2.5	99
022	14.5	60
023	9.0	77
024	8.5	69
025	4.0	80

3. Draw the Diagram
    The first thing you should do is scale the diagram so that both axes are approximately the same length. The length of any axis should be long

enough to accommodate the entire range of values, and the entire length of each axis should be used. In our example, the time per week the students watched TV ranged from less than 2.5 hours to 21 hours. The x-axis usually contains the data believed to be the influencing or independent factor while the y-axis contains the dependent or responding factor. In our example, the teacher believed that the more the students watched TV the less they studied, and, as a result, their grades suffered. Therefore, the independent factor is time watching TV and the dependent factor is the grade.

The diagram should be labeled, dated, and the points should be plotted. The completed diagram is shown below.

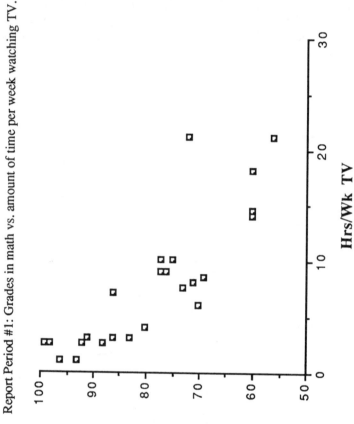

4.   Analyze the Diagram

Although it looks as if there might be a negative correlation between the amount of time the students watched TV and the grade that they received in the mathematics, there may be other factors that influenced the grades, such as the number of absences, etc. Clearly, however, the amount of time the students watch TV might be a possible root cause for poor grades in math.

268

SCENARIO BUILDER

The **Scenario Builder** is a planning tool which roughly quantifies the possible outcomes if one or more proposed changes to a system are implemented. It is a tool that asks "what if?" and concentrates the efforts of team members to propose most likely outcomes, both positive and negative. It is a powerful tool that combines many of the features obtained from an Affinity Diagram, the Nominal Group Process, the Force Field Analysis, and the Systematic Diagram.

Like the Affinity Diagram, it attempts to organize complex issues; like the Nominal Group Process, it forces the group into identifying and ranking the most likely effects that the proposed change may bring; like the Force Field Analysis, it concentrates on both the positive and negative driving and on restraining forces and the action steps that should be taken to overcome the resistance of implementing the change; and, finally, like the Systematic Diagram, it helps to identify possible actions that are necessary in order to achieve a broader goal.

The **Scenario Builder** should not be used until the task force members are familiar with the Affinity Diagram, the Nominal Group Process, the Force Field Analysis, and the Systematic Diagram. The **Scenario Builder** is **not** a replacement for the aforementioned tools, but it is a tool that one may wish to consider **if** the situation under examination requires the use of two or more of the tools. Although the **Scenario Builder** requires a minimum of three hours of concentrated effort to complete, it still may save the task force many hours if, for example, three CQI tools are required to arrive at similar conclusions.

Procedure

1. Spell out the recommended changes

In using the **Scenario Builder**, the group begins by defining the system that requires modification. In fact, the team members should have identified the change(s) that must be implemented in order to improve the system.

The recommended change ("C") is placed in the middle of the hexagon (see **Scenario Builder** Figure). The task force members should assume that the appropriate recommendations will be accepted in order to implement the change.

2. Record the Perceptions

The task force members should list at least three beneficial outcomes of the proposed change, and, if possible, three undesirable outcomes of the proposed change. The three beneficial outcomes should be listed in the squares labeled 1 through 3; the three undesirable outcomes should be listed in the squares 4 through 6. (Sometimes it is difficult and/or almost impossible to identify three truly unacceptable outcomes as a result of implementing improvements in processes or systems. However, the group should attempt to identify at least two undesirable outcomes.)

Following the above pattern, the group should label four scenarios that are likely to occur as a result of the outcomes identified in the squares labeled 1 through 6. If possible, two should be positive and two should be negative scenarios. In any event, at least one should be either positive or negative.

The aforementioned pattern should be repeated within the triangles and the ellipsoids. At least one of the perceived outcomes should be either positive or negative at any of the levels.

Scenario Builder To Determine The Effect of Change

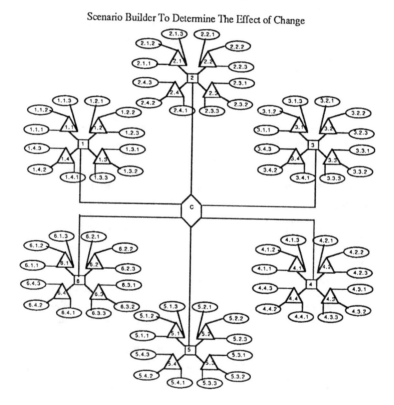

Scenario Builder tally sheet for estimating perceived effects of change on a process or a system and the prospect that a given event will occur.

1. ____	1. ____	1. ____	1. ____
1.1 ____	1.2 ____	1.3 ____	1.4 ____
1.1.1 ____	1.2.1 ____	1.3.1 ____	1.4.1 ____
1.1.2 ____	1.2.2 ____	1.3.2 ____	1.4.2 ____
1.1.3 ____	1.2.3 ____	1.3.3 ____	1.4.3 ____
Total ____	Total ____	Total ____	Total ____

2. ____	2. ____	2. ____	2. ____
2.1 ____	2.2 ____	2.3 ____	2.4 ____
2.1.1 ____	2.2.1 ____	2.3.1 ____	2.4.1 ____
2.1.2 ____	2.2.2 ____	2.3.2 ____	2.4.2 ____
2.1.3 ____	2.2.3 ____	2.3.3 ____	2.4.3 ____
Total ____	Total ____	Total ____	Total ____

3. ____	3. ____	3. ____	3. ____
3.1 ____	3.2 ____	3.3 ____	3.4 ____
3.1.1 ____	3.2.1 ____	3.3.1 ____	3.4.1 ____
3.1.2 ____	3.2.2 ____	3.3.2 ____	3.4.2 ____
3.1.3 ____	3.2.3 ____	3.3.3 ____	3.4.3 ____
Total ____	Total ____	Total ____	Total ____

4. ____	4. ____	4. ____	4. ____
4.1 ____	4.2 ____	4.3 ____	4.4 ____
4.1.1 ____	4.2.1 ____	4.3.1 ____	4.4.1 ____
4.1.2 ____	4.2.2 ____	4.3.2 ____	4.4.2 ____
4.1.3 ____	4.2.3 ____	4.3.3 ____	4.4.3 ____
Total ____	Total ____	Total ____	Total ____

5. ____	5. ____	5. ____	5. ____
5.1 ____	5.2 ____	5.3 ____	5.4 ____
5.1.1 ____	5.2.1 ____	5.3.1 ____	5.4.1 ____
5.1.2 ____	5.2.2 ____	5.3.2 ____	5.4.2 ____
5.1.3 ____	5.2.3 ____	5.3.3 ____	5.4.3 ____
Total ____	Total ____	Total ____	Total ____

6. ____	6. ____	6. ____	6. ____
6.1 ____	6.2 ____	6.3 ____	6.4 ____
6.1.1 ____	6.2.1 ____	6.3.1 ____	6.4.1 ____
6.1.2 ____	6.2.2 ____	6.3.2 ____	6.4.2 ____
6.1.3 ____	6.2.3 ____	6.3.3 ____	6.4.3 ____
Total ____	Total ____	Total ____	Total ____

3. Score the Scenarios

Scoring of the scenarios can be done either as they are listed, or afterwards. But all six first-level scenarios should have at least a 70 percent perceived probability of occurring. To score the **Scenario Builder,** the group assigns a number ranging from +1 to +10 to any positive scenario that might occur if the change is implemented, and -1 to -10 for any negative scenario that might occur if the change is implemented.

For example, the group may decide that a positive scenario A, identified and placed in square 1, would surely result if the change were effected. Therefore, they assigned it a value +10. The +10 means that the positive scenario would occur 100 percent of the time if the change were implemented and **IF** nothing were done to stop it. Likewise, a +3 should be assigned a value of 30 percent; +4, 40 percent, etc. The group may decide that positive scenarios B and C should be assigned values of +7 and +5 respectively. Similarly, the task force might decide that negative scenario D would almost definitely occur (100 percent of the time) if the change were implemented. Therefore, they would assign it a value of -10, whereas the negative scenarios E and F were only assigned values of -3 (30 percent) and -4 (40 percent) since they were less likely to occur if the change were implemented.

If a **very positive** scenario would occur if the change was effected, and if its effect could not be altered, it should be assigned a value of +50. If a disaster would occur if the change was implemented, and if its effect could not be altered, it should be assigned a value of -50.

The values for the first level scenarios, 1 through 6, should be recorded on a scenario builder tally sheet as shown below. Likewise, the values for the second level scenarios, 1.1 through 6.4, should be recorded. Finally, the values for the third level scenarios, 1.1.1 through 6.4.3, should be recorded. The scoring guidelines for the Scenario Builder are shown in the following table.

Positive Scenario	Negative Scenario	Would Likely Occur Percent of the Time	Effect Can Be Altered?
+1	-1	10%	Yes
+2	-2	20%	Yes
+3	-3	30%	Yes
+4	-4	40%	Yes
+5	-5	50%	Yes, Requires Effort
+6	-6	60%	Yes, Requires More Effort
+7	-7	70%	Yes, Requires Much Effort
+8	-8	80%	Yes, With Difficulty
+9	-9	90%	Yes, But Unlikely
+10	-10	100%	Not Likely
+50	-50	100%	Never

Scenario Builder tally sheet for estimating perceived effects of change on a process or a system and the prospect that a given event will occur.

4. Interpret the Scores

    The team should examine the first-level scenarios, labeled 1 through 6. They should have values ±7—all should have a greater than 70 percent chance of occurring if the changes were implemented.

    The task force should continue to build upon the **major** positive and negative scenarios through levels two and three. As before, they should concentrate their efforts on only the scenarios with values of ±7 or greater.

5. Describe what will likely happen to each event and then what **action step** needs to be taken to accentuate the positive and minimize the negative outcomes as well as the **desired outcome.**

    Your recommendations to change the system should be evaluated and quantified. Action steps can now be identified to either recommend the change and to minimize the possible negative outcomes, or even abandon the change as it might be disastrous to the classroom or school.

6. List and analyze any scenario that has a number greater than ±100

    The scenarios that have a high score usually mean that if the recommended changes were implemented and if the perceptions of the task force members are representative of the institutional culture, then the scenarios would take place.

7. Suggest what one or two systems should be improved to maximize the positive and minimize the negative

Case Study

Here is an example of how the **Scenario Builder** was effectively used with students performing poorly in Ms. Amie Mosier's twelfth-grade English class.

A task force consisting of five students and Ms. Mosier was formed. After conducting a Nominal Group Process session with the class, they arrived at the conclusion that the students would learn more and do better quality work if the students could work cooperatively in groups.

Following that decision, the group:

1. Spelled out the recommended change(s)

    The recommended change ("C") is: **Students will work in groups on all classroom assignments in order to receive better grades in English.**

2. Recorded the Perceptions

    The task force members listed an almost equal number of beneficial outcomes and undesirable outcomes of the proposed change. These are shown below along with the task force's scoring.

3. Score the Scenarios

    Scoring of the scenarios can be done either as they are listed, or afterwards. As noted earlier, all six, first-level scenarios should have at least a 70 percent perceived probability of occurring. To score the **Scenario Builder**, the group assigned a number of +1 to +10 to any positive scenario that might occur if the change is implemented, and -1 to -10 to any negative scenario that might occur if the change is implemented. If a **very positive** scenario would occur if the change is affected, and if its effect could not be altered, it should be assigned a value of +50. Likewise, if a disaster would occur if the change is implemented, and if its effect could not be altered, it should be assigned a value -50. The table was used, and the following numbers were assigned to the scenarios if the recommended change ("C") was implemented: **Students will work in groups on all classroom assignments in order to receive better grades in English.**

1. Students will get along well and will work effectively in the groups. (+7)
   - 1.1 Students will realize the importance of group success. (+7)
     - 1.1.1 Self esteem will rise because the group will be successful. (+9)
     - 1.1.2 Students will bond with a different group of students. (+6)
     - 1.1.3 Some will be frustrated because there will be less individual recognition.(-3)
   - 1.2 Students will achieve a quality group product. (+8)
     - 1.2.1 Students will take pride in workmanship realizing they've produced a quality product. (+10)
     - 1.2.2 Students will recognize excellence and know they can achieve it. (+10)
     - 1.2.3 Students will be frustrated at the amount of work involved in achieving quality work.(-2)
   - 1.3 Students will spend too much time chatting/gossiping and little time working on the assignment. (-2)
     - 1.3.1 Students will broaden their circle of friends. (+5)
     - 1.3.2 Students will practice better communication skills. (+5)
     - 1.3.3 Students will not achieve quality work because they will not focus on the assignment. (-8)
   - 1.4 Students will broaden the assignment , causing them to be inefficient in their use of time. (-3)
     - 1.4.1 Students will become so enthusiastic they will continue to find new ways to explore the assignment. (+4)
     - 1.4.2 Students will learn many different off-shoots about the assignment, thus broadening their knowledge base. (+4)
     - 1.4.3 Students will not finish the assignment on time. (-6)

2. After Ms. Mosier trains students in cooperative learning, groups will work effectively producing quality assignments. (+10)

    2.1   Students will enjoy cooperative learning and will agree to work in groups. (+8)

          2.1.1 Students will become active learners and have fun in the classroom. (+8)

          2.1.2 Students will expand their friendships. (+7)

          2.1.3 Students will not focus on the assignment. (-3)

    2.2   Students will feel good about being helpful to their classmates. (+50)

          2.2.1   Self-esteem will increase. (+10)

          2.2.2   Students will realize how working together increases success. (+10)

          2.2.3   Some students will do the work of others rather than helping them. (-7)

    2.3   Training students will take up a great deal of class time. (-8)

          2.3.1   Ms. Mosier will consider this is important. (+10)

          2.3.2   Students will learn how to work cooperatively. (+7)

          2.3.3   Training will take away valuable class time, causing Ms. Mosier to feel stressed. (-8)

    2.4   Students who are not in groups with their friends will not put all their focus and energy into accomplishing the assignment. (-5)

          2.4.1   Students will get to know other students. (+5)

          2.4.2   Factions within the classroom will begin to break down as students work together with others. (+4)

          2.4.3   Some students will become angry and refuse to work together. (-7)

3. Students will appreciate individual differences in their classmates and will recognize how each contributes to the success of the group. (+9)

    3.1   Students will recognize that people learn differently. (+50)

          3.1.1   Students will learn that some are "smart" in other subjects but "slow" in English. (+50)

          3.1.2   Teaming will become more important than individual success. (+7)

          3.1.3   Racial tension will be reduced as students work together. (+10)

    3.2   Students will be frustrated with those who not contribute to the project. (-10)

          3.2.1   Clicks will form within the group. (-10)

          3.2.2   Hard feelings will result. (-10)

          3.2.3   Racial tension will increase. (-10)

    3.3   Leaders will evolve to direct the group. (-50)

          3.3.1   All members of the group will develop significant leadership qualities. (+7)

          3.3.2   Some of the leaders will become pushy. (-50)

          3.3.3   Some students will ignore the leaders. (+10)

4. Students will resist working together and will do individual projects within the group. (-8)
- 4.1 Students will work harder for their own gain than they otherwise would. (+3)
  - 4.1.1 The quality of each person's work will be higher than normal. (+2)
  - 4.1.2 Students will learn about independent study. (+3)
  - 4.1.3 There will be an overlap among student's work. (-7)
- 4.2 The group assignment will not be cohesive. (-7)
  - 4.2.1 The individual parts of the assignment will good quality. (+3)
  - 4.2.2 Students have will not learn to work cooperatively. (-10)
  - 4.2.3 The group assignment will not be completed since the group will not tie it all together. (-9)
- 4.3 Students will become angry because each thinks s/he is doing all the work. (-8)
  - 4.3.1 Adrenaline will make all students work harder. (+2)
  - 4.3.2 Some students will quit because they will feel unappreciated. (-4)
  - 4.3.3 Groups will break apart because students will refuse to work together. (-9)

5. Some students will simply not participate in the group, and a few students will undertake responsibility for completing the group assignment. (-7)
- 5.1 Some students will get the assignment done. (+3)
  - 5.1.1 The assignment will be completed. (+3)
  - 5.1.2 The goal of working together in a group will be achieved. (-10)
  - 5.1.3 Students will be angry with other group members for not helping. (-8)
- 5.2 There will be dissension between the students. (-10)
  - 5.2.1 Natural tension will cause students to practice communication skills. (+2)
  - 5.2.2 Students will break into factions...those working and those not. (-7)
  - 5.2.3 Students will complain to Ms. Mosier that the assignment is unfair. (-8)
- 5.3 Some students will not do any work. (-10)
  - 5.3.1 Some students will relax. (+1)
  - 5.3.2 Working students will be angry with those who are not. (-9)
  - 5.3.3 Group goals will not being met since students will not learn to work together. (-10)

6. Tensions will be high since students will refuse to work with anyone other than their friends. (-8)

The task force entered the scores of each scenario into the table that follows.

Scenario Builder tally sheet for estimating perceived effects of change on a process or a system and the prospect that a given event will occur.

1. +7	1. +7	1. +7	1. +7
1.1 +7	1.2 +8	1.3 -2	1.4 -3
1.1.1 +9	1.2.1 +10	1.3.1 +5	1.4.1 +4
1.1.2 +6	1.2.2 +10	1.3.2 +5	1.4.2 +4
1.1.3 -3	1.2.3 -2	1.3.3 -8	1.4.3 -6
Total +26	Total +33	Total +7	Total +6

2. +10	2. +10	2. +10	2. +10
2.1 +8	2.2 +9	2.3 -8	2.4 -5
2.1.1 +8	2.2.1 +50	2.3.1 +10	2.4.1 +5
2.1.2 +7	2.2.2 +10	2.3.2 +7	2.4.2 +4
2.1.3 -3	2.2.3 -7	2.3.3 -8	2.4.3 -7
Total +30	Total +72	Total +11	Total +7

3. +9	3. +9	3. +9	3. +9
3.1 +50	3.2 -10	3.3 -50	3.4 ND
3.1.1 +50	3.2.1 -10	3.3.1 +7	3.4.1 ___
3.1.2 +7	3.2.2 -10	3.3.2 -50	3.4.2 ___
3.1.3 +10	3.2.3 -10	3.3.3 -9	3.4.3 ___
Total +126	Total -39	Total -74	Total ___

4. -8	4. -8	4. -8	4. -8
4.1 +3	4.2 -7	4.3 -8	4.4 ND
4.1.1 +2	4.2.1 +3	4.3.1 +2	4.4.1 ___
4.1.2 +3	4.2.2 -10	4.3.2 -4	4.4.2 ___
4.1.3 -7	4.2.3 -9	4.3.3 -9	4.4.3 ___
Total -7	Total -31	Total -27	Total ___

5. -7	5. -7	5. -7	5. -7
5.1 +3	5.2 -10	5.3 -10	5.4 ND
5.1.1 +3	5.2.1 +2	5.3.1 +1	5.4.1 ___
5.1.2 -10	5.2.2 -7	5.3.2 -9	5.4.2 ___
5.1.3 -8	5.2.3 -8	5.3.3 -10	5.4.3 ___
Total -19	Total -30	Total -35	Total ___

6. -8			
6.1 ND	6.2 ND	6.3 ND	6.4 ND
6.1.1 ___	6.2.1 ___	6.3.1 ___	6.4.1 ___
6.1.2 ___	6.2.2 ___	6.3.2 ___	6.4.2 ___
6.1.3 ___	6.2.3 ___	6.3.3 ___	6.4.3 ___
Total ___	Total ___	Total ___	Total ___

4. Interpret the Scores

   4.1 Examine the scores of the six, first level scenarios

   The team should examine the first level scenarios, labeled 1 through 6. They should have values ±7—all should have a greater than 70 percent chance of occurring if the changes were implemented. All scenarios did have a score greater than ±7.

   4.2   Build upon the second-level scenarios that have a 70 percent chance or greater perceived probability of occurring

   The task force continued to build upon the **major** positive and negative scenarios through levels two and three. As before they concentrated their efforts on only the scenarios with values of ±7 or greater.

   The task force, therefore, had to consider the following scenarios: 1.1, 1.2, 2.1, 2.2, 2.3, 3.1, 3.2, 3.3, 4.2, 4.3, 5.2, and 5.3.

5. Describe what will likely happen to each event and then what **action step** needs to be taken to accentuate the positive and minimize the negative outcomes as well as the **desired outcome.**

   Action steps can now be identified to either recommend the change and to minimize the possible negative outcomes, or to abandon the change as it might be disastrous to the organization.

SCENARIO 1: The students will get along well and work effectively in groups (+7) since they will realize the importance of group success (+7). Therefore self-esteem will rise because the group will be successful (+9) and this will cause the students to bond together (+6).

   While working together to produce a quality "product (+8)," the individuals will take pride-in-workmanship (+10) and will recognize excellence and know they can achieve it (+10).

   ACTION STEP: The task force will report its finding and recommendations back to the class.

   DESIRED OUTCOMES: The students will realize that cooperative learning and teaming is the way things are done in real life situations.

SCENARIO 2: After Ms. Mosier trains the students in cooperative learning, groups will work effectively together (+10). After the training, the students will enjoy working in groups (+8) as they will become active learners (+8). In addition, they will expand their friendships (+7). Group projects will make students feel good about helping their classmates (+50) and self-esteem will increase (+10). Students will realize the importance of group success, although some students may end up doing the work of others rather than showing them how the work should be done (-7).

   Ms. Mosier knows that it will take time to train the students in CQI tools (-8) and that this time will come from regular class time (-8), but the training is very important (+10) if the students are to learn how to work as a team (+7).

   ACTION STEP: Ms. Mosier will take time from the regular classes to teach the appropriate CQI tools which encourage teaming.

DESIRED OUTCOMES: The students will begin to work as a team and realize success in English.

SCENARIO 3: Students will appreciate individual differences in their classmates and will recognize how each contributes to the success of the group (+9). As a result students will recognize different learning styles (+50) and the differences in preferences for subjects (+50). Since teaming will become more important than individual success (+7), racial tension will be reduced as the students work together (+10).

The possibility exists that the students will become frustrated with those who do not contribute to the project (-10) and various subunits will result (-10) which will increase hard feelings (-10) and increase racial tension (-10).

As in any group project, leaders will emerge and direct the group project (-50). Actually, this may be a +50 if the leaders help group members realize their own potential and don't become pushy (-50). Some students will totally ignore pushy leaders (+10).

ACTION STEP: Each group will have to constantly remind its members about the benefits of team work.

DESIRED OUTCOMES: The students will realize the importance of leadership in helping the group obtain success.

SCENARIO 4: Students will resist working together and will do individual projects within the group (-8). The group will not be cohesive (-7) since most students will not learn to work cooperatively (-1). As a result, the group assignments will not be completed (-9). Students will become angry as each student will think that they are doing the majority of the work (-8) and the group will break apart because they will refuse to work together (-9).

ACTION STEP: Ms. Mosier must instill into the students the importance of teaming and how to use the CQI tools in order to achieve success.

DESIRED OUTCOMES: The students will learn the necessary skills to work together as a group.

SCENARIO 5: Some students will simply not participate in the group, and a few students will undertake responsibility for completing the group assignment (-7). (The task force members concluded that this scenario was so similar to #4 that it did not need to be discussed further, since it would be resolved by the action step taken under scenario 4.)

SCENARIO 6: Tensions will be high since the students will refuse to work with anyone other that their friends (-8). No action step is recommended since this may fade after the work teams are formed and success is achieved.

6. List and analyze any scenario that has a number greater than ±100

The scenarios that have a high score usually means that if the recommended changes were implemented and if the perceptions of the task force members were representative of the institutional culture, then the scenarios would take place.

One scenario has a number greater than ±100 , namely 3.1, which reads:

3. Students will appreciate individual differences in their classmates and will recognize how each contributes to the success of the group. (+9)

3.1 Students will recognize that people learn differently. (+50)

    3.1.1 Students will learn that some are "smart" in other subjects but "slow" in English. (+50)

    3.1.2 Teaming will become more important than individual success. (+7)

    3.1.3 Racial tension will be reduced as students work together. (+10)

(It should be mentioned that before the end of the year Scenario 3 did occur.)

7. Suggest what one or two systems should be improved to maximize the positive and minimize the negative

After analyzing the results of the scenarios and the results that were obtained by the end of the school year, the action team decided that a major dysfunctional system was at the root of poor learning in their high school— the students were not taught how to work together in order to obtain quality results. In a letter to the school board and the principal, the students suggested that a course in CQI procedures be taught at the ninth- grade level, if not sooner.

SYSTEMATIC DIAGRAM

The **Systematic Diagram** is used as a planning tool to determine the specific action steps that are necessary to accomplish a broader goal, especially if a number of people, departments, or units are involved. The **Systematic Diagram** is best used with an Affinity Diagram or a Relations Diagram.

Procedure

1. Statement of the Problem/Goal

We will build upon the example presented in the Relations Diagram section when a task force consisting of drama students and their teacher was attempting to establish a set design and construction shop. The goal is drawn on the left side of the paper. This can be done using an overhead projector or a large sheet of flip chart paper.

END

Establish a Set Design and Construction Shop

2. Generate Levels of Events and Actions Necessary to Accomplish the Ends

The first level of events and actions are usually broad, but as you move from left to right, the tasks become very specific as one level builds upon the other. In the example that follows, the task force members know that if they are to accomplish their goal, they will ultimately require approval and support from the principal, parents, business community, and students. In order for that to occur, however, the task force recognized that it would need to develop a rationale, a design, and informational materials. The steps are incorporated in the completed **Systematic Diagram** below.

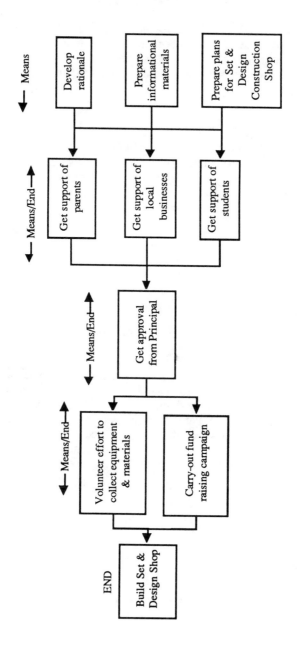